Karen Brown's
Ireland
Charming Inns & Itineraries

Written by
JUNE BROWN

Illustrations by Barbara Tapp
Cover Painting by Jann Pollard

Karen Brown's Guides, San Mateo, California

Karen Brown Titles

Austria: Charming Inns & Itineraries

California: Charming Inns & Itineraries

England: Charming Bed & Breakfasts

England, Wales & Scotland: Charming Hotels & Itineraries

France: Charming Bed & Breakfasts

France: Charming Inns & Itineraries

Germany: Charming Inns & Itineraries

Ireland: Charming Inns & Itineraries

Italy: Charming Bed & Breakfasts

Italy: Charming Inns & Itineraries

New England: Charming Inns & Itineraries

Portugal: Charming Inns & Itineraries

Spain: Charming Inns & Itineraries

Switzerland: Charming Inns & Itineraries

Beneta,
you live on in the hearts of everyone
you touched and loved while you were here.

Editors: Anthony Brown, Karen Brown, June Brown, Clare Brown, Iris Sandilands, Lorena Aburto.

Illustrations: Barbara Tapp; Cover painting: Jann Pollard; Web designer: Lynn Upthagrove.

Maps: Susanne Lau Alloway—Greenleaf Design & Graphics; Inside cover photo: W. Russell Ohlson.

Distributed by Fodor's Travel Publications, Inc., 280 Park Avenue, New York, NY 10017, USA.

Distributed in Canada by Random House Canada, 2775 Matheson Boulevard. East, Mississanga, Ontario, Canada L4W 4P7, phone (905) 624 0672, fax (905) 624 6217

Distributed in the United Kingdom, Ireland and Europe by Random House UK, 20 Vauxhall Bridge Road, London, SW1V 2SA, phone: 44 20 7840 4000, fax: 44 20 7840 8406.

Distributed in Australia by Random House Australia, 20 Alfred Street, Milsons Point, Sydney NSW 2061, Australia, phone: 61 2 9954 9966, fax: 61 2 9954 4562.

Distributed in New Zealand by Random House New Zealand, 18 Poland Road, Glenfield, Auckland, New Zealand, phone: 64 9 444 7197, fax: 64 9 444 7524.

Distributed in South Africa by Random House South Africa, Endulani, East Wing, 5A Jubilee Road, Parktown 2193, South Africa, phone: 27 11 484 3538, fax: 27 11 484 6180.

A catalog record for this book is available from the British Library.

Library of Congress Cataloging-in-Publication Data

Brown, June, 1949-
   Karen Brown's Ireland : charming inns & itineraries / written by June Brown ; illustrations by Barbara Tapp.
     p. cm. -- (Karen Brown's country inn series)
   ISBN 1-928901-07-7
   1. Bed and breakfast accommodations--Ireland Guidebooks. 2. Hotels--Ireland--Guidebooks. 3. Ireland--Guidebooks. I. Brown, Karen, 1956- II. Title. III. Series.

TX907.5.I73 B74 2001
647.94415'01--dc21   00-037931

Contents

An Irish Blessing

May the road rise to meet you,
May the wind be always at your back,
May the sun shine warm upon your face,
May the rains fall soft upon your fields,
And, until we meet again,
May God hold you in the palm of his hand.

Introduction

Writers wax lyrical about Ireland's spectacular scenery: ever-changing landscapes, splendid seascapes, purple moorlands, monastic ruins, enchanting lakes, towering fortresses, and vast, spreading patchworks of fields in every shade of green—believe every word they say. But realize that it's the people with their open friendliness and warmth of welcome that make a visit to Ireland special. This guide is all about Irish hospitality and staying in places where you are a houseguest rather than a customer. Ireland is not conducive to rushing: the narrow country roads lend themselves to exploration at a leisurely pace where you return the smile and wave of greeting of those you pass. Take time to stop at a pub and be drawn into conversation, and when you get lost, ask directions and learn a bit of history or folklore as a bonus, along with the directions.

About This Guide

Ireland: Charming Inns & Itineraries is written specifically for independent travelers who want to experience a slice of Irish life staying as guests in country houses, farms, and family-run hotels. Our guide is not written for those who want the symmetry of worldwide hotel chains with their identical bathrooms and mini bars. The fondest memories of a visit to the Emerald Isle are those of its warm-hearted, friendly people, and there can be no better way to meet the Irish than to stay with them in their homes.

In the title the term "inn" is generic for all types of lodgings ranging from a simple farmhouse bed and breakfast to a luxurious country estate, owned and run by a welcoming family. These are often the kinds of places where you are expected to carry your own bags: service may not be the most efficient and occasionally the owners have their eccentricities, which all adds to the allure. There are enough recommendations in every price category to enable you to tailor your trip to your budget. Rates are quoted in Irish punts in the Republic of Ireland and pounds sterling in Northern Ireland. We have recommended accommodation in the widest of price ranges, so please do not expect the same standard of luxury at, for example, Foxmount Farm, as The Park Hotel Kenmare—there is no comparison—yet each is outstanding in what it offers.

To keep you on the right track we have formed itineraries linking the most interesting sightseeing, enabling you to spend from a few weeks to a month exploring this fascinating island. In addition, we have designed a walking tour of Dublin's fair city that blends culture, history, shopping, and Guinness.

Please supplement this book with the Karen Brown website (*www.karenbrown.com*). Our site contains not only a wealth of information for planning your vacation but also post-press updates on our guides, and is a handy source for Michelin maps. A great many of the properties in this guide are featured there (their web addresses are on their description pages) with photos and direct links to their email and website.

About Ireland

The following pointers are given in alphabetical order, not in order of importance.

CLIMATE

It has been said that there is no such thing as climate in Ireland—only weather, and no such thing as bad weather—only the wrong clothes. This is because the changes in conditions from day to day and even from hour to hour seem greater than the changes from one season to the next. The Atlantic Ocean and the air masses moving east give Ireland very little seasonal variation in temperature, producing mild winters and cool summers. The ocean's influence is strongest near the coast, especially in winter when areas bordering the sea are milder than those inland. Coastal areas, particularly in the west, also have less variation in temperature between day and night. Even when it rains, and it does, it never pours—it's just soft Irish rain that keeps the isle emerald. The best thing is to be prepared for sun and sudden squalls at all times.

CLOTHING

Ireland is an easygoing place and casual clothes are acceptable everywhere, even at the fanciest restaurants. Because the weather is changeable, layers of sweaters and shirts that can be added to and removed are recommended. A lightweight, waterproof jacket with a hood is indispensable. Do not haul huge suitcases into bed and breakfasts: rather, we suggest that you have a small suitcase (of the size that fits under your airline seat) that you take into the places you stay, leaving larger luggage in the car.

CURRENCY

The unit of currency in the Republic of Ireland is the punt, in Northern Ireland the pound sterling. The two currencies do not have equal value. Both are abbreviated to "£."

DRIVING

It is to the countryside that you must go, for to visit Ireland without driving through the country areas is to miss the best she has to offer. Driving is on the left-hand side of the road, which may take a little getting used to if you drive on the right at home, so avoid driving in cities until you feel comfortable with the system. If your arrival city is Dublin, do not pick your car up until you are ready to leave for the countryside. A valid driver's license from your home country is required. Your car will not be an automatic unless you specifically reserve one. If you intend to travel in Northern Ireland and rent your car in the Republic, make certain that the car company permits its car to be taken into Northern Ireland. Petrol (gasoline) is extremely expensive.

In the Republic, people by and large do not use road numbers when giving directions: they refer to roads as where they might lead to, e.g., the Cork road. To add to the confusion, new road signs quote distances in kilometers, while old signposts are in miles. The Irish seem to use neither, always quoting distances in the number of hours it takes them to drive.

The distances in Ireland are not great, but then the roads are not great either—though they are getting a lot better. Estimate your journey on the basis of an average of 30 miles (about 50 kilometers) per hour.

The types of roads found in Ireland are as follows:

MOTORWAYS: The letter "M" precedes these fast roads which have two or three lanes of traffic either side of a central divider. Motorways are more prevalent in Northern Ireland though they are becoming more common between larger towns in the Republic.

NATIONAL ROADS: The letter "N" precedes the road number in the Republic, while in Northern Ireland the road number is preceded by the letter "A." They are the straightest and most direct routes you can take when motorways are not available.

REGIONAL ROADS: The letter "R" precedes the road number on maps, but their numbers rarely, if ever, appear on signposts. They are usually wide enough for two cars or one tractor.

Off the major routes, road signs are not posted as often as you might wish, so when you drive it's best to plan some extra time for asking the way. Asking the way does have its advantages—you get to experience Irish directions from natives always ready to assure you that you cannot miss your destination—which gives you the opportunity of asking another friendly local the way when you do. One of the joys of meandering along sparsely traveled country roads is rounding a bend to find that cows, sheep, and donkeys take precedence over cars as they saunter up the middle of the road. When you meet someone on a country road, do return his salute.

DRIVING–CAR RENTAL

Readers frequently ask our advice on car rental companies. We always use Auto Europe, a car rental broker that works with the major car rental companies to find the lowest possible price. They also offer motor homes and chauffeur services. Auto Europe's toll-free phone service from every European country connects you to their US-based, 24-hour reservation center (ask for the card with European phone numbers to be sent to you). Auto Europe offers our readers a 5% discount, and occasionally free upgrades. Be sure to use the Karen Brown ID number 99006187 to receive your discount and any special offers. You can make your own reservations via our website, *www.karenbrown.com* (select Auto Europe from the home page under Travel Center), or by phone (800-223-5555).

Introduction: About Ireland

INFORMATION

The Irish Tourist Board and Northern Ireland Tourist Board are invaluable sources of information. They can supply you with details on all areas of Ireland and, at your request, specific information on accommodation in homes, farmhouses, and manors as well as information on festivals, fishing, and the like. In Ireland, the tourist offices, known as *bord failte*, have specific information on their areas and will, for a small fee, make lodging reservations for you. Their major offices are located as follows:

BELFAST:
Irish Tourist Board: 53 Castle Street, Belfast BT1 1GH
Tel: (028) 9032 7888, Fax: (028) 9024 0201
Northern Ireland Tourist Board: 59 North Street, Belfast BT1 1NB
Tel: (028) 9024 6609, Fax: (028) 9031 2424

DUBLIN:
Irish Tourist Board: Baggot Street Bridge, Dublin 2
Tel: (01) 602 4000, Fax: (01) 602 4100
Northern Ireland Tourist Board: 16 Nassau Street, Dublin 2
Tel: (01) 679 1977, Fax: (01) 679 1863

FRANKFURT:
Irish Tourist Board: Untermainanlige 7, D60329 Frankfurt/Main
Tel: (069) 923 1855, Fax: (069) 923 1858
Northern Ireland Tourist Board: Westendstrasse 16-22, 60329 Frankfurt/Main
Tel: (069) 234504, Fax: (069) 233480

LONDON:
All Ireland Tourism: British Travel Centre, 150 New Bond Street, London, W1Y OAQ
Tel: (020) 7493 3201

NEW YORK:
Irish Tourist Board: 345 Park Avenue, New York, NY 10017
Tel: (800) 223 6470, Fax: (212) 371 9052, Website: *www.irelandvacations.com*

Introduction: About Ireland

Northern Ireland Tourist Board: 551 Fifth Avenue, Suite 701, New York, NY 10176
Tel: (800) 326 0036 or (212) 922 0101, Fax: (212) 922 0099

SYDNEY:
Irish Tourist Board: 36 Carrington Street (3rd Level), Sydney, NSW
Tel: (02) 9299 6177, Fax: (02) 9299 6323

TORONTO:
Northern Ireland Tourist Board: 2 Bloor Street West, Suite 1501, Toronto, ON M4W 3E2,
Tel: (416) 925 6368, Fax: (416) 925 6033

MAPS

Each of our driving itineraries is preceded by a map showing the route, and each hotel listing is referenced to a map at the back of the book. These are an artist's drawings and although we have tried to include as much information as possible, you will need a more detailed map to outline your travels. Our preference is for the Michelin map of Ireland, map 923, where the scale is 1 centimeter to 4 kilometers, i.e., 1 inch to 6.30 miles (available in our website store *www.karenbrown.com*).

PUBS

Ireland's pubs will not disappoint—if you do not expect sophisticated establishments. Most of the 12,000 pubs where the Irish share ideas over frothing pints of porter have a contagious spirit and charm. Stop at a pub and you'll soon be drawn into conversation. At local pubs musicians and dancers perform for their own enjoyment, their audience being those who stop by for a drink. If this kind of entertainment appeals to you, ask someone wherever you are staying to recommend a local pub that will have live music that night.

ROOTS

The Potato Famine of the 1840s cut population by a fourth. Through the lean decades that followed, the Irish left by the thousands to make new lives, primarily in the United States, Canada, Australia, and New Zealand. The first step in tracing your Irish roots is to collect together as much information on your Irish antecedent as possible and to find out from relatives or documents (death or marriage certificates) just where he or she came from in Ireland. Armed with this information, your choices are several:

DO IT YOURSELF: If your ancestors hailed from Southern Ireland, visit the genealogical office on Kildare Street in Dublin. If your ancestors came from Northern Ireland, visit the Public Record Office of Northern Ireland, 66 Balmoral Avenue, Belfast BT9 6NY, which is open for visitors to do their own research.

HAVE SOMEONE DO IT FOR YOU: The genealogical office charges a small fee, but often has a backlog so it takes time to do a general search. Write to Chief Herald, General Office of Ireland, 2 Kildare Street, Dublin 2, tel: (01) 603 0200, enclosing whatever information you have on your ancestors.

If your ancestors came from Northern Ireland, send information about them, along with a letter, to one of the following: General Register Office, Oxford House, 49 Chichester Street, Belfast BT1 4HL; Presbyterian Historical Society, Church House, Fisherwick Place, Belfast BT1 6DU.

The major tourist offices have brochures on tracing your ancestors that give more detailed information and provide information on publications that may be of interest to those of Irish descent.

SHOPPING

Prices of goods are fairly standard throughout Ireland, so make your purchases as you find items you like since it is doubtful that you will find them again at a less expensive price. The most popular items to buy are hand-knitted sweaters, tweeds, crystal, china, and hand-embroidered linens.

Value Added Tax (VAT) is included in the price of your purchases. There is usually a minimum purchase requirement, but it is possible for visitors from non-EU countries to get a refund of the VAT on the goods they buy in one of two ways:

1. If the goods are shipped overseas direct from the point of purchase, the store can deduct the VAT at the time of sale.

2. Visitors taking the goods with them should ask the store to issue a VAT refund receipt. A passport is needed for identification. On departure, **before** you check in for your flight, go to the refund office at Shannon or Dublin airport. Your receipts will be stamped and they may ask to see your purchases. You will be given a cash refund in the currency of your choice.

About Itineraries

To keep you on the right track, we have created driving itineraries covering the most interesting sightseeing. If time allows, you can link the four itineraries together and travel around Ireland. Each itinerary explores a region's scenic beauty, history, and culture, and avoids its large cities. Along the way we suggest alternative routes and side trips (indicated in italics). At the beginning of each itinerary we suggest our recommended pacing to help you decide the amount of time to allocate to each region. Do not try to see all of Ireland in a week—this is frankly impossible. You will enjoy yourself much more if you concentrate on a smaller number of destinations and stay for at least a couple of nights in each, rather than spending most of your precious vacation rushing from place to place. Each itinerary map shows all of the towns and villages in which we have a recommended place to stay. The capricious changes in the weather mean that often what appears sparkling and romantic in sunshine appears dull and depressing under gathering storm clouds. If the weather is stormy, find a nice place to stay with good company. Once the rain clears, there is much to see. Each itinerary is preceded by an artist's impression of the proposed route. We suggest that you outline this on a commercial map: our preference is the Michelin map of Ireland where the scale is 1 centimeter to 4 kilometers (1/400,000).

Overview Map
Driving Itineraries

The North

Rosgull Peninsula

Tory Island

Giant's Causeway

Glencolumbkille

Donegal

Belfast

The West

Céide Fields

Sligo

Crossmolina

Lough Gill

Achill Island

Inishbofin Island

Connemara

Clifden

Galway

Dublin

Dublin Walking Tour

Burren

Aran Islands

Kilkenny

Limerick

Cashel

Waterford

The Southeast

Dingle Peninsula

Killarney

Blarney

Ring of Kerry

Kenmare

Cork

Skellig Michael

Kinsale

Beara Peninsula

The Southwest

Itinerary Route

Alternative Routes & Sidetrips

11

About Places to Stay

This book does not cover the many modern hotels in Ireland with their look-alike bedrooms, televisions, and direct-dial phones. Rather, it offers a selection of personally recommended lodgings that cover the widest range from a very basic, clean room in a simple farmhouse to a sumptuous suite in an elegant castle hotel. In some, the decor is less than perfect, but the one thing they all have in common is that their owners offer wholehearted hospitality. We have inspected each and every one, and have stayed in a great many. The accommodations selected are the kind of places that we enjoy. We have tried to be candid and honest in our appraisals and to convey each listing's special flavor so that you know what to expect and will not be disappointed. To help you appreciate and understand what to expect when staying at listings in this guide, the following pointers are given in alphabetical order, not in order of importance.

CHILDREN

The majority of listings in this guide welcome children. A great many places offer family rooms with a double and one or two single beds in a room. If you want to tuck your children up in bed and enjoy a leisurely dinner, many of the listings will with advance notice provide an early supper for children.

CHRISTMAS

If the information section indicates that the listing is open during the Christmas holiday season, there is a very good chance that it offers a festive Christmas package.

CLASSIFICATION OF PLACES TO STAY

To help you select the type of accommodation you are looking for, the bottom of the description gives one of the following classifications:

B&B: A private home, not on a farm, that offers bed and breakfast.

B&B WITH STABLES: Accommodation and the opportunity to ride.

CITY HOTEL: A hotel in Dublin or Belfast.

COUNTRY HOUSE: More up-market than a farmhouse or a B&B, a home of architectural interest without all the amenities offered by a country house hotel.

COUNTRY HOUSE HOTEL: A home or establishment of architectural interest with a restaurant, bar, and staff other than the proprietors.

FAMILY HOTEL: A small, family-run hotel.

FARMHOUSE B&B: A private home on a farm that offers bed and breakfast.

GUESTHOUSE: A small, usually family-run hotel corresponding roughly to a Continental *pension*.

INN: A pub with rooms.

LUXURY RESORT: An architecturally interesting hotel that is a destination in itself. It usually offers such facilities as gymnasium, swimming pool, golf course, riding, fishing, and shooting.

RESTAURANT WITH ROOMS: A restaurant that also offers bed-and-breakfast accommodation.

SELF-CATERING: Fully furnished accommodation with laundry and limited cooking facilities. No meals are included. These are typically rented by the week but shorter stays are often available. See *Self-Catering Accommodation* on page 19 and the list on page 251.

CREDIT CARDS

Whether an accommodation accepts payment by credit card is indicated in the accommodation description as follows: none, AX—American Express, MC—MasterCard, VS—Visa, or simply, all major.

DIRECTIONS

We give concise driving directions to guide you to the listing, which is often in a more out-of-the-way place than the town or village in the address. We would be very grateful if you would let us know of cases where our directions have proved inadequate.

ELECTRICITY

The voltage is 240. Most hotels, guesthouses, and farmhouses have American-style razor points for 110 volts. If you are coming from overseas, it is recommended that you take only dual-voltage appliances and a kit of electrical plugs. Your host can usually loan you a hairdryer or an iron.

HANDICAP FACILITIES

We list at the back of the book all the places to stay that have ground-floor rooms or rooms specially equipped for the handicapped. Please discuss your requirements when you call your chosen place to stay to see if they have accommodation that is suitable for you.

HIDDEN IRELAND

Several of the listings are members of Hidden Ireland, a consortium of private houses that open their doors to a handful of guests at a time. All houses are of architectural merit and character with owners to match. These are the kinds of houses where you can indulge yourself by staying with people who have mile-long driveways, grand dining rooms watched over by redoubtable ancestors, four-poster beds that you have to climb into, and vast billiard rooms. The kinds of places most of us can only dream of living in,

but where you are very welcome as guests because you are the ones who help the owners pay their central heating bills, school fees, and gardeners. Guests become a part of the household and family life carries on around you—you are not expected to scuttle up to your room. Everyone usually dines together round a polished table and, unless you make special requests, you eat what is served to you. The conversation flows and you meet people you might never have met elsewhere. Early or late in the season you may find that you are the only guests and you can enjoy a romantic candlelit dinner in a house full of character and charm. There are lakes full of salmon and stylish modern bedrooms at Delphi, gigantic old-fashioned bedrooms at Temple House, homey friendliness at Lorum Old Rectory, and a rhododendron forest at Ardnamona. We have listed members of this group at the back of the book. A brochure containing information on all members of Hidden Ireland is available from Irish tourist offices or from Hidden Ireland, P.O. Box 5451, Dublin 2, Ireland. From the USA: (800) 688-0299, tel: (01) 662-7166, fax: (01) 662-7144, email: info@hidden-ireland.com, website: *www.hidden-ireland.com.*

IRELAND'S BLUE BOOK

Several of our listings are members of the Irish Country Houses Association, usually referred to as The Blue Book because of the distinctive blue color of its brochure. This is an association of owner-managed country houses, hotels, and restaurants. The majority are country house hotels offering accommodation in charming surroundings with restaurants, bars, and room service. However, there are several members who welcome guests to their ancestral homes on house-party lines (much as members of Hidden Ireland) with no bar and a set dinner menu. We have listed members of this group at the back of the book. Ireland's Blue Book, listing all members, is available in the USA: (800) 323-5463 or (800) 223-6510, from Irish tourist offices, and Ardbraccan Glebe, Navan, Co Meath, Ireland, tel: (046) 23416, fax: (046) 23292, email: bluebook@iol.ie, website: *www.irelands-blue-book.ie.*

MAPS

At the back of the book are four regional maps showing each recommended place to stay's location. The pertinent regional map number is given at the right on the top line of each accommodation's description. To make it easier for you, we have divided each location map into a grid of four parts, a, b, c, and d, as indicated on each map's key.

MEALS

Owners of guesthouses, farmhouses, and bed and breakfasts are often happy to serve an evening meal if you make arrangements 24 hours in advance. Country houses offer a set menu of more elaborate fare and most offer interesting wines—again, arrangements to dine must be made 24 hours in advance. **You cannot just arrive and expect dinner.** Hotels offer menus and wine lists, giving you more dining choices. Our suggestion is that you make arrangements for dinner on the night of your arrival at the same time as you make reservations for accommodation.

RATES

Rates are those quoted to us either verbally or by correspondence for the 2001 high season (June, July, and August). The rates given generally cover the least expensive to the most expensive double room (two people sharing a room) inclusive of taxes and, in most cases, breakfast. **Otherwise**, we quote the cost of bed and breakfast per person per night in a room that has en-suite facilities (whenever these are available), based on two people sharing a room. We do not quote rates for single people occupying a room. When a listing does not include breakfast in its rates, we mention this in the description. We feel a great deal of resentment when an obligatory service charge of 10–15% is added to the bill and feel that establishments often use this as a way of padding their rates. Forewarned is forearmed, so we have stated if an establishment adds a service charge. Please **always check** prices and terms when making a reservation. Rates are quoted in Irish punts in the Republic of Ireland and pounds sterling in Northern Ireland. Prices vary considerably and on the whole reflect the type of house in which you will be staying. From the charm of a simple farmhouse to the special ambiance of a vast sporting estate, each listing reflects the Irish way of life.

RESERVATIONS

When making your reservations, be sure to identify yourself as a "Karen Brown traveler." The hotels appreciate your visit, value their inclusion in our guide, and frequently tell us they take special care of our readers. We hear over and over again that the people who use our guides are such wonderful guests!

Reservations should always be made in advance for Dublin accommodation. In the countryside space is not so tight and a nice room can often be had simply by calling in the morning. July and August are the busiest times and if you are traveling to a popular spot such as Killarney, you should make advance reservations. Be specific as to what your needs are, such as a ground-floor room, en-suite shower, twin beds, family room. Check the prices, which may well have changed from those given in the book (summer 2001). Ask what deposit to send or give your credit card number. Tell them about what time you intend to arrive and request dinner if you want it. Ask for a confirmation with brochure and map to be sent to you. There are several options for making reservations:

EMAIL: This is our preferred way of making a reservation. If the hotel/bed and breakfast is on our website we have included their email in the listing, and added a direct link on their Karen Brown website. (Always spell out the month as the Irish reverse the American month/day numbering system.)

FAX: If you have access to a fax machine, this is a very quick way to reach a hotel/bed and breakfast. If the place to stay has a fax, we have included the number in the listing. (See comment above about spelling out the month.)

LETTER: If you write for reservations, you will usually receive your confirmation and a map. You should then send your deposit. (See comment on email about spelling out month.)

TELEPHONE: By telephoning you have your answer immediately, so if space is not available, you can then decide on an alternative. If calling from the United States, allow for the time difference (Ireland is five hours ahead of New York) so that you can call during their business day. Dial 011 (the international code), 353 (Republic of Ireland's code) **or** 44 (Northern Ireland's code), then the city code (dropping the 0), and the telephone number.

SELF-CATERING ACCOMMODATION

An excellent way to explore an area is to rent self-catering accommodation on a weekly basis. You can unpack your bags, put your feet up and make yourself at home, come and go as you please, and eat what you like when you like. Tir Na Fiúise in Terryglass is our only exclusively self-catering property. Several of the country houses that operate as bed and breakfasts can be rented in their entirety as luxurious homes. The Quay House has apartments that can be let on either a self-catering or bed-and-breakfast basis. A great many listings have additional houses, cottages, and converted outbuildings that range from former coach houses to a onetime hen house. Because our primary focus is on beds, breakfasts, and evening meals we do not have space to discuss self-catering accommodation at length. Also, because this is a new feature of our guide for 2001, we have not yet had the opportunity in all cases to determine rates for weekly stays. To assist you in finding self-catering accommodation, we list at the back of the book all the places in this guide that provide it. Please discuss your requirements when you contact them and see if they have accommodation that is suitable for you.

SIGHTSEEING

We have tried to mention sightseeing attractions near each lodging to encourage you to spend several nights in each location.

Introduction: About Places to Stay

19

WEBSITE

Please utilize the Karen Brown website (*www.karenbrown.com*) in conjunction with this book. It provides comments, feedback, and discoveries from you, our readers, information on our latest finds, post-press updates, drawings for free books, and one-stop shopping for our guides and associated Michelin maps. Most of our favorite places to stay are featured on our website (their web addresses are on their description pages in this book) with color photos and, through direct links to their own websites, even more information. You can email them directly, making reservations a breeze.

Waterford, Foxmount Farm

Dublin Walking Tour

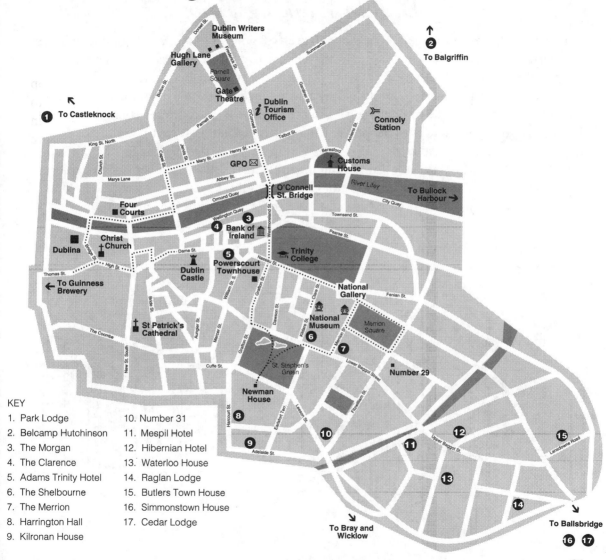

KEY

1. Park Lodge
2. Belcamp Hutchinson
3. The Morgan
4. The Clarence
5. Adams Trinity Hotel
6. The Shelbourne
7. The Merrion
8. Harrington Hall
9. Kilronan House
10. Number 31
11. Mespil Hotel
12. Hibernian Hotel
13. Waterloo House
14. Raglan Lodge
15. Butlers Town House
16. Simmonstown House
17. Cedar Lodge

Dublin Walking Tour

"In Dublin's fair city where the girls are so pretty," goes the popular old ballad. The girls are certainly pretty and the city fair if you can overlook the rash of modern office developments begun in the 1960s and the areas that have been razed and seemingly abandoned. Dublin now appears to have seen the error of its ways and efforts are being made to restore what the bulldozers have spared. A car is more trouble than it is worth in Dublin. If your visit here is at the outset of your trip, we suggest that you not get your car until you are ready to leave or, if Dublin is a stop on your trip, park it for the duration of your stay. Dublin is a walking town, so don comfortable shoes and set out to explore the buildings, streets, and shops of this bustling, friendly city. If you feel weary along the way, there is no shortage of pubs where you can revive yourself with a refreshing drink.

Recommended Pacing: If you select a few museums that appeal to you and simply skirt the exterior of the others, this walking tour can be accomplished in a day, which means that you will need two nights' accommodation in Dublin. (*For further information, visit the Dublin Tourist Office website: www.visitdublin.com.*)

A convenient place to begin your tour, at the southern end of O'Connell Street, is **O'Connell Bridge**, spanning the River Liffey, which divides the north from the south of Dublin. (It is also just by the city center terminus for buses: those displaying "*An Lar,*" meaning city center, usually end up here.) Turn south into **Westmoreland Street** past the somber, windowless **Bank of Ireland**, which began life in 1729 as the seat of the Irish parliament. Cross the street and enter through the front arch of **Trinity College** into the cobbled square. Founded in 1591 by Elizabeth I, it contains a fine collection of buildings from the 18th to the 20th centuries. Cross the square to the library where a display center houses the jewel of Trinity College, the ***Book of Kells,*** a Latin text of the Four Gospels. A page of this magnificent illuminated manuscript is turned every month and if you are not overly impressed by the page on display, return to the library bookshop and browse through a reproduction. (*Open daily.*) While at the college visit **The Dublin Experience**, a sophisticated audio-visual presentation that orients you to the main events of Irish history. (*Open end of May–Sep.*)

Retrace your steps to the front gate and turn south into pedestrians-only **Grafton Street**, teeming with people and enlivened by lots of street musicians and entertainers. Its large, modern department store, **Brown Thomas**, is popular with visitors. **Bewley's Café** is a landmark, old-fashioned tea and coffee shop frequented by Dubliners. Upstairs, genteel waitress service is offered while downstairs it's self-service tea, coffee, sticky buns, sausages, chips, and the like. The food is not outstanding, but the atmosphere is very "Dublin."

If you take Johnson Court, a narrow lane off Grafton Street, you'll find yourself in **Powerscourt Townhouse**. This was a courtyard house built between 1771 and 1774 which has been converted into a shopping center by covering the courtyard with a glass roof and building balconies and stairways against the brick façades forming the quadrangle. The center space and balconies are given over to café tables and chairs—secure a balcony table and watch Dubliners at their leisure. The surrounding maze of narrow streets is full of trendy restaurants, cafés, and interesting shops—search out **Magill's** delicatessen on Clarendon Street: it's packed with cheeses, breads, meats, and all kinds of appetizing foods.

At the end of Grafton Street dodge the hurrying buses and cross into the peaceful tranquillity of **St. Stephen's Green**, an island of flowers, trees, and grass surrounding small lakes dotted with ducks. On the far side of the square at 85 and 86 St. Stephen's Green is **Newman House**, once the home of the old Catholic University (later University College Dublin), which boasted James Joyce amongst its distinguished graduates. Number 85 is restored to its pristine, aristocratic years of the 1740s. On the ground floor are wall reliefs of the god Apollo and his nine muse daughters, done elaborately in stucco. A staircase of Cuban mahogany leads to a reception room with more riotous plasterwork figures on the ceiling. Number 86 has some rooms with interesting associations with the Whaley family and Gerard Manley Hopkins, and the Bishop's Room has been restored to its Victorian splendor. (*Open Jun, Jul, Aug, tours on the hour from noon, tel: 01 706 7422.*) **The Commons**, in the basement of Newman House, is an elegant restaurant where you can enjoy a drink out on the terrace before or after your meal.

Return to the north side of the square past the landmark **Shelbourne Hotel**, a perfect place to enjoy a sedate afternoon tea of dainty sandwiches, buttered scones with whipped cream, and homemade cakes and pastries (3–5:30 pm). Follow **Merrion Row** and turn left into **Merrion Street** passing the back of **Leinster House**, the Irish Parliament. It consists of two chambers—the *Dáil*, the lower house, and the *Seanad*, the upper house or senate. You can tour the building when parliament is not in session. Adjacent to the parliament building is the **National Gallery of Ireland**, which is a Victorian building with about 3,000 works of art. There's a major collection of Ireland's greatest painter,

Jack Yeats, and works by Canaletto, Goya, Titian, El Greco, Poussin, Manet, Picasso, and many others. (*Open daily, tel: 01 661 5133, website: www.nationalgallery.ie.*)

Merrion Square is one of Dublin's finest remaining Georgian squares and the onetime home of several famous personages—William Butler Yeats lived at 82 and earlier at 52, Daniel O'Connell at 51, and Oscar Wilde's parents occupied number 1. The jewel of Merrion Square is **Number 29** Lower Fitzwilliam Street (corner of Lower Fitzwilliam Street and Upper Mount Street), a magnificently restored, late-18th-century townhouse. From the basement through the living rooms to the nursery and playrooms, the house is meticulously furnished in the style of the period (1790–1820)—real *Upstairs, Downstairs* stuff. You can tour the house along with a tape telling you all about it. (*Closed Mon, tel: 01 702 6165.*)

Merrion Square

Stroll into **Clare Street**, stopping to browse in **Greene's Bookstore** with its lovely old façade and tables of books outside.

Detour into **Kildare Street** where you find the **National Museum** displaying all the finest treasures of the country. There are marvelous examples of gold, bronze, and other ornaments as well as relics of the Viking occupation of Dublin—the 8th-century Tara Brooch is perhaps the best-known item here.

Follow the railings of Trinity College to the **Kilkenny Design Centre** and **Blarney Woolen Mills**, fine places to shop for Irish crafts and clothing.

With your back to the front gate of Trinity College, cross into **Dame Street** where the statue of Henry Grattan, a famous orator, stands with arms outstretched outside the parliament building. (If you want to visit the **Dublin Tourism Centre**, take the first left off Dame Street into Church Lane, a one-block street that brings you to the center located in a sturdy granite church on Suffolk Street. Here you can book sightseeing tours, purchase ferry, train, and bus tickets, arrange lodgings, find out what is on in Dublin, make accommodation reservations throughout Ireland, and enjoy a cup of coffee.) Walk along Dame Street past one of Dublin's more controversial modern buildings, the **Central Bank**, which looks like egg boxes on stilts. Go under the bank and you are in **Temple Bar**, the energetic, "in place to be" for Dublin's youth. Its narrow streets are full of clubs, youth-oriented stores, and cafés that come alive at night. Returning to Dame Street and a more sedate side of Dublin, you come to **Dublin Castle**, built in the early 13th century on the site of an earlier Danish fortification. The adjoining 18th-century **State Apartments** with their ornate furnishings are more impressive inside than out. (*Open daily, tel: 01 677 7129.*)

Returning to Dame Street, you pass **City Hall** and on your right the impressive **Christ Church Cathedral** comes into view. Dedicated in 1192, it has been rebuilt and restored many times. After the Reformation when the Protestant religion was imposed on the Irish people, it became a Protestant cathedral (Church of Ireland). The large crypt remained as a gathering spot and marketplace for the locals (Catholics) who used it for many years until a rector expelled them because their rowdiness was interrupting church services. Another point of interest is **Strongbow's Tomb**: he was one of the most famous Norman lords of Ireland and by tradition debts were paid across his tomb. When a wall collapsed and crushed the tomb a replacement, unknown crusader's tomb was conscripted and named Strongbow's Tomb. (*Open daily, tel: 01 677 8099.*)

Joined to the cathedral by a covered bridge that arches across the street is **Dublina** where you learn the history of Dublin through an audio-visual display. You conclude your tour at the large-scale model of the city and the gift shop. (*Open daily, tel: 01 679 4611.*)

At the junction of High Street and Bridge Street, pause to climb the restored remains of a portion of **Dublin's Walls**. When they were built in 1240, the walls fronted onto the River Liffey.

If you feel like walking the distance along **Thomas Street**, now is the time to detour about 1.5 kilometers to that thriving Dublin institution, the **Guinness Brewery**, whence flows the national drink. Be aware that this is a seedier area of town. As you near your goal the smell of roasting grains permeates the air. When you enter the Guinness hop store, your reward for watching an audio-visual show on the making of the world-famous Irish brew is a sample (pints if you wish) of the divine liquid and the chance to purchase souvenirs of all things Guinness. The two million gallons of water a day that the brewery uses do not come from the Liffey, but from St. James's well on the Grand Canal—it is this limestone water that gives Guinness its characteristic flavor. (*Open weekdays, tel: 01 453 6700, ext. 5155, fax: 01 454 6519.*)

If you are not up to the walk to the Guinness Brewery, cross diagonally from the walls to the **Brazen Head** in **Bridge Street** where you can enjoy that same brew in Dublin's oldest pub. There has been a tavern on this site since Viking times, though the present, rather dilapidated premises date from 1688. It's always a crowded spot that really comes alive late in the evening when musicians gather for impromptu traditional music sessions.

Cross the River Liffey and strolling along the **Inns Quay**, you come to **The Four Courts**, the supreme and high courts of Ireland. You can look inside the fine circular waiting hall under the beautiful green dome which allows light through its apex. If it is early morning, you may see barristers in their gowns and wigs on their way to court.

Turn left up **Capel Street** and third right into **Mary Street** (a rather seedy area) where little shops sell all manner of goods and lead to the busiest pedestrian shopping street in Dublin, **Henry Street**. Hardy ladies wrapped in warm woolen coats stand before their prams and bawl in Dublinese, "Bananas six for a pound" and "Peaches a pound a basket." Policemen regularly move the ladies on but within a few minutes, they are back hawking their wares.

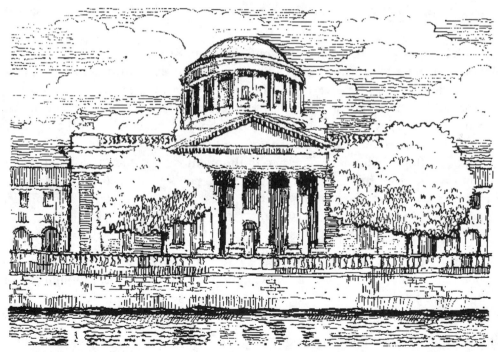

The Four Courts

Dublin Walking Tour

A short detour down **Moore Street** takes you through Dublin's colorful open-air fruit, vegetable, and flower market.

On reaching **O'Connell Street**, turn left. O'Connell Street has its share of tourist traps and hamburger stores, but it's a lively bunch of Dubliners who walk its promenades: placard-carrying nuns, nurses collecting for charity, hawkers of fruit, flowers, and plastic trinkets. All are there for you to see as you stroll along this wide boulevard and continue past the **Gate Theatre** into **Parnell Square** where at the north end of the square you find the **Dublin Writers Museum** in a restored 18th-century mansion. You go on a tour of the paintings and memorabilia with a tape telling you all about it. Among those featured are George Bernard Shaw, William Butler Yeats, Oscar Wilde, James Joyce, and Samuel Beckett. (*Open daily, tel: 01 872 2077.*) Just a few doors away is the **Hugh Lane Gallery** of modern art that ranges from works by Impressionists to contemporary Irish artists. (*Closed Mon, tel: 01 874 1903.*)

Retrace your steps down O'Connell Street to the **General Post Office**. The GPO, as it is affectionately known, is a national shrine as the headquarters of the 1916 revolution. Pass the statues of those who fought for Irish freedom and you are back at your starting point, O'Connell Bridge.

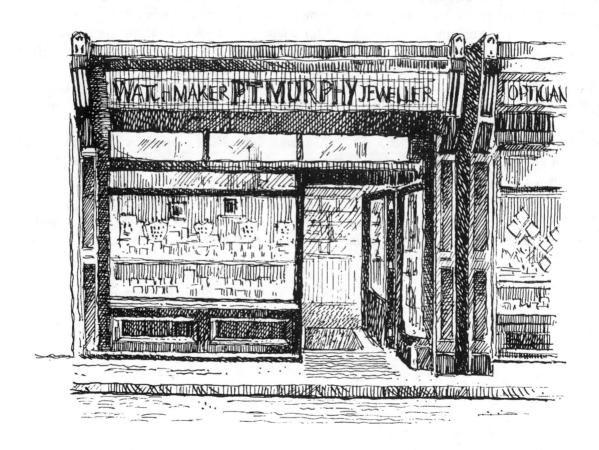

The Southeast

Legend

- ● Places to Stay
- ○ Orientation/ Sightseeing
- ▨ Itinerary Route
- — Roads
- ▨ Alternative Route & Sidetrips
- ✈ Airport

Belfast

Dublin

Dublin

Straffan

Powerscourt Gardens & Waterfall

Dunlavin

Sally Gap

Ashford

Rathnew

Glendalough

Annamoe

Wicklow

Vale of Avoca

Avoca

Arklow

Killinierin

Gorey

Thurles

R693

Kilkenny

Bagenalstown

Ferns

Freshford

Borris

N9

Enniscorthy

Maddoxstown

Dualla

Thomastown

Ballymurn

Cashel

N8

Inistoge

Bansha

Newcastle

Wexford

Cahir

N24

New Ross

Campile

Four Mile Water

Nire Valley

Waterford

John F. Kennedy Park

Arthurstown

Cappoquin

Passage East

The Vee

Glencairn

Lismore

N25

Tramore

Annestown

Castlelyons

N72

Dungarven

N11

Killeagh

Castlemartyr

Youghal

Cork

N25

Shanagarry

Ballinacurra

31

The Southeast

All too often visitors rush from Dublin through Waterford and on to western Ireland, never realizing that they are missing some of the most ancient antiquities and lovely scenery along the seductive little byways that traverse the moorlands and wind through wooded glens. This itinerary travels from Dublin into the Wicklow mountains, pausing to admire the lovely Powerscourt Gardens, lingering amongst the ancient monastic ruins of Glendalough, visiting the Avoca handweavers who capture the subtle hues of heather and field in their fabric, and admiring the skill of the Waterford crystal cutters.

Glendalough

Recommended Pacing: If you are not a leisurely sightseer, and leave Dublin early, you can follow this itinerary and be in Youghal by nightfall. But resist the temptation—select a base for two nights in two places and explore at leisure. If you are not continuing westward and return to Dublin via The Vee, Cashel, and Kilkenny, select a place to stay near Cashel or Kilkenny.

Leave Dublin following the N11 in the direction of Wexford. (If you have difficulty finding the correct road, follow signs for the ferry at Dun Laoghaire and from there pick up signs for Wexford.) As soon as the city suburbs are behind you, the road becomes a dual carriageway. Watch for signs indicating an exit signposted **Enniskerry** and **Powerscourt Gardens**. Follow the winding, wooded lane to Enniskerry and bear left in the center of the village: this brings you to the main gates of Powerscourt Gardens. As you drive through the vast, parklike grounds, the mountains of Wicklow appear before you, decked in every shade of green. Powerscourt House was burnt to a ruin in 1974: a rook's nest blocked one of the chimneys, and when a fire was lit in the fireplace, the resultant blaze quickly engulfed this grand home. Restoration is under way and while there are no grand rooms to visit, you can enjoy refreshments at the restaurant and shopping at the Avoca knitwear store. The gardens descend in grand tiers from the ruined house, rather as if descending into a bowl—a mirror-like lake sits at the bottom. Masses of roses adorn the walled garden and velvet, green, grassy walks lead through the woodlands. Many visitors are intrigued by the animal cemetery with its little headstones and inscriptions—not an uncommon sight in Irish stately homes. (*Open mid-Mar–Oct, tel: 01 204 6000, email: gardens@powerscourt.ie, website: www.powerscourt.ie/gardens.*) Leaving the car park, turn left for the 6-kilometer drive to the foot of **Powerscourt Waterfall**, the highest waterfall in Ireland and a favorite summer picnic place for many Dubliners.

Turn to the left as you leave the waterfall grounds to meander along narrow country lanes towards **Glencree**. As you come upon open moorland, take the first turn left for the 8-kilometer uphill drive to the summit of **Sally Gap**. This road is known as the old military road because it follows the path that the British built across these wild

Powerscourt Gardens

mountains to aid them in their attempts to suppress the feisty men of County Wicklow. Neat stacks of turf are piled to dry in the sun and the wind. Grazing sheep seem to be the only occupants of this vast, rolling moorland. Below **Glenmacnass Waterfall** the valley opens up to a patchwork of fields beckoning you to **Laragh** and Glendalough.

Glendalough, a monastic settlement of seven churches, was founded by St. Kevin in the 6th century. After St. Patrick, St. Kevin is Ireland's most popular saint. He certainly picked a stunning site in this wooded valley between two lakes to found his monastic order. Amidst the tilting stones of the graveyard, the round tower—still perfect after more than a thousand years—punctuates the skyline. A 15-minute movie and display on the history of the area is available at the Interpretive Centre. (*Open all year, tel: 0404 45325.*) Take time to follow the track beyond Glendalough to the Upper Lake (you can also drive there). Tradition has it that St. Kevin lived a solitary life in a hut near here. Farther up on a cliff face is a cave known as St. Kevin's Bed. Here, so the story goes,

Kathleen, a beautiful temptress, tried to seduce the saint who, to cool her advances, threw her into the lake.

Retrace the road to Laragh, turn right, and travel south through the village of Rathdrum where sturdy stone cottages line the street and continue across the crossroad following signposts for **Avondale House**, the home of Charles Stewart Parnell. Parnell was born into the ruling Anglo-Irish gentry but, due in part to the influence of his more open-minded mother, an American, he became the leading light in Ireland's political fight for independence. His downfall was his long-term affair with a married English lady. The house is sparsely furnished and takes just a few minutes to tour. You can also wander around the estate with its wonderful trees. (*Open mid-Mar–Oct, tel: 0404 46111.*)

Leave Avondale to the left and you soon join the main road that takes you through the **Vale of Avoca** to the "Meeting of the Waters" at the confluence of the rivers Avonmore and Avonbeg. Detour into **Avoca** to visit the **Avoca Handweavers**. You are welcome to wander amongst the skeins and bobbins of brightly-hued wool to see the weavers at work and talk to them above the noise of the looms. An adjacent shop sells tweeds and woolens. (*Open daily all year, tel: 01 286 7466.*)

At **Arklow** join the N11, a broad, fast road taking you south through Gorey and Ferns to **Enniscorthy**. Amidst the gray-stone houses built on steeply sloping ground by the River Slaney lies a Norman castle. Rebuilt in 1586, the castle houses a folk museum that includes exhibits from the Stone Age to the present day, with the emphasis on the part played by local people in the 1798 rebellion against English rule. (*Open all year, tel: 054 35926.*)

On the outskirts of Wexford take the N25 in the direction of Waterford. Before reaching **New Ross** the N25 merges with the N30 where you turn left for Arthurstown and the **John F. Kennedy Park**. The great-grandfather of American President John F. Kennedy emigrated from nearby Dunganstown, driven from Ireland by the terrible potato famine of the 1840s. Row upon row of dark evergreens stand before you like an honor guard to the slain president as you climb to the panoramic viewing point atop Slieve Coillte. (*Open all year, tel: 051 388171.*)

Return to the main road and continue south to **Arthurstown** (see listing) where the **Passage East ferry** takes you across the estuary to **Passage East**, the tiny village on the western shores of Waterford harbor. Arriving at the N25, you turn right to visit the town of **Waterford** (see listings) fronting the River Suir, and left to arrive at the **Waterford Crystal Factory**. This is a very worthwhile excursion as the tours give you an appreciation for why these hand-blown and -cut items are so expensive. It takes many years to become a master craftsman and one little mistake in the intricate cutting means the painstaking hours of work are wasted and the item is simply smashed and recycled— there are no seconds (Waterford crystal items are uniformly priced throughout the country). While appointments are not necessary, if you are visiting in the busy summer months, either arrive at 9 am or make a tour reservation in advance and avoid waiting while seemingly endless coachloads of tourists go ahead of you. I thoroughly enjoyed touring with a guide (weekends) but the weekday tours have the advantage of enabling you to go at your own pace and linger beside skilled workmen. The showroom displays the full line of Waterford's production from shimmering chandeliers to glassware. The visitors' center also has a gift shop, tourist information center, and café. (*Open daily, tel: 051 373311, fax: 051 356821.*)

If the weather is inclement, stay on the N25 in the direction of Cork but otherwise meander along the coast road by doubling back in the direction of Waterford for a **very short** distance, turning to the right to **Tramore**, a family holiday town, long a favorite of the "ice-cream-and-bucket-and-spade" brigade. Skirting the town, follow the beautiful coastal road through **Annestown** (see listing) to **Dungarven**.

Where the coastal road meets the N25, make a detour from your route, turning sharp left to **Shell House**. Like it or hate it, there is nothing quite like it on any suburban street in the world—a cottage where all available wall surfaces are decorated with colored shells in various patterns.

Returning to the main road after crossing Dungarven harbor, the N25 winds up and away from the coast, presenting lovely views of the town and the coast. If you haven't eaten, try **Seanachie** (a restored thatched farmhouse, now a traditional restaurant and bar) which sits atop the hill and serves good Irish and Continental food.

After passing through several kilometers of forests, turn left on the R673 to **Ardmore**, following the coastline to the village. Beyond the neatly painted houses which cluster together lies the **Ardmore Monastic Site**. The well-preserved round tower used to have six internal timber landings joined by ladders, and at the top was a bell to call the monks to prayer or warn of a hostile raid. The round tower is unique to Ireland, its entrance door placed well above the ground: entry was gained by means of a ladder which could be drawn up whenever necessary. Early Christian monks built round towers as protection against Vikings and other raiders. Leaving the ruins, turn left in the village for **Youghal** (see listing) where this itinerary ends. Sightseeing in Youghal is outlined in the following itinerary. From Youghal you can continue west to follow *The Southwest* itinerary, or take the following alternative route back to Dublin via The Vee, Cashel, and Kilkenny.

Youghal

ROUTE FROM YOUGHAL TO DUBLIN VIA THE VEE, CASHEL, AND KILKENNY

From Youghal retrace your steps towards Waterford to the bridge that crosses the River Blackwater and turn sharp left (before you cross the river) on **Blackwater Valley Drive**, a narrow road which follows the broad, muddy waters of the Blackwater through scenic wooded countryside. The "drive" is well signposted as "Scenic Route." Quiet country roads bring you into **Lismore**. Turn left into town and right at the town square. Cross the river and take the second road to the left, following signs for **Clogheen** and **The Vee**. As the road climbs, woods give way to heathery moorlands climbing to the summit where the valley opens before you—a broad "V" shape framing an endless patchwork of fields in every shade of green.

Continue on to **Cahir Castle**, which has stood on guard to defend the surrounding town of **Cahir** since 1375. A guided tour explains the elaborate defensive system, making a visit here both interesting and informative. A separate audio-visual presentation provides information about the castle and other monuments in the area. (*Open Oct–May, closed Mon, tel: 052 41011.*)

Leaving the castle, continue through the town square for the 16-kilometer drive to **Cashel**. The **Rock of Cashel** seems to grow out of the landscape as you near the town and you can see why this easily defensible site was the capital for the kings of Munster as long ago as 370 A.D. In the course of converting Ireland to Christianity, St. Patrick reached the castle and, according to legend, jabbed his staff into the king's foot during the conversion ceremony. The king apparently took it all very stoically, thinking it was part of the ritual. Upon reaching the summit of the rock, you find a 10th-century round tower, a 13th-century cathedral, and a 15th-century entrance building or Hall of Vicars Choral, a building which was sensitively restored in the 1970s and now houses some exhibits including St. Patrick's Cross, an ancient Irish high cross of unusual design. (*Open all year, tel: 062 61437.*)

If you overnight in or near Cashel, be sure to enjoy **Brú Ború**, a foot tapping evening of traditional Irish entertainment in the theater below the Rock. (*Jun–Sep, Tue–Sat, 9 pm,*

Rock of Cashel

tel: 062 61122, fax: 062 62700.) As an alternative to the show and dinner package, enjoy dinner next door at **Legends Restaurant** (see listing) and then go on to the show.

Leave Cashel on the N8 for the 40-kilometer drive northeast to **Urlingford** where you bear right through **Freshford** (see listing) for the 27-kilometer drive to **Kilkenny** (see listing). Kilkenny is quite the loveliest of Irish towns and it is easy to spend a day here sightseeing and shopping. Entering the town, turn left at the first traffic lights along the main street and park your car outside the castle.

Kilkenny Castle was originally built between 1195 and 1207. The imposing building as it now stands is a mixture of Tudor and Gothic design and is definitely worth a visit. The east wing picture gallery is flooded by natural light from the skylights in the roof and displays a collection of portraits of the Ormonde family, the owners of Kilkenny Castle from 1391 until 1967. (*Open all year, tel: 056 21450.*)

Opposite the castle entrance, the stables now house the **Kilkenny Design Centre**, a retail outlet for goods of Irish design and production: silver jewelry, knits, textiles, furniture, and crafts.

Undoubtedly the best way to see the medieval buildings of Kilkenny is on foot. A walking tour starts from the tourist office in the **Shee Alms House** just a short distance from the castle. Stroll up High Street into Parliament Street to **Rothe House**. The house, built in 1594 as the home of Elizabethan merchant John Rothe, is now a museum depicting how such a merchant lived. You should also see **St. Canice's Cathedral** at the top of Parliament Street. The round tower dates from the 6th century when St. Canice founded a monastic order here. Building began on the cathedral in 1251, though most of the lovely church you see today is an 1864 restoration.

Alleyways with fanciful names such as The Butter Slip lead you from the High Street to St. Kieran Street where you find **Kylters Inn**, the oldest building in town. This historic inn has a lurid history—supposedly a hostess of many centuries ago murdered four successive husbands, was then accused of witchcraft, and narrowly escaped being burnt at the stake by fleeing to the Continent.

This is an area noted for its craftspeople (leatherworkers, potters, painters) and culinary artists, which means that the surrounding villages have a plethora of restaurants and craft shops that make this a very interesting area in which to spend several days. I always head for the **Nicholas Mosse Pottery** in Bennetsbridge where you can purchase quality seconds as well as watch skilled potters making and decorating this classic spongewear. (*Open all year, tel: 056 27105, fax: 056 27491, website: www.nicholasmosse.com.*)

The Southwest

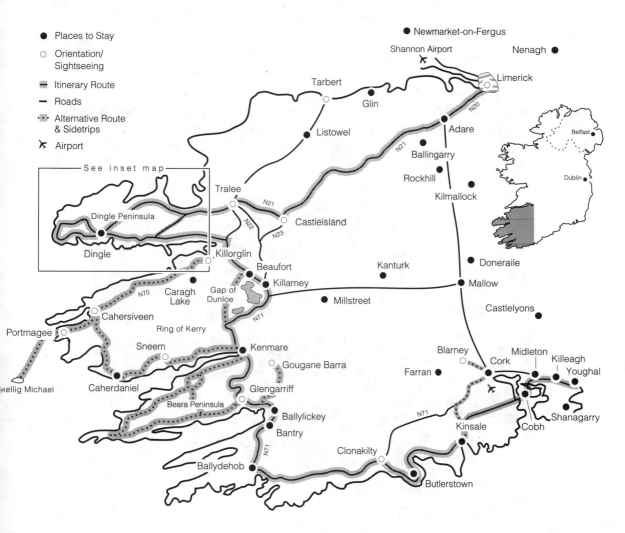

- ● Places to Stay
- ○ Orientation/ Sightseeing
- ▨ Itinerary Route
- — Roads
- ▧ Alternative Route & Sidetrips
- ✈ Airport

See inset map

Newmarket-on-Fergus

Shannon Airport

Nenagh

Limerick

Tarbert

Glin

Adare

Listowel

Ballingarry

Rockhill

Kilmallock

Tralee

Dingle Peninsula

Dingle

Castlelsland

Killorglin

Beaufort

Killarney

Kanturk

Doneraile

Caragh Lake

Gap of Dunloe

Mallow

Millstreet

Castlelyons

Cahersiveen

Ring of Kerry

Portmagee

Sneem

Kenmare

Gougane Barra

Blarney

Cork

Midleton

Killeagh

Youghal

Skellig Michael

Caherdaniel

Farran

Beara Peninsula

Glengarriff

Cobh

Shanagarry

Ballylickey

Bantry

Kinsale

Clonakilty

Ballydehob

Butlerstown

Belfast

Dublin

41

The Southwest

The scenery of the southwest is absolutely magnificent: the mellow charm of Kinsale Harbor, the rugged scenery that winds you towards Glengarriff and its island filled with subtropical vegetation, the pretty 19th-century town of Kenmare, the translucent lakes of Killarney, and the ever-changing light on spectacular seascapes on the Dingle Peninsula. Relish the fabled beauties of this lovely part of Ireland. Take time to detour to Blarney to take part in the tradition of climbing atop Blarney Castle to kiss the stone that is said to confer "the gift of the gab." Do not hurry: allow time to linger over breakfast, enjoy a chat over a glass of Guinness, sample freshly caught salmon and scallops, and join in an evening singsong in a local pub.

Kinsale

Recommended Pacing: For this portion of the itinerary select two places to stay near the coast, one in either Kenmare or Killarney, and one in Dingle. Allow one or two nights in each spot.

Your journey to the southwest begins in **Youghal** (pronounced "yawl"). Sir Walter Raleigh, who introduced the potato and tobacco from the New World, was once its mayor. It's a pleasant old town, dominated by the clock tower, which was built in 1776 and served as the town's jail. The one-way traffic system makes it impossible to explore without parking the car and walking. Several of the Main Street shops have been refurbished, but the town still has an "ungussied-up" look to it. Make your first stop the **Heritage Centre** with its displays on the town, where you can pick up a brochure that outlines a walking tour of the old buildings.

Traveling the N25, a 30-kilometer drive brings you to the heart of **Midleton** where you find the **Jameson Heritage Centre** in the old whiskey distillery. Marvel at the world's largest pot distillery in the courtyard (capacity 143,872 liters), learn about whiskey production, visit the huge waterwheel, and be rewarded by a sample of the golden liquor. There's also a shop and café. (*Open Mar–Oct, tel: 021 631821.*)

Nearby **Cobh** (pronounced "cove") was renamed Queenstown to mark the visit of Queen Victoria in 1849 and reverted back to Cobh in 1922. There's a long tradition of naval operations here, as its large harbor is a safe anchorage. The **Cobh Experience**, an audio-visual display housed in the restored Victorian railway station, tells the story of this port. Cobh was the point of departure for many emigrants off to seek a better life in America and Australia. For many it was the last piece of Irish soil they stood on before taking a boat to a new life. The ill-fated *Lusitania* was torpedoed not far from Cobh and survivors were brought here. It was also the last port of call of the *Titanic*. There's an excellent shop and café—an enjoyable place to spend a couple of hours on a rainy day. (*Open May–Sep, tel: 021 813591, fax: 021 813595.*)

Retrace your steps a short distance to the **Carriagaloe-Glenbrook ferry**, which transports you across Cork harbor and eliminates the hassle of driving through Cork city.

A short countryside drive brings you to **Kinsale**, its harbor full of tall-masted boats. Narrow, winding streets lined both with quaint and several sadly derelict houses lead up from the harbor. Flowers abound, with small posies tucked into little baskets and overflowing windowboxes planted artistically at every turn. As well as for its floral extravaganza, Kinsale is noted as being the gourmet capital of Ireland and twelve restaurants have come together to form a good food circle. It's a pleasant pastime to check some of the menus on display as you inhale mouth-watering aromas and peek at happy people enjoying their food.

There has been a fortress in Kinsale since Norman times. A great battle nearby in 1601 precipitated the flight of the earls and sounded the death knell of the ancient Gaelic civilization. It was from Kinsale that James II left for exile after his defeat at Boyne Water. Bypassed by 20th-century events, Kinsale has emerged as a village full of character, attracting visitors who find themselves seduced by its charms.

About 3 kilometers east of Kinsale, the impressive, 17th-century **Charles Fort** stands guard over the entrance to its harbor. It takes several hours to tour the five bastions that make up the complex. The ordnance sheds are restored and hold a photographic and historical exhibition about the fort. (*Open mid-Mar–Oct, tel: 021 772263.*)

Across the estuary you see the 1603 **James Fort** where William Penn's father was governor of Kinsale, while William worked as a clerk of the Admiralty Court. Later William was given a land grant in America on which he founded the state of Pennsylvania.

SIDE TRIP TO BLARNEY

About a half-hour drive north of Kinsale lie **Blarney Castle** *and its famous tourist attraction, the* **Blarney Stone**. *Kissing the Blarney Stone, by climbing atop the keep and hanging upside-down, is said to confer the "gift of the gab." Even if you are not inclined to join in this back-breaking, unhygienic pursuit, the castle is worth a visit. (Open all year, tel: 021 385252.)* **Blarney Castle House** *next door has been home to the Colhurst family for over a hundred years and they open up their doors in the afternoon to visitors. The light, airy rooms are furnished in exquisite taste. (Open Jun–Sep, closed Sun, tel: 021 385252.) Just up the street,* **Blarney Woolen Mills** *is an excellent place to shop for all things Irish, particularly knitwear.*

Blarney

Leave Kinsale along the harbor, cross the River Bandon, and follow country lanes to the sleepy little village of **Ballinspittle**. As you drive through the village, it is hard to imagine that in 1985 it was overwhelmed by pilgrims. They came to the village shrine after a local girl reported seeing the statue of the Virgin Mary rocking back and forth. You pass the shrine on your right just before you come to the village. Follow country lanes to **Timoleague**, a very small coastal village watched over by the ruins of a Franciscan abbey, and on to the N71 and **Clonakilty** and **Skibbereen**. As you travel westwards, rolling fields in every shade of green present themselves.

Arriving at the waterfront in **Bantry** you come to **Bantry House**. Like so many other Irish country houses, it has seen better days, but the present owner, Egerton Shelswell-White, makes visitors welcome and gives a typed information sheet, in the language of your choice, that guides you room-by-room through the house. The house has a wonderful collection of pictures, furniture, and works of art, brought together by the second Earl of Bantry during his European travels in the first half of the 19th century. In contrast to his ancestors' staid portraits, Egerton is shown playing his trombone. (*Open all year, tel: 027 50047.*)

Apart from furnishing the house, the second Earl, inspired by the gardens of Europe, laid out a formal Italian garden and a "staircase to the sky" rising up the steep terraces to the crest of the hill behind the house. If you are not up to the climb, you can still enjoy a magnificent, though less lofty view across the boat-filled bay from the terrace in front of the house. A very pleasant tea and gift shop occupies the old kitchen. One wing of the house has been renovated and modernized to provide up-market bed-and-breakfast accommodation (see listing).

In the stable block next to the house the **1796 Bantry French Armada Centre** relates the story of the French Armada's attempt to invade Ireland in 1796. It failed and a model of one of the armada's ships that sank in Bantry Bay is on display—a very interesting look at a little-known piece of Irish history. (*Open Apr–Oct, tel: 027 51796.*)

Eight kilometers north lies **Ballylickey**.

SIDE TRIP TO GOUGANE BARRA LAKE

*From Ballylickey an inland excursion takes you to **Gougane Barra Lake**, a beautiful lake locked into a ring of mountains. Here you find a small hotel where you can stop for a snack or a warming drink, and a little church on an island in the lake, the oratory where St. Finbarr went to contemplate and pray. The road to and from the lake takes you over a high pass and through mountain tunnels.*

Continue along the N71 and just before you enter **Glengarriff** turn left for the harbor to take a ferryboat for the ten-minute ride to Garinish Island, a most worthwhile trip. (*Harbour Queen Ferryboats, tel: 027 63116, fax: 027 63298.*) **Garinish Island**, once a barren rock where only gorse and heather grew, was transformed into a miniature botanical paradise at the beginning of this century by a Scottish politician, Arran Bryce. The sheltered site of the island provides perfect growing conditions for trees, shrubs, and flowers from all over the world. It took a hundred men over three years to sculpt this lovely spot with its formal Italian garden, caseta, and temple. (*Open Apr–Oct, closed Sat, tel: 027 63081.*)

From Glengarriff the road winds upwards and, glancing behind, you have a spectacular view of **Bantry Bay** lying beyond a patchwork of green fields. Rounding the summit, the road tunnels through a large buttress of rock and you emerge to stunning views of sparse, rocky hillsides.

Cross the River Kenmare into **Kenmare**. This delightful town of gray-stone houses, with gaily-painted shop fronts lining two broad main streets, is a favorite with tourists who prefer its peace and charm to the hectic pace of Killarney. Kenmare is full of excellent shops: **Cleo's** has outstanding knitwear, **Quills** has vast quantities of woolens, **Brenmar Jon** sells top-of-the-line fine knitwear, **The Craft Shop** offers souvenirs and pottery, and **Nostalgia** offers antique and new linen and lace. The town also has some delightful restaurants: **The Purple Heather**, a daytime bistro, **Packies**, a lively restaurant, the charming **Lime Tree** restaurant in the Old Schoolhouse, and **The Park Hotel** with its opulent afternoon silver-service teas and superb restaurant. Visit the **Heritage Centre** with its displays of locally made lace (*tel: 064 41233*). Just a short walk from the Heritage Centre, the **Kenmare Stone Circle** is the largest in the southwest of Ireland. Walks abound, from strolling along the broad river estuary to strenuous hill hikes. Kenmare is a perfect base for exploring both the Iveragh (Ring of Kerry) and Beara peninsulas and for visiting Killarney. It also serves as a stepping-off point for a side trip to Skellig Michael.

SIDE TRIP TO THE BEARA PENINSULA

*If you do not stop along the way, it will take you between two and three hours to drive the **Beara Peninsula** where the scenery is wild, but gorgeous. From Kenmare a minor road (R571) takes you along the north shore of the peninsula to **Ardgroom**, a picturesque village nestling beside a little harbor at the foot of the mountains. Farther west, **Eyeries** village looks out over the Skellig Rocks and several rocky inlets. Behind the village, the mountain road rises up through the Pass of Boffickle for a fantastic view back over the bay. In the 19th century **Allihies** was a center of the copper-mining industry, but now it is a resort with a magnificent beach curving along the bay. At the most westerly point of the peninsula lies **Garinish** where a cable car takes visitors over to **Dursey Island**.*

Dursey is a long, mountain island encircled by high cliffs. Offshore are several other islands, the most interesting of which is Bull Rock, a roosting place for gannets. A cave passes right through it, creating a massive rock arch.

*Skirting the southern shore of the peninsula, the narrow road hugs the ocean through **Castletownbere** and **Adrigole** from where you can follow the coastal road into Glengarriff or take the opportunity for a spectacular view by turning left and ascending the **Healy Pass**. It's hard to turn and admire the vista of **Bantry Bay** as the road gently zigzags up the pass, so stop at the top to relish the view before continuing down to **Lauraugh**, where you turn right for Kenmare.*

The Southwest

SIDE TRIP TO IVERAGH PENINSULA—RING OF KERRY

Instead of following the itinerary, you can use the Ring of Kerry as a route to Dingle or Killarney, or as a daytrip from Kenmare to Kenmare—you will have traveled the complete "Ring" if you go from Kenmare to Kenmare.

*The drive round the **Iveragh Peninsula** is, in my opinion, somewhat overrated, but if you want to see the much-publicized **Ring of Kerry**, hope that the fickle Irish weather is at its best, for when mists wreathe the Ring, it takes a lot of imagination to conjure up seascapes as you drive down fog-shrouded lanes. Even if the weather is dull, do not lose heart because at any moment the sun could break through. Driving the Ring can be a trial during the busy summer months when the roads are choked with tourist coaches but your trip will be more enjoyable if you take advantage of some local knowledge before starting your journey. The coaches leave Killarney between 10 and 11 am and travel around the Ring in an anticlockwise direction, arriving back in Killarney by 5 pm. I prefer to meet the coaches head on (see below) rather than inhale their exhaust fumes and suggest an early start to meet them later in the day. If you prefer to avoid them totally, make an early start, travel anticlockwise, and make certain that you are beyond Killarney before 9:30 am.*

*Beginning the Ring, a pleasant drive takes you along the Kenmare river estuary and you get tempting glimpses of water and the Beara Peninsula. Arriving at **Sneem**, enjoy the most picturesque village on the Ring, with its tiny, gaily painted houses bordering two village greens. (The most beautiful coastal scenery lies between Sneem and Waterville.)*

*Continuing your journey westward you come to **Caherdaniel** village where you turn left for **Derrynane House**, the home of Daniel O'Connell "The Liberator," a title he earned for winning Catholic emancipation. If the weather is inclement, concentrate on the house with its furnished rooms, audio-visual presentation, museum, and tea rooms. But if the weather is fine, spend your time outdoors walking along the sandy beach of Derrynane Bay and crossing the narrow strip of sand that separates the mainland from **Abbey Island** where St. Fionan founded a monastic order over 1,000 years ago. Just round the* point lies **Iskeroon** (see listing) and **Bunavalla** pier where boats leave for the Skellig Islands (see "Side Trip to Skellig Michael"). A panoramic view of Derrynane Bay can be enjoyed form the **Scariff Inn**—you cannot miss the landmark bright-yellow pub sitting beside the road three kilometers above the seashore.

Cresting the Coomakesta Pass, you turn north for **Waterville**, an aptly named town surrounded by water. Its main street with several colorfully painted houses is built along the shore. From here a pleasant drive takes you to **Cahersiveen,** a classic Irish town with a long main street made up of shops and pubs. Onwards you go to **Killorglin** and thence to **Killarney** and back to **Kenmare** (see Kenmare to Killarney drive on next page). However, our suggested route for your return to Kenmare is to take a right-hand turn to **Caragh Lake** (5 kilometers before your reach Killorglin) and follow the narrow lanes around this beautiful lake and across the rugged **Macgillycuddy's Reeks** (Ireland's highest mountains) to Blackwater Bridge (on the Ring) and Kenmare—a trip to be undertaken only on a clear day.

SIDE TRIP TO SKELLIG MICHAEL

Skellig Michael is a very special place, a rocky island topped by the ruins of an ancient monastery lying 12 kilometers off the coast of the Ring of Kerry. Boats run daily between Easter and October and you need to call at least two days in advance to make a reservation. However, the trip to the island cannot be counted upon until the actual day because it depends on calm seas. Boat service operates from several harbors on the Ring of Kerry—Bunavalla: Seamus Shea, tel: 066 9475129; Portmagee: Des Lavelle, tel: 066 9476124, fax: 066 9476309; or Brendan O'Keefe, Fisherman's Bar, tel: 066 9477103. Remember to wear flat-heeled shoes and take a waterproof jacket, an extra sweater, and lunch. The morning departure for the island and the late afternoon return necessitate your spending two nights on the Ring of Kerry (see listings Caragh Lake, Derrynane, and Kenmare).

View to Little Skellig from Skellig Michael

After you arrive at the cove beneath the looming rock, the first part of your ascent follows the path to the abandoned lighthouse, past seabirds' nests clinging to tiny crevasses in the steep rock slopes. As you round a corner, the monks' stairway appears and you climb up hundreds and hundreds of hand-hewn stone steps to the monastery perched on a ledge high above the pounding ocean. Pausing to catch your breath, you wonder at the monks who set out in fragile little boats to establish this monastery and toiled with crude implements to build these steps up the sheer rock face.

At the summit six little beehive huts, a slightly larger stone oratory, and the roofless walls of a small church nestle against the hillside, some poised at the edge—only a low stone wall between them and the churning ocean far below. The windowless interiors of the huts hardly seem large enough for a person to lie down. Remarkably, the monks' only water source was rainwater runoff stored in rock fissures. The Office of Public Works is maintaining and restoring the site and there may be someone there to impart information.

It is reputed that the monks arrived in 600 A.D. According to annals, the Vikings raided in 812 and 823 and found an established community. It is documented that the last monks departed in the 13th century. When it is time to leave this spot, you feel a sense of wonder at the men who toiled in this rocky place, enduring deprivation, hardship, and solitude to achieve a state of grace.

*As a complement (or an alternative) to visiting Skellig Michael, visit the **Skellig Heritage Centre** on Valencia Island. The center is found where the road bridge meets the island, directly opposite Portmagee. An audio-visual presentation, "The Call of the Skelligs," takes you to the Skellig Michael monastery while displays show the bird and sea life of the islands. (Open Apr–mid-Nov, tel: 066 9476306.)*

From Kenmare travel over one of Ireland's most beautiful roads (N71) for the twisty 34-kilometer drive over mountains to Killarney, stopping at **Ladies' View** to admire a spectacular panorama with the lakes of Killarney spread at your feet.

In amongst the woodlands you find the car park for **Torc Waterfall**. Following the stream, a short uphill walk brings you to the celebrated 20-meter cascade of water.

Muckross House and Gardens are 5 kilometers out of Killarney on the Kenmare road. (Be sure to choose the entrance gate that enables you to take your car to the car park beside the house). Tudor-style Muckross was built in 1843 in an enviable position beside the lake. The main rooms are furnished in splendid Victorian style and the remainder of the house serves as a folk museum with various exhibits. There's also a bustling gift shop and tea room. (*Open daily, Mar–Nov, tel: 064 31440, fax: 064 33926.*) The gardens surrounding the house are lovely, containing many subtropical plants, and there is no more delightful way to tour the grounds than by horse and trap. Take a step back in time and visit **Muckross Traditional Farms** (the entrance is on the opposite side of the car park to the house). Stroll up the lane (or ride the old bus) to visit three farms that demonstrate what Kerry farming was like in the 1930s before the advent of electricity and farming machinery. Chat with the farmers and their wives as they go about their daily work. Muckross House and its vast estate were given to the Irish nation by the Bourne family of California who had a smaller lakeside estate, Filoli, just south of San Francisco.

Believe everything you ever read about the magnificent beauty of the Killarney lakes, but realize that **Killarney**, not an attractive town, is absolutely packed with tourists during the summer season. If you would like additional views of the lakes, then a tour to Aghadoe Hill or a boat trip from Ross Castle should give you what you are looking for. Leave Killarney on the road to Tralee (N22) and turn left for the 5-kilometer drive to **Aghadoe** where Killarney town, lakes, and mountains can all be seen from this vantage point. If you prefer a close look at the lake and its island, take the 90-minute boat tour of the Lower Lake, which leaves from the jetty alongside Ross Castle. Tickets for this trip can be purchased from the tourist office in town. **Ross Castle** has been restored and you can climb its steep stone stairs to see what living in a castle was like.

SIDE TRIP UP THE GAP OF DUNLOE

*The road through the **Gap of Dunloe** (signposted from the Killorglin road just past the golf course) is a single-lane dirt track up a 6-kilometer ravine carved by glaciers. **Kate Kearney's Cottage** sits at the entrance to the ravine. Legend has it that Kate was a beautiful witch who drove men wild with desire—now her home is greatly enlarged as a coffee and souvenir shop. As you travel up the gap the dramatic setting is enhanced by the purple mountains on your left and **Macgillycuddy's Reeks** on your right.*

In the past I have recommended an evening drive up the gap to emerge on the N71 just west of Moll's Gap and returning to Killarney with a quick stop at Ladies' View to admire the unparalleled views of the lakes of Killarney. Signs have been posted to discourage motor traffic, so as alternatives I recommend that you either park your car near Kate Kearney's cottage and walk; arrange for a jaunting car to take you up the gap; or purchase a ticket at the tourist office for the Dero Tours day trip. This includes a shuttle service from your lodging to the gap, horse or jaunting car rides up the ravine, transportation by electric boat through the lakes of Killarney, and transportation back to your lodging.

Ladies' View, Killarney

The Dingle Peninsula

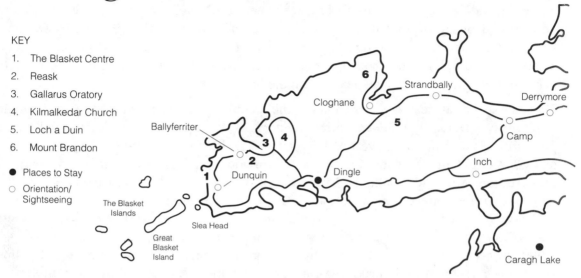

KEY

1. The Blasket Centre
2. Reask
3. Gallarus Oratory
4. Kilmalkedar Church
5. Loch a Duin
6. Mount Brandon

● Places to Stay
○ Orientation/Sightseeing

Leaving Killarney, a two-hour drive will bring you to Limerick, but rather than taking a direct route, take the time to explore the lovely **Dingle Peninsula**. It's a very special place, a narrow promontory of harshly beautiful land and seascapes where the people are especially friendly and welcoming to strangers. The road from Killarney to Dingle town takes you northwest to **Castlemaine** where you follow the coast road west through **Inch** to Dingle town, the largest settlement on the peninsula (it's only an hour-and-a-half drive from Killarney to Dingle).

Colorfully painted pubs, shops, and houses welcome you to **Dingle** (*An Daingean*) where fishing boats bob in the harbor unloading bountiful catches of fish and shellfish. It is not surprising that you find a great many excellent seafood restaurants here: **The Half Door** and adjacent **Doyle's** (see listing) are two up-market favorites. After dinner ask where you can go to hear traditional Irish music. Dingle's population is under 2,000 yet it has over 50 pubs, some of which double as shops—for example, **Dick Mack's** in Green Lane, where you can buy a pair of shoes while enjoying a drink, and **James Flahive's** cluttered, old-fashioned pub by the harbor. There are several interesting shops—**Brian de Staic's** jewelry store contains exquisite gold and silver jewelry inspired by Dingle's flora and ancient Celtic motifs. The town's most famous resident is **Fungi**, a playful bottle-nosed dolphin who took up residence in the harbor in 1985 and who loves to perform for visitors (tour boats leave from the harbor).

Plan to spend at least two nights on the peninsula to experience the beauty and tranquillity offered by the unspoiled scenery of the spectacular beaches and rocky promontories that lie to the west of Dingle town. Take time to wander along the beaches or walk along the lanes where fuchsia hedges divide the fields and friendly locals wave a salute of welcome and to take the trip to the Blasket Islands. Because Irish is the official language of the peninsula, signposts are in Irish (though commercial maps are in English) so we give the Irish in parentheses to aid you in finding your way. We outline a route that will take you on a half-day drive around Slea Head but for a real appreciation of the 2,000 archaeological sites of the Dingle Peninsula (peppered with lots of interesting stories) we recommend forsaking your car and taking one of **Sciuird's** mini-van or walking tours. Michael and his dad Timothy offer tours that range from an hour's walk round Dingle town to visiting ancient Ogham stones, wedge tombs, standing stones, and ring forts. (*Sciuird, Holyground, Dingle, Co Kerry, tel: 066 9151606, fax: 066 9151937.*)

The road to Slea Head signposted as **Slea Head Drive** (*Ceann Sléibhe*) twists and turns, following the contours of the increasingly rocky coast. Stunning seascapes present themselves, demanding that you pause just to admire the view. Several of the farms along the way have beehive stone huts and for a small fee the farmers will let you climb up to visit them. Conjecture has it that these small huts were used by early pilgrims traveling the St. Brendan's pilgrimage route. A large white crucifix marks **Slea Head**, which affords the first view of the **Blasket Islands** (*Na Blascaodaí*), alternately sparkling like jewels in the blue ocean and disappearing under dark clouds a moment later.

Around the point the scattered village of **Dunquin** (*Dún Chaoin*) and the **Blasket Island Centre** come into view. The building is impressive, with exhibits lining a long corridor that leads to an observatory overlooking the island's abandoned village. Remarkably, this tiny, isolated island abode produced an outpouring of music and writing. Three classics of Irish literature emerged with Peig Sayers' *Peig,* Thomas Crohan's *The Islandman*, and Maurice O'Sullivan's *Twenty Years a'Growing.* The islands have been uninhabited since 1953 when the last islanders evacuated their windswept homes. The center's large, airy dining room serves food and provides enticing island views. (*Open all year, tel: 066 9156444.*)

Before you visit the center, park on the cliff-top (opposite the two yellow bungalows) and walk down to **Dunquin's pier**, which sits away from the scattered village and is reached by a steep path that zigzags down the cliff. As you round the last twist, you see curraghs turned upside down looking like giant black beetles stranded high above the water line. Curraghs are fragile boats made of tarred canvas stretched over a wooden skeleton. St. Brendan is reputed to have discovered America in such a boat. In clear weather a ferry takes day-trip visitors to and from **Great Blasket Island**. The little village on the island is mostly in ruins and paths wander amongst the fields where the hardy islanders struggled to earn a living—a café offers the only shelter. (*Ferry sails every hour 10 am–6 pm in summer, tel: 066 9156444.*)

On the road to **Ballyferriter** (*Balle an Fheirtearaigh*), an attractive little village with a couple of pubs and a little museum, the pottery of **Louis Mulcahy** makes an interesting stop. Shortly after the pottery (just beyond Bracks pub) watch for a small signpost indicating a right-hand turn to **Reask** (*Riasc*), an ancient monastic settlement with its large slab cross, foundations of beehive huts, and slab stone with a contract ring, a small hole through which people touched fingers to seal agreements.

Returning to the main road, a short drive brings you to the **Gallarus Oratory** (*Séipéilín Ghallarais*). Over 1,000 years ago many of St. Brendan's contemporaries lived on the Dingle Peninsula in unmortared, beehive-shaped stone huts called clochans. The most famous example is the Gallarus Oratory, a tiny church built not as a circle, but in the shape of an upturned boat. It has a small window at one end, a small door at the other, and is as watertight today as when it was built over 900 years ago. The little visitors' center shows a video and has a café.

Arriving in the nearby village of **Múirioch,** turn right at the Y for **Kilmalkedar Church** (*Séipéal Chill Mhaolcéadair*). This now-roofless place of worship was built in the 12th century on the site of a 7th-century church. However, it dates back even further, for within the graveyard is a magnificent early-Christian cross, an ancient Ogham stone, and an intricately decorated sundial. Within the church stands a rare alphabet stone, which the monks used for teaching the alphabet. Locals refer to the little slit east window as the eye of the needle and folklore has it that if you climb through the window, you will surely marry within a year and a day.

Continuing uphill, the field to your right contains the ruins of the Chancellor's house. Park your car by the gate on the right that follows the little lane (not signposted) and walk into the farmer's field to examine the waist-high foundations of the **Caher Dorgan** *(Cathar Dairgáin)* ring fort with its beehive huts. On a clear day you get a magnificent view of the Three Sisters, a line of three mountains that tumble into the sea.

Cresting the rise, you travel 5 kilometers of the Dingle Peninsula's straightest road, known as *An Bóthar Fada*—The Long Road. It must have seemed a very long road for farmers walking to town. In the distance the entrance to Dingle's harbor is guarded by **Esk Tower**, built in 1847 by an English landlord to give paid work to the men of Dingle. Its giant wooden hand serves as a marker for fishermen to the entrance to the protected harbor.

NOTE: If you get lost on the peninsula's little lanes, ask a friendly local or follow signposts for *An Daingean*, Dingle town.

There are lots of interesting walks on the Dingle Peninsula. Two of the more unusual ones are following the **Way of St. Brendan** and exploring the **Loch a Duin Valley**. The Way of St. Brendan is laid out on a map that you obtain at **Cloghane's** tiny tourist office.

The route begins in nearby Brandon and follows a well-marked route that the saint supposedly took to the top of Mount Brandon (about five hours of walking). Cloghane's tourist office also sells a booklet that takes you on a self-guided tour through the Loch a Duin Valley (Sciuird also leads a walking tour). Beginning at the hut beside the road at the bottom of Connor Pass, this route leads you on a well-marked three-hour walk through the valley's boglands. Structures associated with prehistoric habitation (2,000 B.C.), ritual, and agriculture, along with several kilometers of prehistoric field wall, still survive. The valley is also of interest to birdwatchers, botanists, and geologists.

Leaving the Dingle Peninsula (signposted Tralee), the **Connor Pass** twists you upward to the summit where a backward glance gives you a magnificent view of Dingle and its harbor. The view is spectacular, but there is no guarantee that you will see it—all will be green fields and blue sea and sky until the mists roll in and everything vanishes. Follow the coast road through **Ballyduff, Stradbally**, and **Camp** to **Tralee**. (If you are heading for the Cliffs of Moher, take the N69 to the **Tarbert ferry**, which takes you across the River Shannon.) At Tralee you join the main road (N21) for the drive to **Castleisland** and on to **Adare** with its charming row of thatched cottages and tree-lined streets. Less than an hour's drive will find you in **Limerick** whose traffic-crowded streets can be avoided by taking the ring road signposted Ennis and Shannon Airport.

Dingle

The West

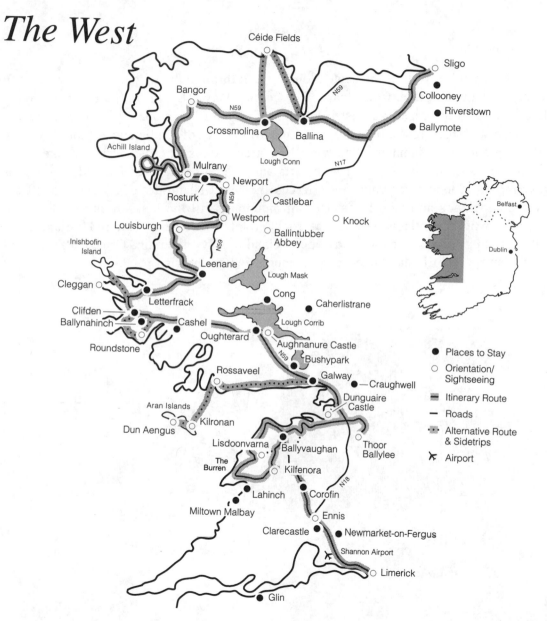

- Céide Fields
- Sligo
- Bangor
- Collooney
- N59
- Riverstown
- Crossmolina
- Ballina
- Ballymote
- Achill Island
- Mulrany
- Newport
- Lough Conn
- N17
- Rosturk
- N59
- Castlebar
- Westport
- Knock
- Louisburgh
- Ballintubber Abbey
- Inishbofin Island
- N59
- Leenane
- Lough Mask
- Cleggan
- Cong
- Caherlistrane
- Letterfrack
- Lough Corrib
- Clifden
- Ballynahinch
- Cashel
- Oughterard
- Aughnanure Castle
- Roundstone
- Bushypark
- N59
- Rossaveel
- Galway
- Craughwell
- Aran Islands
- Dunguaire Castle
- Dun Aengus
- Kilronan
- Lisdoonvarna
- Ballyvaughan
- Thoor Ballylee
- The Burren
- Kilfenora
- Lahinch
- Corofin
- Miltown Malbay
- Ennis
- Clarecastle
- Newmarket-on-Fergus
- N18
- Shannon Airport
- Limerick
- Glin

Belfast

Dublin

- Places to Stay
- Orientation/ Sightseeing
- Itinerary Route
- Roads
- Alternative Route & Sidetrips
- ✈ Airport

61

The West

This itinerary takes you off the beaten tourist track through the wild, hauntingly beautiful scenery of County Clare, Connemara, and County Mayo. Lying on the coast of County Clare, The Burren presents a vast landscape of smooth limestone rocks whose crevices are ablaze with rock roses, blue gentians, and all manner of Arctic and Alpine flowers in the spring and early summer. Otherwise there are no trees, shrubs, rivers, or lakes—just bare moonscapes of rocks dotted with forts and ruined castles, tombs, and rock cairns. Traveling to Connemara, your route traces the vast, island-dotted Lough Corrib and traverses boglands and moorlands. Distant mountains fill the horizon and guide you to the coast where gentle waves lap at rocky inlets sheltering scattered villages, and whitewashed cottages dot the landscape. Ireland's holy mountain, Croagh Patrick, and the windswept Achill Island leave a deep impression on the visitor.

Cliffs of Moher

Recommended Pacing: It is possible to tour the west in just a few days, but this beautiful area calls for you to linger. Our ideal would be one or two nights on or near The Burren, two or three nights in Connemara, and two or three nights near either Crossmolina or Sligo.

Leave **Limerick** in the direction of Ennis and Shannon airport and you soon arrive at **Bunratty Castle and Folk Park**. An interesting history and guide to the castle is available at the entrance. As the majority of castles in Ireland stand roofless and in ruins, it is a treat to visit a 15th-century castle that has been restored so beautifully. The authentic 14th- to 17th-century furniture in the rooms gives the castle a really lived-in feel. In the evenings firelit banquets, warmed with goblets of mead, whisk visitors back to the days when the castle was young. In the castle grounds a folk park contains several cottages, farmhouses, and a whole 19th-century village street of shops, houses, and buildings furnished appropriately for their era. The community is brought to life by costumed townspeople who bake, make butter, and tend the animals. (*Open daily, tel: 061 360788, fax: 061 472523.*) **Bunratty Cottage**, opposite the castle, offers a wide range of handmade Irish goods, and just at the entrance to the park is **Durty Nelly's**, one of Ireland's most popular pubs, dating from the 1600s.

Just to the northwest lies the strangest landscape in Ireland, **The Burren**. Burren means "a rocky place" and this is certainly the case for as far as the eye can see, this is a wilderness. A wilderness that is rich in archaeological sites (megalithic tombs, ring forts, and the remains of ancient huts) and strange rock formations whose tiny crevices are a mass of Arctic, Mediterranean, and Alpine flowers in springtime. Ludlow, one of Cromwell's generals, passing through the area in 1649, wrote, "There is not enough wood to hang a man, nor water to drown him, nor earth enough to bury him in."

Base yourself at either **Corofin** or **Ballyvaughan** (see *Places to Stay*) to explore this unique area. To help you appreciate this unusual landscape, first visit **The Burren Display Centre** at **Kilfenora**, which offers a 15-minute lecture and 10-minute film on the geology and rare flora and fauna of the area. Models explain the pattern of settlement and the geological makeup of the area and silk flowers show the non-botanist what to look for. Next to the display center an old churchyard contains some interesting high crosses with symbolic carvings.

Turn right as you leave the interpretive center and left as you come to the main road to reach the **Cliffs of Moher**, the most spectacular section of the coastline, where towering cliffs rise above the pounding Atlantic Ocean. These majestic cliffs stretching along 5 kilometers of the coast are one of Ireland's most popular sights. The cliffs face due west which means that the best time to see them is on a bright summer evening. The visitors' center offers welcome shelter on cool and windy days. A short distance from the visitors' center, **O'Brien's Tower** (built in 1835 by Sir Cornelius O'Brien, Member of Parliament, for "strangers visiting the magnificent scenery of this neighborhood") marks the highest and most photographed point along the clifftops.

On leaving the cliffs, head north towards, but not into, Lisdoonvarna and follow the coastal road around Black Head where the rocky Burren spills into Galway Bay to Ballyvaughan where you turn right following signs for the **Ailwee Caves** on the bluff above you. The visitors' center is so cleverly designed that it is hard to distinguish it from the surrounding gray landscape. Beneath the eerie moonscape of The Burren lie vast caves, streams, and lakes. You can take a tour through a small section of these underground caverns. The first cave is called Bear Haven because the bones of a brown bear that died long ago were found here. In other chambers you see limestone cascades, stalactites, and stalagmites before the tour ends at the edge of an underground river. Remember to dress warmly, for it's cool in the caves. (*Closed Jan–Feb, tel: 065 7077036.*)

Retrace your steps a short distance down the road towards Ballyvaughan and take the first turn left, passing Gregans Castle hotel and up Corkscrew Hill, a winding road that takes you from a lush green valley to the gray, rocky landscape above. Take the first turn to the left and you come to **Cahermacnaghter**, a ring fort that was occupied until the

18th century. You enter via a medieval two-story gateway, and the foundations of buildings of similar date can be seen inside the stone wall.

Some 7 kilometers farther south, you come to another ring fort, **Ballykinvarga**. You have to walk several hundred meters before you see the Iron-Age fort surrounded by its defensive pointed stones known as *chevaux de frise*, a term derived from a military expression describing how Dutch Frisians used spikes to impede attackers. Ireland has three other such forts, of which the two most impressive are found on the Aran Islands.

When you leave The Burren head directly for the coast and follow it east (N67) to **Kinvarra**, a pretty village with boats bobbing in the harbor and small rocky islands separating it from the expanse of Galway Bay. On the outskirts of the village, the restored **Dunguaire Castle** has a craft shop and on summer evenings hosts medieval banquets. (*Open May–Oct, tel: 091 637108.*)

From the castle car park, turn towards the village and immediately take a left-hand turn (opposite the castle entrance) for the 5-kilometer drive to **Ardrahan** where you turn right on the N18, and after 6 kilometers left for the 2-kilometer drive to **Thoor Ballylee**. William Butler Yeats bought this 13th-century tower house and cottage in 1917, and it was his summer home for 11 years. The cozy thatched cottage is now a bookshop and the adjacent tea room with its three-legged bog chairs and welcoming fire provides an excellent excuse to linger over tea and scones or enjoy lunch. An audio-visual presentation tells of Yeats's artistic and political achievements. Two floors of the tower are sparsely furnished as they were in his occupancy. By pressing a green button on each room's wall you receive information and hear excerpts of his poetry. (*Open May–Sep, tel: 091 631436.*) Leaving Thoor Ballylee, retrace your steps to the N18 for a 24-kilometer drive to **Galway**.

SIDE TRIP TO THE ARAN ISLANDS

*If you are planning to visit the **Aran Islands**, take the coastal route through Spiddal to **Rossaveel** where two ferry companies operate a shuttle service to **Kilronan** on **Inishmore**, the largest of the three Aran Islands. (Aran Ferries, tel: 091 68903; Island Ferries tel: 091 561767 and 091 568903.) Until a decade or so ago, time had stood still here and the way of life and the culture of the islanders had changed little. Now their traditional dress comes out only for TV cameras and special occasions, and their traditional way of life has been replaced by a more profitable one—tourism. In the summertime more than double the population of the islands arrives on Inishmore as day-trippers. When you arrive, visit the Tourist Information Centre by the harbor to discuss the cost of horse and trap, bicycle (there are plenty of shops where you can rent bikes), and mini-bus transportation. The barren landscape is closely related to that of The Burren: sheer cliffs plunge into the pounding Atlantic Ocean along the southern coast while the north coast flattens out with shallow, rock-ringed sandy beaches. You will have no difficulty obtaining transportation to **Dún Aengus** (about 8 kilometers from the harbor), the best known of the island's stone forts, believed to date from the early Celtic period some two- to three-thousand years ago. It has sheer cliffs at its back and is surrounded by pointed boulders designed to twist ankles and skin shins. Despite the hordes of visitors scrambling over its walls and stones, Dún Aengus is remarkably well preserved. With four stone forts, stone-hut remains, high crosses, and ruined churches to examine, the archaeologically minded could spend many days with detailed map in hand exploring the islands.*

Those who are not island-bound should follow signs for Clifden (N59) around Galway. Leaving the town behind, the road is straight and well paved, but a tad bouncy if you try to go too fast. Accommodation signs for nearby Oughterard alert you to watch for a right-hand turn to **Aughnanure Castle**. Approaching the castle, you may be greeted, as we were, by a friendly family of goats snoozing on the wooden footbridge before the castle gates. Aughnanure Castle was the stronghold of the ferocious O'Flahertys who launched attacks on Galway town until their castle was destroyed by English forces in

Clifden

1572. The clan regained their castle for a period of time until wars with Cromwell and William of Orange saw them expelled again. (*Open Jun–Sep, tel: 091 552214.*) Nearby **Oughterard** (see listing) is a pleasant, bustling town ("the gateway to Connemara") whose main street has several attractive shops. A stay here affords the opportunity for fishing and exploring the island-dotted Lough Corrib by boat.

Beyond Oughterard you plunge into Connemara past the **Twelve Bens** mountains which dominate the wild, almost treeless landscape of bogs, lakes, and rivers, a landscape that is ever being changed by the dashing clouds that rush in from the Atlantic. Apart from the occasional craft shop, there are no houses until you reach **Clifden** (see listing) on the Atlantic coast (N59, 80 kilometers). Clifden is the major market town of Connemara and the home of the annual Connemara Pony Show (*third week in August*). The town presents a gay face with shopfronts painted in bright hues of red, blue, yellow, and green. Craft and tourist shops alternate with the butchers, the hardware store, pubs, and restaurants. On Market Street you find **Connemara Walking Centre** where you can buy booklets on the locale and sign up for one of the walking tours that vary from an interesting stroll through the Roundstone bogs—great walking amongst lakes full of otters and interesting plant life—to the demanding climb up one half of the great Glanhoaghan Horseshoe in the stark Twelve Bens mountains. (*Contact Michael Gibbons, Connemara Walking Centre, Island House, Market Street, Clifden, Co Galway, tel: 095 21379, fax: 095 21845, email: walkwest@indigo.ie, website: www.walkingireland.com.*)

SIDE TRIP TO ROUNDSTONE

*To the south of Clifden the road has more views of sea than land as little boats bob in rocky inlets and cottages gaze westward across tiny islands. The road passes the marshy area where Alcock and Brown crash-landed after the first transatlantic flight in 1919 (commemorated by a monument about 500 meters from the main road). Via **Ballinaboy**, **Ballyconneely**, and **Roundstone**, the sweeping seascapes that this route presents are so compelling that it is difficult to concentrate on the driving.*

SIDE TRIP TO INISHBOFIN ISLAND

*If the weather is fine, a delightful day trip can be taken to **Inishbofin Island**. The Inishbofin boat leaves from Cleggan pier at 11:30 am, returning at 5 pm (the crossing takes less than an hour). Be at **Cleggan** pier half an hour before sailing time and buy your ticket at the Pier Bar. Sailings depend on weather conditions so it's best to phone ahead to verify departure times. (Kings Ferries, Cleggan, tel: 095 44642/21520 or The Inishbofin Experience, the O'Halloran family, tel: 095 45903/45806/45831.) The boat sails into the sheltered harbor presided over by the remains of a Cromwellian castle, and you wade ashore at a cluster of houses that make up the island's main settlement. Many islanders have left in search of greener pastures and their cottages have fallen into disrepair, but those who remain eke out a hard living from the land and the sea. As you walk down lanes edged with wild fuchsias and brightly-colored wildflowers, whitewashed farmhouses appear and you see fields dotted with handmade haystacks. (Regrettably, the odd long-abandoned rusting car spoils the scene.) At the far side of the island a row of cottages fronts the beach, one of them housing a welcoming little café* *where you can have lunch or tea before walking back to the harbor to take the evening boat back to Cleggan.*

Clifden stands just outside the **Connemara National Park**, which covers 5,000 acres of mountain, heath, and bog—there are no pretty gardens or verdant woodlands. The video in the visitors' center gives a beautiful introduction to the park, which has wonderful hiking trails. If you want to tackle the smaller paths leading into the Twelve Bens mountains, consider joining one of the guided walks that begin at the visitors' center (four of the Twelve Bens, including Benbaum, the highest, are found in the park). Two signposted nature trails start at the center: one leads you through Ellis Wood while the other takes you into rougher terrain. (*Open Apr–Sep.*)

Leaving Clifden to the north, the N59 passes the much-photographed **Kylemore Abbey**. Originally built by a wealthy Englishman in the 19th century, this grand home, surrounded by greenery and fronting a lake, passed into the hands of Benedictine nuns who have a school here. You'll find ample parking (lots of coaches) and a large restaurant and gift shop. You can walk beside the lake to the abbey where in summer the library is open to visitors. In the grounds you can visit the restored Gothic chapel with its pretty sandstone interior and different-colored marble pillars. (*Open all year, tel: 095 41146.*) Follow the shore of **Killary Harbor**, the longest and most picturesque fjord in Ireland, to **Leenane**, a little village nestled at the head of the inlet. Continue along the shoreline and take the first turn to the left, signposted as a scenic route to Westport via Louisburgh. This interesting side road gently winds you along the sea lough to **Delphi**, an area of pools and loughs amongst some of the highest and wildest mountains in the west. Acres of woodlands offer shelter and there is not a bungalow in sight. The Marquis of Sligo built a lodge here in 1840 and called it "Delphi" because it reminded him of Delphi in Greece. After falling into dereliction, the house and estate were bought by the Mantles who welcome guests to their restored home (see listing under Leenane).

Leaving Delphi, the isolated mountain road takes you along the shore of **Doo Lough** at the foot of **Mweelrea Mountain** and on through wild, remote scenery to **Louisburgh**, where, turning towards Westport, the summit of the conical-shaped **Croagh Patrick** (Ireland's most famous mountain) comes into view. Swirling mists substantiate its mystical place in Irish history. It was after St. Patrick spent the 40 days of Lent atop its rocky summit in 441 that the mountain became sacred to Christians. Every year thousands of penitential pilgrims begin their climb to the oratory at the summit at dawn on the last Sunday in July, several going barefoot up the stony track. The ritual involves stopping at three stations and reciting prayers. No climbing skills are needed as it's a well-worn path to the top and on a clear day a walk to the summit affords a panoramic view across Clew Bay to Achill Island.

Nearby **Westport** lies on the shore of Clew Bay and is unique amongst Irish towns because it was built following a pre-designed plan. The architect walled the river and lined the riverside malls with lime trees and austere Georgian homes, forming a most delightful thoroughfare. There's a buzz to the town and on a sunny day you can enjoy a drink at the tables and chairs outside **Geraghtey's Bar** and **Grand Central**, on the Octagon (the heart of the town with a granite pillar in the center of the square). At **Clew Bay Heritage Centre** on Westport Quay, postcards and old photographs show the town as it was at the turn of the century. There is also a genealogical research center and a display on the maritime traditions of Westport. (*Open May–Sep, tel: 098 26852.*)

From Westport the most direct route to Sligo is by way of the broad, well-paved, fast N5, and N17. However, if the weather is clear and bright, it is a delightful drive from Westport to Sligo via **Newport**, **Achill Island**, **Crossmolina** (see listing), and **Ballina** (see listing).

Croagh Patrick

Achill Island is Ireland's largest offshore island. Traditionally the Achill islanders traveled to Scotland as migrant farmworkers during the summer, but now what population has not been enticed away by emigration remains to garner a meager living from a harsh land. This was the home of the infamous British Captain Boycott who gave his name to the English language when tenants "boycotted" him for his excessive rents during the potato famine. Today this island holds the allure that belongs to wild and lonely places: in sunshine it is glorious, but in torrential rain it is a grim and depressing place. On the island take the first turn to your left, signposted for the windswept **Atlantic Drive**, where you drive along the tops of rugged cliffs carved by the pounding Atlantic Ocean far below. The "drive" ends at **Knockmore** where scattered houses shelter from the biting winds.

Returning to Mulrany, turn north on the N59 for the 32-kilometer drive across boglands, where vast quantities of turf are harvested by mechanical means, to **Bangor** and on to **Crossmolina, Ballina,** and **Sligo**. The many sightseeing opportunities in the Sligo area are outlined in the following itinerary.

SIDE TRIP TO CÉIDE FIELDS

*From Ballina you can detour north 20 kilometers to Ballycastle and drive another 8 kilometers east to the great cliffs of **Downpatrick Head** where the Stone-Age settlements at **Céide Fields** (pronounced "kay-jeh") are being excavated. Under the peat has been unearthed the most extensive Stone-Age settlement in the world, with walls older than the pyramids, a vast site which once supported a community of over 10,000 people. Wander round a portion of the archaeological dig and enjoy an audio-visual presentation and a cup of tea in the pyramid-shaped visitors' center. (Open mid-Mar–Nov, tel: 096 43325.) The surrounding cliffs are amongst the most magnificent you will see in Ireland. Retrace your steps to Ballycastle and take the R314 through **Killala** (a workaday village whose skyline is punctuated by an ancient round tower) to **Ballina** where you turn left for **Sligo**.*

From the Sligo area you can go into Northern Ireland, continue north on the following itinerary, or return south. If you travel south, consider visiting either **Ballintubber Abbey**, a beautifully restored church dating back to 1216, or the village of **Knock**. A religious apparition seen on the gable of the village church in 1879 and some hearty promotion has led to the development of Knock as a religious pilgrimage site and a tourist venue. A giant basilica stands next to the little church, a large complex of religious souvenir shops sits across the road, and nearby Knock airport has a runway capable of providing landing facilities for large jets. Surrounded as it is by narrow country lanes, this sophisticated complex seems very out of place in rural Ireland.

The North

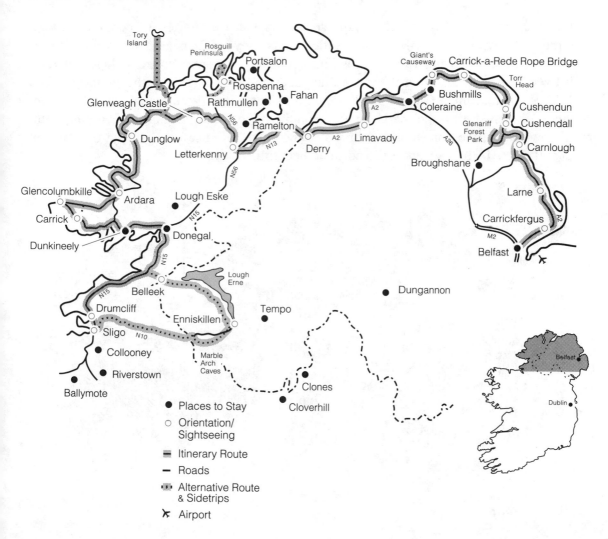

Legend:
- ● Places to Stay
- ○ Orientation/Sightseeing
- ▨ Itinerary Route
- — Roads
- ▨ Alternative Route & Sidetrips
- ✈ Airport

Map labels:
Tory Island, Rosguill Peninsula, Portsalon, Giant's Causeway, Carrick-a-Rede Rope Bridge, Rosapenna, Torr Head, Fahan, Glenveagh Castle, Rathmullen, Bushmills, Cushendun, Coleraine, Cushendall, Ramelton, Glenariff Forest Park, Dunglow, Carnlough, Letterkenny, Derry, Limavady, Broughshane, Larne, Glencolumbkille, Ardara, Lough Eske, Carrickfergus, Carrick, Dunkineely, Donegal, Belfast, Dungannon, Lough Erne, Belleek, Drumcliff, Tempo, Enniskillen, Sligo, Collooney, Marble Arch Caves, Riverstown, Clones, Ballymote, Cloverhill, Dublin

Route labels: N56, N13, N15, N10, A2, A26, A5, M2

The North

The northernmost reaches of Ireland hold special appeal. Herein lies the countryside that inspired the moving poetry of William Butler Yeats. Beyond Donegal narrow roads twist and turn around the wild, rugged coastline of County Donegal where villagers weave their tweeds and Irish is often the spoken language and that written on the signposts. The Folk Village Museum at Glencolumbkille, with its authentically furnished, thatch-topped cottages, demonstrates the harsh living conditions of the far north. Crossing into Northern Ireland, the honeycomb columns of the Giant's Causeway signpost the Antrim coast full of cliffs, lush green headlands, and beautiful views.

Dunluce Castle

The North

Recommended Pacing: Two or three nights around Sligo and Donegal, a night near Glenveagh National Park (to permit a leisurely visit), and two nights along the Antrim coast will give you time to explore this lovely area.

The county and town of **Sligo** are ever mindful of William Butler Yeats, and the whole area is promoted as being Yeats country. If you are an ardent admirer of the poet, you will want to visit the **County Museum**, which has a special section about his poetry and writing. Base yourself near the town for several days—**Ballymote**, **Riverstown**, and **Collooney** are our accommodation choices in the *Places to Stay* section. The countryside is very pretty and there is enough sightseeing to keep you busy for a week.

SIDE TRIP TO CARROWMORE AND CARROWKEEL

Seven kilometers to the southwest of Sligo town, sitting in fields on either side of a narrow country lane, are the megalithic tombs of **Carrowmore***. Wander amongst the cows and explore the little stone circles and larger dolmens reputed to be the largest Bronze-Age cemetery in Europe. Farther inland take the Boyle road (N4) 30 kilometers south of Sligo to Castlebaldwin where you turn right following signposts for Carrowkeel. At the end of a mountain track you come to* **Carrowkeel***, a 4,000-year-old passage tomb cemetery. There are 13 cairns covering passage tombs while the 14th is a long cairn. One of the tombs can be entered (backwards) and it is claimed that, on the summer solstice, the setting sun lights up the main chamber.*

SIDE TRIP AROUND LOUGH GILL

A half-day sightseeing trip from Sligo can be taken by driving around Lough Gill, visiting Parke's Castle and enjoying a meal at Markree Castle. Leave Sligo to the north and follow signposts for Enniskillen, Lough Derg, and Dromohair, which bring you to the northerly shore of **Lough Gill**. *Glimpses of the lough through the trees give way to stunning lough views as the road hugs the shore and arrives at* **Parke's Castle**, *a fortified manor house whose ramparts and cottages (tea rooms) have been restored. (Open Easter–Oct, tel: 071 64149.) In summer you can take a boat trip on the lake which takes you around* **Inishfree Island**. *Leaving the castle, follow the lough into* **Dromohair** *where you pick up the Sligo road. After 5 kilometers, when the road divides, take a single-track lane to the right, which leads you down to the lakeside where John O'Connel's rowboat is tied to the pier. He lives by the lake and is sometimes available to row you to Inishfree Island. Returning to the main road, it's a short drive to* **Collooney** *where you can partake of lunch or afternoon tea at* **Markree Castle** *(see listing).*

Leaving Sligo, travel north along the N15 to **Drumcliff Churchyard**, which has to be the most visited graveyard in Ireland—William Butler Yeats is buried here under the epitaph he composed, "Cast a cold eye on life, on death. Horseman, pass by!" In the background is the imposing **Benbulben Mountain**. Beyond the village a left turn leads to **Lissadell,** home of the Gore-Booth sisters with whom Yeats was friendly. The 1830s Greek-Revival-style house is full of curiosities and quite a sight to behold, but in need of an injection of capital to prevent its decay. The room where Yeats stayed is over the porch. While the sisters belonged to the landed gentry, Eva went on to become a poet and Constance a suffragette commander in the 1916 uprising and a minister of labor in the first Irish government. Sir Henry Gore-Booth went off with his butler to explore the Antarctic in the 1880s. (*Open intermittently, usually Jun–Sep, closed Sun, tel: 071 63150.*)

Leaving Lissadell, continue north on the N15 for the 60-kilometer drive to Donegal or follow a more circuitous route through Northern Ireland.

ALTERNATIVE ROUTE TO DONEGAL

*From Drumcliff churchyard, return towards Sligo and at **Rathcormack** turn left through the village of **Drum** to join the N16 as it travels east towards **Enniskillen**. After checking with the guard at the border post, take the first turn to your right and follow signposts to **Marble Arch Caves**. This extensive network of limestone chambers (billed as "over 300 million years of history") is most impressive. The tour includes an underground boat journey, walks through large illuminated chambers, galleries hung with remarkable stalactites, and a "Moses Walk" along a man-made passage through a lake where your feet are at the bottom of the pool and your head is at the same level as the water. Remember to dress warmly and take a sweater. It is best to telephone in advance because if there has been a lot of rain, the caves are closed. (Open Mar–Oct, tel: 01365 348855.)*

*Leaving the hilltop cave complex, follow signposts for Enniskillen for 7 kilometers to **Florence Court**, an 18th-century mansion that was once the home of the Earls of Enniskillen. The opulent mansion is elegantly furnished and famous for the impressive Rococo plasterwork on the ceilings. (Open Apr–Oct, tel: 01365 348249.) On leaving Florence Court, do **not** go into Enniskillen, but turn left onto the A46, following the scenic southern shore of **Lough Erne** for the 38-kilometer drive to Belleek.*

***Belleek**, on the far north shore of the lough, is famous for its ornate, creamy pottery: porcelain festooned with shamrocks or delicate, spaghetti-like strands woven into trellis-like plates. You can tour the visitors' center and then browse at the factory shop. (Open May–Sep.) Crossing back into the Republic, head for **Ballyshannon** and follow the wide N15 north for 23 kilometers to Donegal.*

Glencolumbkille

Donegal (see listing) is a busy, bustling place, laid out around a diamond-shaped area surrounded by shops. Donegal is one of the best places to buy tweed goods—**Magees** sells a variety—and the **Four Masters Bookshop** is a handy place to stock up on reading material. The ruins of **Donegal Castle** (open to the public), built in the 16th century by Hugh O'Donell, stand beside the Diamond.

Take the N56 west, hugging the coast, through **Dunkineely** (see listing) and **Bruckless** to **Killybegs**, Ireland's major fishing port. Large trawlers from all over the world have replaced family fishing boats in the working harbor of this most enjoyable town. As you move west from Killybegs, the roads become more difficult, the landscape more rugged, and the signposts less frequent, and, to complicate things, they are often written in Irish (Irish names are referenced in parentheses).

If the weather is fine, you can enjoy some spectacular scenery by following the brown signs that indicate a coastal route from **Kilcar** to **Carrick** (*An Charraig*) where you turn left (in the center of the village opposite the pub) for **Telin** (*Teilean*) and follow the brown signs for **Bunglar** and The Cliffs. As the narrow road winds up, down, and around the rocky, rolling landscape you see several examples of traditional Irish cottages with small thatched pony-cart barns huddled next to them. The road narrows to a single track and takes you along the very edge of the headlands to a viewpoint that overlooks the spot where the **Slieve League Cliffs** plummet into the sea. Walkers will love the magnificent walks along the headlands. This is not a trip to be taken in inclement weather.

Retrace your steps to Carrick and turn left towards **Glencolumbkille** (*Gleann Cholaim Cille*). The road enters the Owenwee Valley where you climb before descending into the glen. Drive through the scattered village to **Glencolumbkille Folk Village Museum** at the water's edge. Glencolumbkille is a very special place that gives an appreciation of the survival of a people who endured hardship, famine, and debilitating emigration. By the 1960s, emigration was threatening to turn Glencolumbkille into a ghost town. In an effort to try to create some jobs, the parish priest, Father McDyer, formed a cooperative of the remaining local residents to develop a tourist industry by building a folk museum and holiday homes and by encouraging local crafts. Tucked against a rocky hillside, the cottages that comprise the folk museum are grouped to form a traditional tiny village, or *clachan*. Each cottage is a replica of those lived in by local people in each of three successive centuries. The thick, thatched roofs are tied down with heavy rope and anchored with stones, securing them from the harsh Atlantic winds. Inside, the little homes are furnished with period furniture and utensils. Friendly locals guide you through the houses and give you snippets of local history. A handicraft shop sells Irish cottage crafts and the adjacent tea room serves oven-fresh scones and piping hot tea on lovely Irish pottery. (*Open Apr–Oct, tel: 073 30017.*)

Leaving Glencolumbkille, the narrow road climbs and dips through seemingly uninhabited, rugged countryside where the views are often obscured by swirling mists as you climb the Glengesh Pass before dropping down into **Ardara**.

The road skirts the coast and brings you to the twin fishing villages of **Portnoo** and **Nairn**, set amongst isolated beaches that truly have an "end-of-the-earth" quality about them. A short drive brings you to **Maas** whence you travel an extremely twisty road to the Gweebarra bridge which brings you to **Lettermacaward** (*Leitir Mhic An Bhaird*) and on to **Dungloe** (*An Globhan Liath*). Nearby in **Burtonport** (*Ailt An Chorain*) more salmon and lobster are landed than at any other port. From here you drive north to **Kincasslagh** and then it's on to **Annagary**, both tiny little communities that pride themselves on speaking the Irish language. A combination of wild, untamed scenery, villages that seem untouched by the 20th century, and narrow, curving roads in general disrepair gives the feeling that the passage of time stopped many years ago in this isolated corner of Ireland.

Rejoin the N56 just south of **Gweedore** (*Gaoth Dobhair*) and follow it for a short distance as it swings inland paralleling a sea loch. As the main road swings to the right, continue straight up the mountain, following a narrow, winding road that brings you across peat bogs and purple, heather-covered moorlands inhabited only by sheep to **Glenveagh National Park**, Ireland's largest, most natural, and most beautiful park. At its center lies a sheltered glen with a lake and mighty castle. The **Glenveagh Visitors' Centre** is well signposted and well disguised, being sunk into the ground with its roof camouflaged by peat and heather. There are displays, an audio-visual program, and a café (there's another at the castle) and it is here that you leave your car to take the mini-bus around the lake to **Glenveagh Castle** and its gardens. The heather and rose gardens, the rhododendrons, the laurels and pines, busts, and statues are all lovingly maintained, but the walled kitchen garden is especially memorable, with its profusion of flowers and tidy rows of vegetables divided by narrow grass walkways. Surrounding this oasis of cultivated beauty are thousands of acres of wild countryside where the largest herd of red deer in Ireland roam. Glenveagh Castle was built in 1870 by John Adair, using his American wife's money, in a fanciful Gothic design that was popular in the later part of the century. The rooms have been beautifully restored and for a small fee you can tour the house (arrive by 2 pm if you're traveling in July and August). The Glenveagh estate was sold to the nation by the castle's second owner, Henry McIlhenny, who is largely responsible for the design of the gardens. (*Open Apr–Oct, tel: 074 37090.*)

Leaving the national park, turn right across the desolate boglands and heather-clad hills—your destination is **Glebe House and Gallery** (6 kilometers away) near the village of **Churchhill**. Derek Hill gave his home, Glebe House, and his art collection to the state, which remodeled the outbuildings to display his fine collection of paintings. Among the 300 paintings are works by Picasso, Bonnard, Yeats, Annigoni, and Pasmore. The decoration in the house includes William Morris papers and textiles, Victoriana, Donegal folk art, and Japanese and Islamic art. There is a tea room in the courtyard. (*Open May–Sep, closed Fri, tel: 074 37071.*)

SIDE TRIP TO THE ROSGUILL PENINSULA AND TORY ISLAND

If you would like to experience more Donegal coastal landscape, you can do no better than tour the **Rosguill Peninsula** *whose 25-kilometer Atlantic drive traces a wild coastal route from* **Rosapenna** *through* **Downies** *and* **Doagh** *to* **Tranarossan Bay** *and back to Rosapenna. The road goes up and down, most of the time high above the ocean, then sweeps down to white sandy beaches.*

If you follow the coastal road west through **Gortahawk***, you come to* **Meenlaragh** *where you take the ferry to* **Tory Island***, a windswept island where the inhabitants eke out a hard life farming and fishing. Sailing times of the ferryboat depend on the weather. If you want to visit the island, contact the Post Office in Meenlaragh.*

Giant's Causeway

From Glebe House it is a 16-kilometer drive to **Letterkenny**. From the town, your route into Northern Ireland is well signposted to **Derry**. The N13 becomes the A2 as you cross the border and the pound sterling becomes the currency. Skirt Derry city on the **Foyle Bridge**, then follow the A2 to **Limavady** and the A37 for 21 kilometers to **Coleraine**.

Bushmills and the Giant's Causeway are well signposted from the outskirts of Coleraine. (One of the delights of traveling in Northern Ireland is that the roads are well paved and the signposting frequent and accurate.) **Bushmills** (see listing) is famous for its whiskey—a whiskey spelled with an "e"—of which Special Old Black Bush is the best. A tour of the factory demonstrates how they turn barley and water into whiskey and rewards you with a sample of the classic drink to fortify you for your visit to the nearby Giant's Causeway. (*Open weekdays*.)

In the last century the **Giant's Causeway** was thought to be one of the wonders of the world. Formed from basaltic rock, which cooled and split into regular prismatic shapes, it stepped out to sea to build an irregular honeycomb of columns some 70,000,000 years ago. More romantic than scientific fact is the legend that claims the causeway was built by the Irish giant, Finn MacCool, to get at his rival in Scotland. Do not expect the columns to be tall, for they are not—it is their patterns that make them interesting, not their size.

The first stop on a visit to the causeway is the **Giant's Causeway Centre** where the facts and legends about the causeway are well presented in an audio-visual theater. (*Open all year, tel: 028 2073 1159, email: unavsm@smtp.ntrust.org.uk.*) A mini-bus takes you to the head of the causeway where you follow the path past formations called "Honeycomb," "Wishing Well," "Giant's Granny," "King and his Nobles," "Port na Spaniagh" (where gold and silver treasure from the Spanish Armada ship *Girona* was found in 1967), and "Lovers' Leap" and up the wooden staircase to the headlands where you walk back to the visitors' center along the clifftops. (It's a 5-kilometer walk and you can truly say you have seen the causeway if you complete the circuit.)

Leaving the causeway, turn right along the coast to visit the ruins of the nearby **Dunluce Castle**, a romantic ruin clinging to a wave-lashed cliff with a great cave right underneath. This was the main fort of the Irish MacDonnells, chiefs of Antrim, and fell into ruin after the kitchen (and cooks!) fell into the sea during a storm. (*Open Apr–Sep.*)

Retrace your route down the B146 and at the causeway gates turn left along the coast road. Watch carefully for a small plaque at the side of the road pointing out the very meager ruins of **Dunseverick Castle**. Dunseverick was at the northernmost end of the Celtic road where the Celts crossed to and from Scotland.

Carrick-a-Rede Rope Bridge

Shortly after joining the A2, turn left for **Port Bradon**. The road winds down to the sea where a hamlet of gaily painted houses and a church nestles around a sheltered harbor. As you stand in front of the smallest church in Ireland, the long sandy beaches of **Whitepark Bay** stretch before you.

Farther along the coast a narrow road winds down to the very picturesque **Ballintoy Harbour**, a sheltered haven for boats surrounded by small, jagged, rocky islands. At the first road bend after leaving Ballintoy village, turn sharp left for the **Carrick-a-Rede Rope Bridge**. This is one of the famous things to do in Ireland: walk high above the sea across a narrow, swinging bridge of planks and ropes that joins a precipitous cliff to a rocky island. Hardy fishermen whose cottages and nets nestle in a sheltered cleft on the island and whose fragile wooden boats bob in the ocean below still use the bridge. (*Open mid-Apr–mid-Sep.*)

Life in the nearby holiday town of **Ballycastle** centers around the beach, fishing, and golf. Cross the river and turn onto the A2 to **Ballyvoy**. If the weather is clear, turn left for the scenic drive to Cushendun around **Torr Head**. The narrow road, barely wide enough for two cars to pass, switchbacks across the headlands and corkscrews down the cliffside, offering spectacular views of the rugged coastline and the distant Mull of Kintyre in Scotland.

Nestling by the seashore, the pretty village of **Cushendun** has a National Trust Shop, an excellent place to buy high-quality souvenirs. When you leave Cushendun, the landscape softens and the road, thankfully, returns to a more manageable width. You are now entering the **Glens of Antrim** where lush green fields and a succession of beautiful views present themselves. At **Cushendall** you can detour into **Glenariff Forest Park**, the queen of the glens with a series of waterfalls plunging down a gorge traversed by a scenic path crossing rustic bridges. Thackeray described this glen as "Switzerland in miniature." (*Open all year.*)

After your return to the coast road, **Carnlough**, a pretty seaside and fishing town, soon comes into view, its little white harbor full of bobbing boats. The **Londonderry Arms** was once a coaching inn and now is a very pleasant hotel.

Nearby **Glenarm** is the oldest of the coastal villages, dating back to the time of King John. The pseudo-Gothic castle is the home of the Earl of Antrim, part of whose demesne, **Glenarm Forest**, climbs up from the glen and is open to the public. (*Open all year.*)

Limestone cliffs present themselves as you approach **Larne**, a sizable seaport whose Viking origins are lost amongst more modern commercial developments. Wend your way through this busy port town, following the A2 to **Whitehead**. Nearby **Carrickfergus** is the oldest town in Northern Ireland. **Carrickfergus Castle**, a sturdy Norman castle overlooking the boat-filled harbor, was built as a stronghold in 1178 by John de Courcy after his invasion of Ulster, then taken by King John after a siege in 1210, fell to the Scots in 1316, and was captured by the French in 1760. Life-sized models and a film recreate the castle's turbulent past. (*Open all year.*)

Leaving Carrickfergus, a 12-kilometer drive along the A2 and M2/M1 whisks you through, or into, **Belfast** (see listings), where the A1 will take you south through **Newry** and into the Republic. Or, if you are staying near the Antrim coast for several days of leisurely sightseeing, take the M2 to the A26, which quickly returns you to that area.

Carrickfergus Castle

The North

Places to Stay

Abbeyleix is a little historic gem of a town on the main Cork to Dublin road, the perfect place to break your journey for a couple of days and enjoy Ireland's lovely Midland counties. Amongst the town's treasures is Preston House, the school established in 1834 by Joshua Preston, the M.P. for Cavan, and now a welcoming guesthouse run by the energetic Alison Dowling and her husband Michael. As you enter through the hall door, saddles and riding paraphernalia lead into the inner corridor where, above the hooks that once held pupils' coats, the wall is lined with rosettes and ribbons. The small parlor, formerly the headmaster's drawing room, is country-house cozy and the delightful guests' dining room is full of lovely antiques. A door leads through to the schoolroom, now a country café serving morning coffee, lunch, and well-priced dinners on Thursdays, Fridays, and Saturdays. Alison is as enthusiastic about her cooking as she is about her lively town and taking care of her guests, whom she arms with information on walking in the nearby Slieve Bloom Mountains. Upstairs, the four very spacious bedrooms face a tranquil garden at the back of the house. All have the modern conveniences of TV and phone, and an old-world ambiance created by antique furniture. The entire front section of the house is a huge schoolroom with a raised master dais—just the room for a hunt ball! *Directions*: Abbeyleix is on the N8, Cork to Dublin road, 16 km south of Porlaoise.

PRESTON HOUSE
Owners: Alison & Michael Dowling
Abbeyleix
Co Laois, Ireland
Tel & fax: (502) 31432
4 rooms
£30 per person B&B
Dinner: £20–£30 (not Sun–Wed)
Closed Christmas
Credit cards: MC, VS
Restaurant with rooms

This noble house with ornate Gothic façades stands amidst a vast estate separated from the charming village of Adare by a high stone wall and iron gates. It was rescued from decline by Tom and Judy Kane and transformed into a luxury resort. Built as the elaborate home of the Earls of Dunraven, the house was constructed on a massive scale with a two-story-high paneled reception, over 50 hand-carved fireplaces, and an enormous ornate gallery based on the Hall of Mirrors in Versailles. In the original manor, bedrooms and suites are baronial in size with elaborately carved marble fireplaces, king-sized beds, and seating arrangements. Bathrooms have marble floors and walls, huge tubs, and generous-sized dressing rooms. Bedrooms in the new wing are less opulent. All has been restored to reflect a luxurious, 19th-century country-house atmosphere, yet this is a mix of old and modern. On the grounds are the remains of a Franciscan priory built in 1464, the keep of a feudal castle, a pets' graveyard, and a championship golf course designed by Robert Trent Jones, Sr. Amenities include a luxurious indoor swimming pool, gymnasium, sauna, snooker room, and tack-room bar complete with Irish music. Horse riding, fishing, golf and clay-pigeon shooting are available on the estate. *Directions:* Adare Manor is in Adare, a 30-minute drive from Shannon.

ADARE MANOR
Owners: Judy & Tom Kane
Manager: Stephen Quinn
Adare
Co Limerick, Ireland
Tel: (061) 396566, Fax: (061) 396124
63 rooms
Double: £250–£500*, Dinner: £34.50*
*Plus 15% service
Open all year
Credit cards: all major
Luxury resort

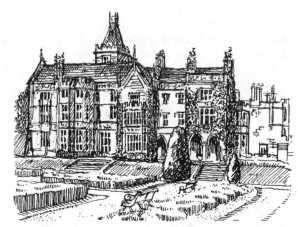

The Dunraven Arms stands on the broad main street of this storybook village. With its uniformed staff and formal restaurant it has more the feel of country house hotel than a hostelry. The hotel is smartly decorated, and attractive antique furniture adds to the old-world feeling. The large, informal bar is the gathering place for locals and residents alike, but if you want a few quiet moments, there is a snug residents' lounge with chintz-covered chairs gathered round a log fire. Request a room in the new wing that stretches down long corridors behind the inn into the peaceful garden. As well as being most attractively decorated, these new rooms enjoy immaculate modern bathrooms. The dining room has quite a reputation for its food—a laden dessert cart sits center stage and waiters hover attentively. If more informal dining is to your taste, visit the hotel's cozy restaurant, The Inn Between, in a quaint thatched cottage across the street. Enjoy the facilities of the fitness center with its swimming pool, steam room, and gymnasium. The hotel specializes in making golfing, equestrian, and fishing arrangements for guests. *Directions:* Adare is on the N21, 40 km from Shannon airport, which makes it an ideal first or last stop in Ireland if you are traveling in the southwest.

DUNRAVEN ARMS
Owners: Louis & Bryan Murphy
Adare
Co Limerick, Ireland
Tel: (061) 396633, Fax: (061) 396541
Email: dunraven@iol.ie
76 rooms
Double: £135*, Suite: £160–£200*, Dinner: £28*
*Breakfast not included: £12, plus 12½% service
Open all year
Credit cards: all major
Inn
www.karenbrown.com/ireland/dunravenarms.html

We have a file of accolades for Margaret Liston's most valued talent—she's a caring hostess who goes the extra mile when looking after her guests. Margaret's home, Glenelg House, one of the simplest lodgings in this guide, is an attractive color-washed bungalow sitting in a pretty garden facing the vast Dunraven estate 2 kilometers from the village of Adare. All is bright and airy, as spic and span inside as out. The simply decorated bedrooms include a family room with one double and one single bed, a double room, and a twin room with its private bathroom across the hall. Guests have their own sitting and breakfast rooms and Margaret is always close at hand making guests tea and scones, answering questions, and sitting down for a chat. Many guests correspond with Margaret and a great many return. Margaret always provides a fruit dish and fresh scones for breakfast as well as traditional cooked food. Breakfast is the only meal served but there is no shortage of places to eat dinner in Adare. The very popular sightseeing venue Bunratty Folk Park is about 20 minutes' drive away, Shannon airport a 30-minute drive. *Directions:* From Adare take the N21, Limerick road for 1 km to the first crossroad. Turn left at Clounanna and Glenelg is the third bed and breakfast on the left.

GLENELG HOUSE
Owner: Margaret Liston
Mondellihy
Adare
Co Limerick, Ireland
Tel: (061) 396077, Fax: none
3 rooms, 2 en suite
£23–£25 per person B&B
Closed Christmas
Credit cards: MC, VS
B&B
www.karenbrown.com/ireland/glenelg.html

Carmel Hawkins, the most hospitable of hostesses, keeps her house as neat as a new pin. When she and Liam were given this plot of land by Liam's family, they, like so many young couples in the 70s, built a bungalow. Carmel subsequently decided to offer bed and breakfast and the builder has hardly been out of the place since, building an addition to the dining room, putting in en-suite bathrooms, enlarging the bedrooms, adding bay windows. She's always at it, improving, decorating, and adding homey little touches that make this a bed and breakfast that stands out against its many competitors. The spacious, welcoming sitting room/breakfast room is well stocked with books, tea, and coffee, and guests can watch a video and learn more about the area. Bathrooms and bedrooms are very spacious—several rooms are large enough to accommodate an extra bed. All are very nicely decorated in soft pastels and Carmel has gone to a lot of trouble to add coordinating bric-a-brac, which makes them feel very cozy. Annamoe is a tiny village in the Wicklow Mountains with a shop, tearoom, antique shop, trout farm, and a scattering of houses. Just up the road is the ancient monastic settlement of Glendalough with its ruined churches and round towers. A little farther afield lie Powerscourt Gardens and the Avoca Handweavers. *Directions:* Annamoe sits between Laragh and Roundwood on the R755, 30 km due south of Dublin. Carmel's is on the east side of the road.

CARMEL'S BED & BREAKFAST   **New**
Owner: Carmel Hawkins
Annamoe, Glendalough
Co Wicklow, Ireland
Tel & fax: (0404) 45297
4 rooms
£19–£20 per person B&B
Open Mar to mid-Nov, Credit cards: none
B&B

Annestown House has a magnificent location high on the cliffs above a picture-perfect crescent of white-sand beach. This impressive 19th-century home, a cluster of cottages, and a little church comprise the village of Annestown—the only village in Ireland without a pub. Pippa, a former restaurateur, and John, whose family has been here since the 1820s, encourage guests to make themselves at home and play the grand piano in the sitting room if they wish. Guests usually congregate in the back kitchen, now a cozy little parlor with comfy chairs drawn round the fire or in the vast billiard room, browsing through the library of books between games. Guests truly do make themselves at home— I found two guests doing press-ups beside the billiard table prior to a run. The ground-floor bedroom is handy for those who have difficulty with stairs but, to get a sweeping view of the sea, request one of the upstairs bedrooms of which the Dressing Room (the largest) and Upper Room offer outstanding views. Dinner is available with 24 hours' notice. John is a keen walker and is happy to equip you with maps, or you can content yourself with a stroll along the beach. Touring the Waterford crystal factory is a great attraction. The Rock of Cashel, Kilkenny, and Lismore castle are all possibilities for day trips. *Directions:* From the roundabout outside the Waterford factory take the coast road through Tramore and on to Annestown. Annestown House is the white house on the cliff.

ANNESTOWN HOUSE
Owners: Pippa & John Galloway
Annestown
Co Waterford, Ireland
Tel: (051) 396160, Fax: (051) 396474
Email: relax@annestownhouse.com
5 rooms
£35–£40 per person B&B
Dinner: £23 (not Sun)
Open Mar to Nov
Credit cards: all major
B&B
www.karenbrown.com/ireland/annestownhouse.html

Dunbrody House boasts the springiest lawn in Ireland—I fairly bounced across it, with labrador and corgi at heel, to the headland while attempting to catch a glimpse of the charming little ferry that plies its way to Waterford across the Barrow estuary. No view of the ferry but a great view of the estuary and a chance to admire Dunbrody from its most attractive vantage point. Catherine and Kevin Dundon have transformed Dunbrody, formerly the home of the Marquis of Donegal, from a private house into a top-class hotel. Kevin produces food that is as exquisite to look at as it is gorgeous to eat—he has been executive chef at the Shelbourne Hotel and in Canada. The house is as delightful as the food, with delicious bedrooms and top-of-the-line bathrooms deserving a special mention. The house is completely wheelchair-accessible and a handicapped room is available. Stretch out your stay and try your hand at equestrian pursuits (a stable yard lies behind the house), explore the wild and beautiful Hook Peninsula, visiting Europe's oldest lighthouse, and take the ferry to Waterford and its famous crystal factory. *Directions:* From Wexford take the R733 to Arthurstown. Dunbrody House is on your left as you approach the village. If arriving from Waterford, take the Passage East Ferry to Ballyhack. Turn right off the ferry and go 2 km (through Arthurstown) to Dunbrody House which is on your right as you go up the hill.

DUNBRODY HOUSE
Owners: Catherine & Kevin Dundon
Arthurstown
Co Wexford, Ireland
Tel: (051) 389600, Fax: (051) 389601
Email: info@dunbrodyhouse.com
20 rooms
Double: £150–£190, Suite: £240
Dinner: à la carte (last orders on Sun 8 pm)
Open all year
Credit cards: all major
Country house hotel
www.karenbrown.com/ireland/dunbrody.html

The Wicklow Mountains offer some of the finest walks in Ireland and while Ballyknocken House has built its reputation on walking holidays, anyone staying here will find that Catherine Fulvio can offer whatever the individual traveler needs. Hospitality is Catherine's keynote (she learnt her trade by watching her mum and in her former career as Marketing Manager for Tinakilly House), with good baking and cooking providing the backbone for fine evening meals and decadent breakfasts. Dad runs the farm and husband Claudio, who hails from Italy, works in Dublin. Catherine has lots of ambitious plans for this delightful Victorian farmhouse but even if it has changed not a jot from when I stayed, you will find that the warm hospitality, good food, and comfortable bedrooms are just your cup of tea. The Wicklow Way, Ireland's oldest and longest hill-walking route, is close by. If you are not up to long tramps, the dogs will take you for a walk in the hills that rise behind the farm—but be sure to have directions with you as they have a habit (as I found out) of depositing you at a neighbor's farm. The remains of the monastic city of Glendalough with its round tower and seven churches are just a few kilometers away and there are spectacular gardens and houses to visit nearby. *Directions:* Take the N11 south from Dublin towards Wicklow for 42 km to Ashford village (just before Rathnew). Turn right immediately after the Texaco station up a steep hill and follow this road for almost 5 km to Ballyknocken House on your right.

BALLYKNOCKEN HOUSE   **New**
Owners: Catherine & Claudio Fulvio
Ashford, Glenealy
Co Wicklow, Ireland
Tel: (0404) 44627, Fax: (0404) 44696
Email: cfulvio@ballyknocken.com
8 rooms
£25–£29.50 per person B&B, Dinner: £18.75
Open Mar to Nov, Credit cards: MC, VS
No-smoking bedrooms & dining room
Farmhouse B&B
www.karenbrown.com/ireland/ballyknocken.html

Bagenalstown is sometimes signposted Muine Bheag, which can lead to a certain amount of confusion in reaching Kilgraney House, but the effort put into finding it is worthwhile, for this is not your run-of-the-mill Irish country house—it's more like *Architectural Digest* than *Country Life*. With its crisp lines and whimsical touches, the decor is the brainchild of your hosts, designers Bryan Leech and Martin Marley. After working abroad, Bryan and Martin returned to Ireland, bringing with them unusual artwork and furniture such as tables and chairs made from coconut shells. Kilgraney House was put together with a touch of whimsy and artistic flair, traditional Irish antiques being added to their overseas treasures, and the same attention to detail was lavished on the spotless modern bathrooms. The final ingredients are the warm welcome offered by your hosts and the lovely food. Martin and Bryan teach design, so their home is open for guests only during June, July, and August and on weekends in March, April, May, June, September, and October. Self-catering accommodation (one- and two-bedroomed) is available in the gate lodge and restored stables, tack room, and coach house. *Directions:* Take the N9 from Dublin to Royal Oak (south of Carlow), turn left into Bagenalstown (Muine Bheag), and right in the village for the 6-km drive to Kilgraney crossroads. Turn right (signposted) and Kilgraney House is the first entrance on the left (a 1½-hour drive).

KILGRANEY HOUSE
Owners: Bryan Leech & Martin Marley
Bagenalstown
Co Carlow, Ireland
Tel: (0503) 75283, Fax: (0503) 75595
Email: kilgrany@indigo.ie
6 rooms, 4 apartments
£35–£55 per person B&B, Dinner: £28
Apartment: from £250 per week
Closed Nov to Feb & see description
Credit cards: all major
Country house & self-catering
www.karenbrown.com/ireland/kilgraneyhouse.html

Ashley House is a large modern bungalow on a quiet country lane just to the north of Ballina town on the River Moy, which is famous for salmon fishing. Carmel Murray, its owner, is a keen gardener and in summer her garden is a profusion of colorful flowers and heathers. The neat-as-a-new-pin look of the garden extends to the home's pristine interior with its daintily papered walls and matching floral drapes. Carmel welcomes her guests with tea and cakes and has compiled a scrapbook of all the things there are to do in the area. Breakfast is served in the sunny dining room overlooking the landscaped back garden. Bedrooms, all on the ground floor, come with one, two, and three beds and while each is different in its decor, they are most attractive, with frilly muslin sheers and flowered drapes, wallpaper, and bedspreads. In summer there are often traditional Irish music and set-dancing locally on Thursdays (Carmel is an enthusiastic set-dancer). Ballina is between two very popular sightseeing venues, Céide Fields and Foxford Woolen Mills. High atop a cliff near Ballycastle, the Stone-Age settlement at Céide Fields has been excavated and a visitors' center shows you how this outpost supported people. Foxford Woolen Mills has been restored and you can see craftspeople produce tweeds, rugs, and blankets and enjoy an audio-visual presentation showing life at Foxford. *Directions:* From Ballina take the N59 in the direction of Belmullet for 1 km and turn right at the signpost.

ASHLEY HOUSE
Owners: Carmel & Michael Murray
Ardoughan
Ballina
Co Mayo, Ireland
Tel: (096) 22799/ (088) 2141889, Fax: none
Email: ashleyhousebb@hotmail.com
4 rooms
£19 per person B&B
Open Mar to Nov, Credit cards: MC, VS
B&B
www.karenbrown.com/ireland/ashley.html

Ballina and Killaloe are two villages connected by a bridge across the River Shannon as it exits Lough Derg on its way to the sea. The large single-story Waterman's Lodge was bought as a home and cleverly converted into a hotel, installing a skylight roof over one of its courtyards, which became the sunny restaurant at the very heart of the building. Bedrooms are off the corridor around the restaurant, making this an ideal place to stay for anyone who has difficulty with stairs. All of the spacious rooms are light and airy, with several of them enjoying views through the trees to the lake. Relax in the sitting room and plan your excursions in this very untouristy part of County Tipperary. Chat with locals and your fellow guests in the clubby bar where conversation often turns to why the hunting rifle is hung above the salmon trophy case—perhaps they shoot fish hereabouts! Walk across the narrow stone bridge to quaint little Killaloe with its narrow main street lined with colorfully painted shops and its small row houses dominated by a huge cathedral where a chamber music festival is held every July. You can rent a boat on the lough, go fishing and walking, or venture farther afield to Bunratty Castle and the Cliffs of Moher. *Directions*: Ballina Killaloe is an hour's drive from Shannon. Coming from Shannon, it is best to avoid the traffic-filled streets of Limerick, so arm yourself with Tom's cross-country directions and come via Sixmilebridge. From Limerick take the N7, Dublin road, go through Birdhill, and turn left for Killaloe. Go through the village of Ballina (do not cross the bridge) and Waterman's Lodge is on your left after 200 meters.

WATERMAN'S LODGE
Manager: Tom Reilly
Ballina Killaloe
Co Clare, Ireland
Tel: (061) 376333, Fax: (061) 375445
Email: info@watermanslodge.ie
11 rooms
Double: £120–£140, Dinner: £18–£30
Closed Christmas to mid-Jan, Credit cards: all major
Country house hotel
www.karenbrown.com/ireland/watermans.html

Beth Hallinan has with flair and imagination created in Rathcoursey House one of the finest places to stay in County Cork. No detail is too small for her to concern herself with, a facet of her personality that served her well when she worked as personal chef for King Constantine of Greece and the Duke and Duchess of Devonshire, ran a successful restaurant, and wrote best-selling cookbooks. A downstairs suite of rooms is outfitted for the handicapped. Upstairs, as I went from room to room each became my absolute favorite—you will be thrilled whichever room you are in. However, I would request the Front Room for its decadent bathroom—plan on candlelight, a crackling fire, champagne on ice, and Gigli on the wind-up gramophone. Beth does not offer evening meals but has researched the finest places to eat (in all price categories) for her guests. Consider renting the entire house on an exclusive basis (minimum of two nights). Below the house the little road meanders along the shore, offering picturesque coastal views and uncrowded beaches. Golfing, sailing, fishing, bird watching, walking, and riding are available close by. Visit the nearby Midleton Jameson Heritage Centre and Cobh with its interesting maritime museum. *Directions:* From Cork take the N25 towards Waterford to the roundabout on the Midleton bypass and turn right for Cloyne. After 4 km turn right towards East Ferry (scenic route), then after 2 km turn left into the avenue for Rathcoursey House. (If you come to the pub you have gone too far.)

RATHCOURSEY HOUSE   **New**
Owner: Beth Hallinan
Ballinacurra
Co Cork, Ireland
Tel: (021) 4613418, Fax: (021) 4613393
Email: beth@rathcoursey.com
4 rooms
£50 per person B&B
Open all year, Credit cards: MC, VS
Country house & self-catering
www.karenbrown.com/ireland/rathcoursey.html

Dan Mullane's famous restaurant, The Mustard Seed, continues to garner rave reviews from our readers. The bold royal-blue dining room with its tables set with crisp white linens affords "foodies" the opportunity to enjoy some of Ireland's finest food and accommodation in a quiet, rural setting. Enjoy tea by the fire in the entrance-hall sitting room, curl up for a good read in the library, work up an appetite for dinner in the exercise room, or enjoy a relaxing massage. The emphasis is very much on a fine dining experience and guests are welcome to pop into the kitchen and chat to the chef and his brigade. The absolutely delightful bedrooms are each named after an aspect of their rather whimsical decor: Black and White, Butterfly, Nostalgia, and Lemon. As I saw each one, it became my favorite. Smokers are directed to "smokers' walk," a pathway through the garden—umbrellas are provided for inclement weather. If you are playing golf at Ballybunion, request an afternoon tee time so you do not have to rush breakfast. Adare is a 15-minute drive away and the surrounding peaceful countryside offers lots of opportunities for horse riding. *Directions:* From Adare take the N21, Killarney road for 2 km and turn left for Ballingarry. In the village take the Newcastle West road for 500 meters and Echo Lodge is on your right.

THE MUSTARD SEED AT ECHO LODGE
Owner: Dan Mullane
Ballingarry
Co Limerick, Ireland
Tel: (069) 68508, Fax: (069) 68511
Email: mustard@indigo.ie
14 rooms
Double: £130–£170, Suite: £170–£200
Dinner: £34
Closed mid-Feb to mid-Mar
Credit cards: all major
Country house hotel
www.karenbrown.com/ireland/echolodge.html

Ballydehob is a colorfully painted village set amongst ruggedly beautiful countryside. Fortunately for visitors to this most attractive spot, there is a charming bed and breakfast, Lynwood, just a short walk from town. Ann is the most welcoming of hostesses and she makes as much effort with her home as she does with her guests—her latest additions to her prettily decorated bedrooms are televisions, hairdryers, and electric blankets. All the guestrooms have tea- and coffee-makings and compact, en-suite shower rooms. A conservatory overlooks a tennis court, which guests are welcome to use. For dinner most visitors go to Annie's Restaurant, because breakfast is the only meal that Ann serves. The road to Mizen Head takes travelers through Schull and past Barley Cove, a flat, sandy beach, to the southwestern tip of Ireland where vertical sandstone cliffs plunge into the sea—the last little bit of Ireland that so many emigrants saw as they sailed for America. The road back along the northern coast of the peninsula is very beautiful. *Directions:* Ballydehob is just off the N71 (Cork to Killarney road). Follow the Schull road through the village and Lynwood is on your right.

LYNWOOD
Owner: Ann Vaughan
Schull Road
Ballydehob
Co Cork, Ireland
Tel & fax: (028) 37124
Email: lynwoodbb@hotmail.com
4 rooms
£20 per person B&B
Open Apr to Oct
Credit cards: none
B&B
www.karenbrown.com/ireland/lynwood.html

This tall, bright-white Victorian house is set amidst lush gardens rimming the shores of Bantry Bay. While it is worth a stay here just to soak up the spectacular scenery, the house has much to offer and Kathleen O'Sullivan is an energetic and caring hostess. The sitting room/bar, pretty in soft pinks and blues with light-wood furniture, offers plenty of places to sit, and for those in search of peace and quiet there is an old-fashioned parlor/TV room. The spacious bedrooms are individually decorated, those at the front of the house having the advantage of views of Bantry Bay through the trees. If you are looking for extra-roomy accommodation, request one of the very reasonably priced suites with two bathrooms. The Garden Room, on the ground floor, has been specially equipped for the handicapped. In addition, Kathleen has a very comfortable cottage on the grounds, just the place for families, friends traveling together, or those who prefer self-catering. The atmosphere is friendly and informal, which accounts, I am sure, for the large number of guests who return here year after year. Wander off the main roads to explore the Beara Peninsula with its views of barren, rocky mountains tumbling into the sea. A "must visit" is nearby Garinish Island, a spectacular garden with trees, shrubs, and plants from every part of the world. Also nearby is Bantry House, a grand mansion. *Directions:* Sea View House Hotel is located in Ballylickey on the N71 between Bantry and Glengarriff.

SEA VIEW HOUSE HOTEL
Owner: Kathleen O'Sullivan
Ballylickey
Co Cork, Ireland
Tel: (027) 50462/50073, Fax: (027) 51555
Email: seaviewhousehotel@eircom.net
17 rooms, 1 cottage
Double: £100–£120, Suite: £120–£130
Dinner: £27 plus 10% service
Open mid-Mar to mid-Nov
Credit cards: all major
Country house hotel & self-catering
www.karenbrown.com/ireland/seaviewhouse.html

Most of my family home would fit into the entrance hall of Temple House, but as a tour of the house subsequently displayed, that was just the tip of the iceberg, for beyond the enormous tiled entry hall with its array of wellington boots, fishing paraphernalia, and inclement weather gear lies a vast home with rooms of gigantic proportions. This is Deb and Sandy's family home and it's remarkable that they have made it into such a comfortable one. Those who are interested in the history of the place and wonderful stories of ancestors' exploits are directed to Sandy (he is extremely chemically sensitive so please refrain from using all scented products and aerosols). An air of warmth and faded elegance pervades this grand home, which did not have electricity until 1962. All of the furniture made for the house is still here along with some of the original carpets and draperies, though Deb has added a lot of her own. Three of the bedrooms are gigantic. Realizing that guests enjoy the modern as well as the historic, bathrooms have been tucked into dressing rooms, good firm mattresses top historic beds, and central heating has been installed. Choose a pair of wellingtons and explore the estate from the vast parklands to the huge, walled vegetable garden. In the evening you can almost always be directed to Irish music and dancing. The Percevals can find enough to occupy your every waking moment—you will be tempted to stay for a month. *Directions:* From Sligo take the N4 to the N17 (Galway road). The house is signposted to the left. From Dublin turn onto N17 at the Collooney roundabout.

TEMPLE HOUSE
Owners: Deb & Sandy Perceval
Ballymote, Co Sligo, Ireland
Tel: (071) 83329, Fax: (071) 83808
Email: guests@templehouse.ie
6 rooms
£42–£45 per person B&B, Dinner: £20
Open Apr to Nov
Credit cards: all major
Country house
www.karenbrown.com/ireland/templehouse.html

Ballinkeele House was built for the Maher family in 1840, and Margaret and John are the fourth generation of Mahers to call this heritage house home. Set amidst 350 acres of parklike grounds, the house has all the solid quality of a grand home built in the early Victorian period: big rooms, fine ceilings, decorative doors, quality in every detail. Apart from the addition of heating and modern bathrooms, the house has not changed over the years. Soft Oriental rugs dress the flagstone entry, which is warmed by a huge, old-fashioned stove, and grand oil paintings and family portraits adorn the walls. Antique furniture graces the cozy drawing room and enormous dining room where guests enjoy delicious candlelit dinners. The Master Bedroom is a particularly large room decorated in soft red and beiges with an impressive four-poster bed sitting center stage. For recreation there are walks through the estate and croquet on the lawn. Settle in for several nights and enjoy County Wexford—historic Wexford's Georgian theater, is home to the October Opera Festival; the Wexford Wildlife Reserve, famous for its wintering wildfowl; and the National Heritage Park with its old Irish buildings. The Mahers have bicycles for guests and often fishing and a gillie can be arranged. The port of Rosslare is a 40-minute drive away. *Directions:* From Dublin take the N11, Wexford road, to Gorey. Turn left opposite the 64 Lounge restaurant for Wexford (R741) for 30 km and Ballinkeele House is signposted on your right.

BALLINKEELE HOUSE
Owners: Margaret & John Maher
Ballymurn, Enniscorthy
Co Wexford, Ireland
Tel: (053) 38105, Fax: (053) 38468
Email: info@ballinkeele.com
5 rooms
£45–£60 per person B&B, Dinner: £26 (not Thu)
Open Mar to mid-Nov
Credit cards: all major
Country house
www.karenbrown.com/ireland/ballinkeelehouse.html

Ballynahinch Castle, once the home of the O'Flahery chieftains, is a gray heap of a building whose architectural ugliness belies its unstuffy warmth and friendliness. The heart of the place is the bar with its old brick floor and little tables surrounded by Windsor chairs. Here a long table displays the "catch of the day" and fisherfolk hang the keys that give them access to the little huts on their fishing beats—no standing out in the rain when fishing at Ballynahinch Castle. The beats are so close to the house that folks return to the bar for lunch (packed lunches are also available). Bar food is served in the evening for those who are not inclined to partake of a more formal meal in the dining room whose windows overlook the river. Bedrooms come in three varieties: "standard," "superior," and "luxury," which at Ballynahinch Castle means "large," "larger," and "largest." I particularly enjoyed my standard room, Oranmore, and preferred its low-ceiling coziness to the more spacious superior rooms with their higher ceilings. However, I was very taken with the new, luxurious riverside rooms with their four-poster and brass beds, walk-through dressing rooms, separate baths and showers, and fireplaces. The natural beauty of Connemara is on your doorstep. Often guests never leave the hotel's property, spending their days wandering on footpaths through the 350 acres of grounds or just curling up with a book beside the fire. *Directions:* From Galway take the N59, Clifden road, for 68 km and turn left for Roundstone. The hotel is on your right after 4 km.

BALLYNAHINCH CASTLE
Manager: Patrick O'Flaherty
Ballynahinch, Recess, Co Galway, Ireland
Tel: (095) 31006, Fax: (095) 31085
Email: bhinch@iol.ie
40 rooms
Double: £140–£200*, Suite: £300*, Dinner: £27.50*
*Plus 10% service
Closed Christmas & Feb
Credit cards: all major
Country house hotel
www.karenbrown.com/ireland/ballynahinch.html

With the bare limestone crags of the Burren sheltering its back and a panoramic view of Ballyvaughan Bay to the towering cliffs of Black Head in front, Drumcreehy House commands an enviable rural position just outside the picturesque fishing village of Ballyvaughan. Bernadette and Armin designed this new house to look as old as possible but with all modern amenities, and to add to the traditional feel they have furnished the sitting room and dining room with antiques and all the bedrooms with old pine and brass-and-wrought-iron bedheads. Spring Gentian and Dog Violet are especially spacious bedrooms, with larger bathrooms, and along with Cowslip and Primrose (which have shower rooms) enjoy spectacular views across the bay to Black Head. Fuschia is also an especially large room with a broad balcony overlooking the garden and the limestone face of the Burren. Enjoy a delectable cooked breakfast in the sunny yellow breakfast room all decked out in pine where a table is laden with fruit, cereal, cheeses, and meats, and a three-course dinner (must be booked in advance) in the attractive dining room with its view to the water. Shannon is an hour's drive away, making this an ideal first or last night on your trip, but stay longer and explore the Burren, the Cliffs of Moher, and the area's charming little towns. *Directions:* From Shannon take the N18 to Ennis, the N85 towards Ennistymon, and the first right (R476) through Corofin and on towards Kilfenora. At the ruined castle turn right onto the R480 for Ballyvaughan where you turn right on the N67, Galway road. Drumcreehy is on your right after 2 km.

DRUMCREEHY HOUSE   **New**
Owners: Bernadette & Armin Grefkes
Ballyvaughan
Co Clare, Ireland
Tel: (065) 7077377, Fax: (065) 7077379
Email: drumcreehyhouse@eircom.net
10 rooms
£28–£30 per person B&B, Dinner: £17
Open Mar to Oct, Credit cards: MC, VS
Guesthouse
www.karenbrown.com/ireland/drumcreehy.html

Gregans Castle is only 57 kilometers from Shannon airport, so if you are heading north, this is the perfect spot to begin your stay in Ireland. This is not an imposing castle, but a sprawling manor house set in a lush green valley completely surrounded by the Burren, with its moonscapes of gray limestone and oasis of Alpine and Arctic plants. The entire house is delightfully decorated. Public rooms include a snug library and a cozy lounge—blazing turf fires add a cheery warmth. In the dining room, where Peter Haden supervises the production of delectable food, windows frame an outstanding view across the Burren to distant Galway Bay. My favorite room is the Corkscrew Bar with its blazing turf fire and blackened beams hung with copper and brass. Lunch is served here, and in the evening guests and locals gather for a drink and a chat. Traditional country house bedrooms are the order of the day and range in size from comfortably cozy to exceedingly spacious. Three large ground-floor suites have private patios. Local attractions include the Ailwee Caves, full of stalactites and stalagmites, and the Cliffs of Moher. *Directions:* From Shannon take the N18 to Ennis, the N85 towards Ennistymon, and the first right (R476) through Corofin and on towards Kilfenora. At the ruined castle turn right onto the R480 towards Ballyvaughan and as you crest the Burren, you see the hotel in the valley below.

GREGANS CASTLE
Owners: Moira, Peter, & Simon Haden
Ballyvaughan
Co Clare, Ireland
Tel: (065) 7077 005, Fax: (065) 7077 111
Email: res@gregans.ie
22 rooms
Double: £146–£198, Suite: £250–£290
Dinner: £26–£37
Open Apr to Oct
Credit cards: all major
Country house hotel
www.karenbrown.com/ireland/gregans.html

This is just the place to stay if you want visit the famous Rock of Cashel, for Mary can send you off down a quiet lane that brings you out in Cashel. While Mary appreciates that guests enjoy Cashel for daytime sightseeing, she also encourages them to go to an evening of Irish dance and music in a sparkling little theater beside Cashel Rock. The foot-tapping entertainment is followed by a party of tea and cake, or a drink at the bar and a chance for the audience to dance and sing along with the professionals. Mary has been offering hospitality for over 25 years, chatting with guests over a cup of tea, making them simply delicious breakfasts and evening meals, and telling them where to go and what to see. The house is in tip-top shape but sadly the larger rooms lack en-suite facilities. If you want to stay for a week, the Marnanes offer Primrose Cottage, a very attractive two-bedroom residence nearby. Countryside drives include The Vee and the nearby Glen of Aherlow where you can enjoy the view, and woodland walks from Christ the King Statue. The Rock of Cashel, Hoare Abbey, Holy Cross Abbey, and Cahir Castle are all within a 19-kilometer radius. *Directions:* From Tipperary take the Waterford road (N24) to Bansha, turn left in the village, and the farm is on your right after 1 km.

BANSHA HOUSE
Owners: Mary & John Marnane
Bansha
Co Tipperary, Ireland
Tel: (062) 54194, Fax: (062) 54215
8 rooms, 5 en suite, 1 cottage
£23–£26 per person B&B, Dinner: £16
Closed Christmas
Credit cards: MC, VS
Farmhouse B&B & self-catering
www.karenbrown.com/ireland/bansha.html

Just as you arrive in Bantry town, you see the entrance gate to Bantry House on your right. Dating from 1750, this stately home has fine views of the bay, and, like so many grand Irish homes, is struggling to keep up its elegant buildings. The current descendant of the Earls of Bantry, Egerton Shelswell-White, has tackled this problem by opening the house to the public who, with information sheets in hand, tour its lofty rooms and admire its elegant furniture, tapestries, and paintings, retiring afterwards to the tea shop in the old refectory. Yet this is a stately home with a difference, for one entire wing of the house and a couple of rooms over the tea shop have been restored in a more modern vein, offering large, bright, airy bedrooms (some with sitting rooms) on a bed-and-breakfast basis. After showing you to your room, the staff fade away until next morning when they prepare breakfast for you in the country-style dining room in what used to be the old cellars. Dinner is available on weekdays during the summer. In the evening you help yourselves to drinks from the honor bar, toast your toes by the fire, or, if you wish, play billiards in the enormous billiard room. A tour of the house is included in the tariff, so you can pop through the concealed door into the long gallery to wander at leisure through the museum-like rooms of this grand old home. *Directions:* Bantry is on the N71 between Skibbereen and Kenmare.

BANTRY HOUSE
Owner: Egerton Shelswell-White
Bantry
Co Cork, Ireland
Tel: (027) 50047, Fax: (027) 50795
9 rooms
Double £150–£170, Dinner: £27
Open Mar to Oct
Credit cards: all major
Country house

Rosemary and Brian McAuley had Dunauley designed to take advantage of the spectacular view of the island-dotted Bantry Bay, aptly framed by a wall of windows in the living/dining room. Three most attractive double-bedded bedrooms, each with en-suite shower rooms, are found on the same level as the living room. Downstairs two additional bedrooms can be combined with a kitchen to form a self-catering unit with its own entrance. Guests enjoy both the living room and its particularly fine view as they sit round the fire in the evening and while tucking into an ample breakfast before setting out on a day's sightseeing. Breakfast is the only meal Rosemary serves, and guests usually drive into town for dinner. The drive from Bantry to Glengarriff gives a taste of the rugged landscape and exotic flora that you find in this part of Ireland. From the town you can take a boat to Garinish Island, a lush collection of interesting shrubs, trees, and flowers from all over the world. For over three years a hundred men worked to make Arran Bryce's garden, caseta, and temple, but financial hardships precluded the building of his home. *Directions:* From the center of Bantry follow white signs for the hospital through the one-way system and up the hill. Pass a church on the right and continue on this road till you see Dunauley signposted to the right—keep going uphill until you come to the house.

DUNAULEY
Owners: Rosemary & Brian McAuley
Seskin, Bantry
Co Cork, Ireland
Tel & fax: (027) 50290
Email: rosemarymcauley@eircom.net
5 rooms
£22–£30 per person B&B
Open May to Sep
Credit cards: none
No-smoking house
B&B & self-catering
www.karenbrown.com/ireland/dunauley.html

110   *Places to Stay*

Staying at Beaufort House in the little village of Beaufort will enable you to enjoy the outstanding beauty of Killarney National Park without having to deal with the crowds that descend on the nearby town of Killarney. Donald came to Beaufort House as a teenager and spent many years in London before he and his wife Rachel decided that they wanted to bring their two young daughters up in Ireland. Their input of capital has restored the family home to a luxurious state that it had probably never known. The decor is country-house perfection—no frayed edges here. Bedrooms come in two sizes: large with very large bathrooms or extra large with smaller bathrooms. Enjoy tea in the snug library or the sitting room and breakfast in the lovely dining room, and bask in the warm hospitality offered by Donald, Rachel, and their young daughters. Enjoy a week-long stay in one of the Camerons' exquisite self-catering cottages, which come with two, three, and four bedrooms where each bedroom is en suite. All are delightfully furnished and kitted out with everything you might need, including good novels. Stroll down to the River Laune and enjoy views of the not-too-distant Gap of Dunloe. Look carefully amongst the bushes and you'll find the ancient Ogham stone that predates the house by several thousand years. Rachel often sends guests on a day trip that includes a jaunting car ride up the Gap of Dunloe and a boat trip across the lakes of Killarney. *Directions:* Beaufort is 8 km west of Killarney on the R562 (Ring of Kerry). Turn left over the bridge and immediately left into Beaufort House.

BEAUFORT HOUSE
Owners: Rachel & Donald Cameron
Beaufort
Co Kerry, Ireland
Tel & fax: (064) 44764
Email: info@beaufortireland.com
4 rooms, 4 cottages
£65–£75 per person B&B
Open mid-Mar to Sep, Credit cards: all major
Country house & self-catering
www.karenbrown.com/ireland/beauforthouse.html

Thomas Andrews who designed the *Titanic* once lived here. Now Ash-Rowan is the relaxed, very friendly, unpretentious home of Sam and Evelyn Hazlett—an excellent choice for a bed and breakfast while staying in the northern capital. A hearty breakfast sets you up for the day—opt for organic porridge flavored with Drambuie and cream followed by an "Irish scramble" with eggs, chopped bacon, and mushrooms, or the "Ulster fry," the ultimate cooked breakfast which the menu warns is not for the faint-hearted. It's a climb to the top of the house (no large cases!) but worth it to secure one of the choice rooms (7 and 8) that offer more spacious quarters. All the rooms have TVs, phones, bathrobes, and hospitality trays with biscuits, teas, and instant soups. Beds are made with linen sheets and pillowcases. The location, near the university, is perfect for strolling into the city and taxis are inexpensive for a night on the town. Peruse the papers and the tourist literature in the wonderfully cluttered front parlor then seek out Sam or Evelyn to set you up with sightseeing venues for the day. Their favorite sightseeing destination, the Folk and Transport Museum, is a train ride or short drive away. *Directions:* From central Belfast take Dublin Road to Shaftesbury Square. Go through Bradbury Place onto University Road. Pass the university on the left and go straight through the traffic lights into Malone Road. Windsor Avenue is the third avenue on your right.

ASH-ROWAN
Owners: Evelyn & Sam Hazlett
12 Windsor Avenue
Belfast BT9 6EE
Northern Ireland
Tel: (028) 9066 1758, Fax: (028) 9066 3227
5 rooms
£33–£42 per person B&B
Closed Christmas & New Year
Credit cards: all major
Guesthouse

112   *Places to Stay*

Set in the most stylish part of Belfast, The Crescent Townhouse has done its best to provide something more chic than the standard hotel. The townhouse is part of a complex that includes an excellent brasserie, Metro, and a lively pub, Bar Twelve. Standard rooms are more spacious than I expected in a city hotel and I was awed by the size of the Empire and Chelsea suites with their king-sized beds. All the rooms have excellent bathrooms. When I visited, the hotel was planning an expansion to add eight more rooms and suites. Reductions are offered on standard rooms at the weekend. Breakfast is taken in the Metro Brasserie and includes bagels with smoked salmon, poached egg, and cream cheese. Bar Twelve offers pub-style lunches and early dinners with the menu of the day posted on the board. More avant-garde lunch and dinner selections are available in the Metro. The Crescent's location is very convenient for walking to the city center. The hotel is opposite the Botanic railway station, which connects to the main railway network, and the Dublin express train. *Directions:* Take Dublin Road then go through Shaftesbury Square into Botanic Avenue. After 250 meters you come to the hotel on the corner of Botanic and Lower Crescent. Parking (two-hour daytime limit) is in the side streets or in a public car park nearby.

THE CRESCENT TOWNHOUSE
Manager: Gertie Burke
13 Lower Crescent
Belfast BT7 1NR
Northern Ireland
Tel: (028) 9032 3349, Fax: (028) 9032 0646
20 rooms
Double: £100–£110, Dinner: £20–£30
Open all year
Credit cards: all major
City hotel

In the late 1800s Belfast was one of Europe's foremost trading cities. To celebrate the success of their seed and grain companies, Samuel McCausland and John Lytle commissioned the building of the most impressive of Italianate waterfront warehouses. The bustling waterfront has long since disappeared, replaced at the end of the 20th century by a network of wide roads that whisk the traffic around the city. McCausland's and Lytle's warehouses have been converted to a stylish hotel, an oasis of comfortable calm where double glazing blocks the noise of traffic whistling past the front door. The original cast-iron pillars supporting the tall ceiling still remain in the reception lounge, the Café Marco Polo, which serves as the hotel's bar and coffee shop, and Merchants Restaurant with its internationally themed menu. The keycard-entry bedrooms have all the modern conveniences such as CD players, modem points, and TVs (sometimes with video). Decorated in warm autumnal shades and furnished with warm-toned wood furniture, each is accompanied by a splendid modern bathroom. King-sized beds are available in the junior suites. *Directions:* The McCausland is situated on Victoria Street between Ann Street and the Albert clock tower. If arriving by car, park to the side of the hotel in Marlborough Street and the hotel staff will take your car to a local car park that offers a 50% overnight discount for hotel patrons.

McCAUSLAND HOTEL
Manager: Joseph Hughes
34–38 Victoria Street
Belfast BT1 3GH
Northern Ireland
Tel: (028) 9022 0200, Fax: (028) 9022 0220
Email: info@mccauslandhotel.com
60 rooms
Double: £150–£170*, Suite: £170–£190*, Dinner: £29.50
*Breakfast not included: £12
Closed Christmas, Credit cards: all major
City hotel
www.karenbrown.com/ireland/mccausland.html

Bobbie Smith is a caring hostess, carrying on the tradition of warm farmhouse hospitality started by her mother many years ago. She is also an unpretentious, fun person and her home reflects her welcoming, easygoing personality. Filled with mellow old furniture, books, pictures, and family mementos, the Old Rectory is very much a lived-in, comfortable family home for Bobbie, her husband Don, and their three daughters. Guests are welcomed with a reviving pot of tea in the drawing room, and it is here that they chat with fellow guests before dinner which is taken by candlelight round the long, gleaming dining-room table. Bedrooms have the same traditional family feel and range from a snug twin to a spacious family room with a carved four-poster and a single bed—ask for the one with the large feather bed: its comfort will surprise you. All have snug en-suite shower or bathrooms. The area is perfect for cycling, so Don organizes cycling holidays that include cycle hire, airport pickup, and baggage transportation. Those who prefer to stick to their car will find Kilkenny with its castle, fine old shops, and lovely buildings just a 20-minute drive away. Day trips can be taken to Waterford, Kildare, and Glendalough. *Directions:* Take the N9 from Dublin to Royal Oak (south of Carlow), turn left into Bagenalstown, and right in the village for the 6-km drive to Lorum Old Rectory.

LORUM OLD RECTORY
Owners: Bobbie & Don Smith
Kilgreaney, Bagenalstown
Borris
Co Carlow, Ireland
Tel: (0503) 75282, Fax: (0503) 75455
Email: lorum@lorum.com
5 rooms
£37.50–£40 per person B&B, Dinner: £27.50
Closed Christmas
Credit cards: all major
Country house
www.karenbrown.com/ireland/lorumoldrectory.html

Since moving into the spacious, rundown farmhouse that was Dunaird House, Sylvia has supervised a complete transformation, adding modern bathrooms and central heating and decorating the entire house in an elegant fashion. The graceful guest sitting room has damask sofas and elegant draperies while, by contrast, there is a country coziness to the pine breakfast room where Sylvia finds guests often sit in the evening to watch the television in spite of there being satellite TV in the bedrooms. The double-bedded pink room has a large bathroom and, like the adjacent double-bedded room, overlooks the front garden. A smaller twin-bedded room has a very fancy bathroom with shower and claw-foot tub just across the hall. Three additional cottagey bedrooms, decorated in an equally refined style, are found across the former farmyard in the old stables. Low-ceilinged beamed rooms are the order of the day here and the two ground-floor rooms have French windows opening onto a patio and the garden. Breakfast is the only meal served and guests often go the short distance into the village for dinner. Broughshane is the entrance to the Glens of Antrim, which lead to the spectacular Antrim coast and the world-famous Giant's Causeway. *Directions:* Leave the M2 motorway at exit 11 for the 2-km drive to Broughshane. Turn right on the B94 (Ballyclare road) and turn first left by the church for the 1-km drive to Dunaird House on your right.

DUNAIRD HOUSE
Owners: Sylvia & John Graham
15 Buckna Road
Broughshane BT42 4NJ
Co Antrim, Northern Ireland
Tel: (028) 2586 2117, Fax: none
6 rooms
£25 per person B&B
Open all year
Credit cards: none
B&B
www.karenbrown.com/ireland/dunaird.html

The Bushmills Inn was in a very sad and sorry state before it was rescued by the present owner who transformed it in 1987 into a traditional Ulster hostelry. A rocking chair sits before an enormous fireplace and displays of old plates adorn the mantle. The ambiance of an old coaching inn continues to the restaurant with its whitewashed stone walls and tall pine settles dividing the room into intimate little areas. The inn's original kitchen, with its flagstone floor and open fire, links the hotel to the Victorian-style bar still illuminated by flickering gas light. Try a "Black Bush" from the distillery up the road—Bushmills is the home of the world's oldest licensed distillery and on weekdays you can take a tour. The bedrooms of the coaching inn are on the small side and each accompanied by a tiny shower room. More generous sized accommodation is found in the Mill House, an extension of 22 rooms built beside the River Bush. You may have the pleasure of seeing your nation's flag flown in your honor as the inn has the charming custom of raising the national flag of their resident who is from farthest away. Nearby are 13th-century Dunluce Castle, the Giant's Causeway and Royal Portrush golf course. *Directions:* From Coleraine take the B19 to Bushmills. As you cross the River Bush, the main entrance to the hotel is on your left.

THE BUSHMILLS INN
Owner: Roy Bolton
Managers: Stella Minogue & Alan Dunlop
9 Dunluce Road
Bushmills
Co Antrim BT57 8QG, Northern Ireland
Tel: (028) 2073 2339, Fax: (028) 2073 2048
Email: mail@bushmillsinn.com
32 rooms
Double: £98–£128, Dinner: £22–£25
Open all year
Credit cards: MC, VS
Inn
www.karenbrown.com/ireland/bushmillsinn.html

Catherine helped her mother in the antique trade for many years and as her interest in furniture grew, so did her collection—a collection large enough for her to theme her rooms depending on the period of the furniture: Art Nouveau, Victorian, Edwardian, and Regency. These bedrooms are very nice but the prize is her latest endeavor, her garden suite, a large room decorated in vivid yellow and royal blue with a bay window large enough to accommodate two armchairs overlooking a sheltered corner of her vast garden. Catherine's style is ornate—lots of different patterns with grand pieces of furniture in the dining room and six high-backed library chairs grouped around the fire in the sitting room. Breakfast is the only meal served, which is no problem as the White Gables restaurant is just down the road in Moycullan, while more adventurous food is offered farther afield at Drimcong House. Guests often go the 6.5 kilometers into Galway city for city life and take day trips to the Aran Islands or to Connemara, an area of wild beauty found beyond Oughterard. *Directions*: From Galway take the N59 towards Clifden for 6.5 km and Killeen House is on your right.

KILLEEN HOUSE
Owner: Catherine Doyle
Bushypark
Galway, Ireland
Tel: (091) 524179, Fax: (091) 528065
Email: killeenhouse@ireland.com
5 rooms
£45–£55 per person B&B
Closed Christmas
Credit cards: all major
B&B
www.karenbrown.com/ireland/killeen.html

Butlerstown House is a lovely building in a delightful rural location with vistas of farms and rolling pastures from almost every window. This Georgian house has been loved and looked after since it was built for Jonas Travers in about 1805. Its present friendly owners, Liz Jones and Roger Owen, have refurbished their jewel of a home to sail into the 21st century with central heating, spanking-new bath and shower rooms, and a complete decorative face-lift. Furnishings and decor strike just the right note so that the lovely architectural details of the house can shine through: the grand staircase sweeping either side of the huge window that lights the hallway; detailed plasterwork cornices full of starfish, shells, ropes, and oak leaves; and grand fireplaces where fires are lit when the Irish weather dictates. While guests are directed elsewhere for dinner, Liz gives new meaning to the term "Irish breakfast"—one of her specialties is cockles and lavabread (seaweed rolled in oatmeal and sautéed—amazingly good). Close at hand are hidden coves and empty beaches, horse riding, fishing, and walking. Use Butlerstown as a base for explorations up and down this coast from the hurly-burly of Kinsale to the wildness of Mizen Head. *Directions:* From Bandon follow N71 out of town and filter left by the Maxol garage on the left. Go 300 meters and turn left for the 10-km drive to Timoleague. Cross the river bridge, turn left by the ruined friary, and go about 8 km towards Barryroe and Timoleague. At Barryroe follow signs to the house about 1.5 km past the church.

BUTLERSTOWN HOUSE
Owners: Elizabeth Jones & Roger Owen
Butlerstown, Bandon
Co Cork, Ireland
Tel: (023) 40137, Fax: (023) 40137
Email: mail@butlerstownhouse.com
4 rooms
£45–£55 per person B&B
Open Mar to Oct
Credit cards: MC, VS
Country house
www.karenbrown.com/ireland/butlerstown.html

Even though it is only just over 4 kilometers from the Ring of Kerry, Iskeroon is one of the most hidden and secluded properties in Ireland. Reached by a precipitous lane that tumbles down to the sea and a narrow farm track, Iskeroon boasts the most spectacular view in Ireland—truly a hidden gem. Geraldine and David are the first family to call this home, for while the house was built in the '30s, it was previously used as holiday home. Snuggling into a sheltered spot, the long, low-lying house captures the sea view from every room, a view so enchanting that it takes you a while to realize that the house is also delightful with its three spacious bedrooms, living room, and dining room decorated in Mediterranean shades of yellow, blue, red, and green and furnished in a most attractive, unfussy way. Robes are provided for nipping across the hall to your private bathrooms. The nearby town of Waterville has a good selection of restaurants for dinner—David and Geraldine are happy to advise. The garden tumbles down to a private jetty and guests are welcome to accompany the Hares as they check their shrimp and lobster pots. Guests often take the boat from Bunavalla pier to the Skelligs, a "must-do" trip if the weather is good. *Directions*: Derrynane is between Waterville and Caherdaniel. Find the Scarriff Inn (large and yellow) between these villages and take the road signposted Bunavalla Pier, all the way to the bottom, bearing left wherever there's a choice of roads. At the pier turn left, drive over the track beside the beach, through two white gateposts, and you arrive at Iskeroon. A minimum stay of two nights is strongly recommended.

ISKEROON
Owners: Geraldine & David Hare
Caherdaniel, Derrynane
Co Kerry, Ireland
Tel: (066) 9475119, Fax: (066) 9475488
Email: info@iskeroon.com
3 rooms
Double: from £38 per person B&B
Closed Oct to Apr, Credit cards: all major
Country house
www.karenbrown.com/ireland/iskeroon.html

Lisdonagh House's last owner, Valda Palmer, discouraged visitors and frequently shot at them on sight. Thankfully a very different welcome is offered today by Finola and John Cooke. A smile, warm handshake, and a restorative cup of tea in the drawing room is their standard prescription for those of us who have wandered around seemingly identical lanes looking for the place (though it's certainly worth getting lost to stay here deep in the countryside). A striking feature of the house is the oval entrance hall with its 1790 murals depicting the virtues of valor, chastity, beauty, and justice. This leads to a grand staircase, which arches up to bedrooms and down to further bedrooms and a stone-faced lounge-cum-bar at the base of the tower. The house has been recently totally restored Walk down to Lough Hackett and take the rowing boat out to the *crannóg*, a man-made island reputedly the home of the High Kings of Connaught over 2,000 years ago. Farther afield lie Galway and Cong with its luxurious Ashford Castle. Horse riding can be arranged in Cong. Lisdonagh can be rented as a whole on a self-catering basis or complete with chef and housekeeping. *Directions:* From the N18 (Galway road) follow signposts for Sligo through Claregalway and keep on the N17 towards Tuam (about 18 km). Turn left on the R333 towards Headford to Caherlistrane. At Quealey's pub turn right towards Shrule and after nearly 2 km turn left to Lisdonagh House.

LISDONAGH HOUSE
Owners: Finola & John Cooke
Caherlistrane
near Headford
Co Galway, Ireland
Tel: (093) 31163, Fax: (093) 31528
Email: lisdonag@iol.ie
10 rooms
Double: £50–£90 per person B&B
Dinner: £30
Open Mar to Nov, Credit cards: all major
Country house hotel & self-catering
www.karenbrown.com/ireland/lisdonagh.html

This is the place to stay if you are a garden buff for this lovely Georgian house, built in 1794, is surrounded by 7 acres of glorious gardens. Started in 1947, the gardens extend from walled formality with trim lawns and herbaceous borders to a magical informal woodland garden complete with millpond and literary corner where you can curl up with a good book. Should the fickle Irish weather interrupt your reading, retire to a plump fireside chair in the elegant drawing room or take partners for a game of billiards. Guests usually dine together round the dining room table but Emma is happy to offer the option of dining alone. Emma loves to cook fresh seafood, of which there's an abundance available locally, and enjoys combining it with herbs and vegetables from the kitchen garden. Desserts are often based on raspberries, rhubarb, and apples fresh from the garden. Bedrooms are sumptuously decorated: one has a *bateau lit* and another a four-poster—all have terrific views of the garden. There are also two lovely self-catering apartments, The Coach House and The Garden Suite, both sleeping four. The garden is open to the public and tea is served in the conservatory. Many guests visit the vast acres of the John F. Kennedy Arboretum just up the road or take the little ferry across the river to Waterford. Close by lies the Hook Peninsula with its beautiful, uncrowded beaches and dramatic lighthouse. Aromatherapy treatments are available in house. *Directions:* From New Ross take the R733 signposted Campile and follow signposts to Kilmokea Gardens. Turn right to Great Island, cross the causeway, and Kilmokea is at the top of the incline.

KILMOKEA
Owners: Emma & Mark Hewlett
Great Island, Campile
Co Wexford, Ireland
Tel: (051) 388109, Fax: (051) 388766
Email: kilmokea@indigo.ie
6 rooms, 2 apartments
£55–£75 per person B&B, Dinner: £28
Open Feb to Oct, Credit cards: MC, VS
Country house & self-catering
www.karenbrown.com/ireland/kilmokea.html

The Deevys have been promoting this off-the-beaten-path corner of Ireland for more than 30 years and are absolutely unflagging in their efforts. Jean and Bill bought this huge house over 30 years ago and quickly realized that it was far too large to maintain as a family home without an army of staff, so Bill pursued his career as a vet while Jean opened their home to guests. The next generation is now in place, with son Paul in the kitchen and wife Clare on duty in the evening. While Bill has retired to take care of the extensive grounds, Jean enthusiastically advises guests on where to go and what to see between breakfast and dinner. Improvements move at a slow and steady pace, with bedrooms and bathrooms that have been remodeled most recently being the most desirable. This steady pace and Paul's flair for cooking are responsible for the hotel's success and the delightful Irish idiosyncrasy of the place that new and old guests revel in. Dinner is from a set four-course menu with the flexibility of guests being able to order from it à la carte. While Jean has enough sightseeing venues to occupy a fortnight, do not miss the opportunity to visit Lismore Castle, Swiss Cottage, and Waterford Crystal and to take a drive over The Vee. *Directions*: From Waterford take the N72 (Killarney road) for about a one-hour drive to Cappoquin. Richmond House is on the left just before you enter Cappoquin.

RICHMOND HOUSE
Owners: The Deevy family
Manager: Paul Deevy
Cappoquin
Co Waterford, Ireland
Tel: (058) 54278, Fax: (058) 54988
Email: richmond@amireland.com
9 rooms
Double £150, Dinner: £32
Open Feb to Dec
Credit cards: all major
Country house hotel
www.karenbrown.com/ireland/richmond.html

The famous Ring of Kerry driving route runs quite close to Caragh Lake whose quiet shores are far enough away from the tourist path for guests to enjoy the tranquil beauty of this one-time Victorian fishing lodge with its acres of manicured gardens spilling down to the lake and its backdrop of rugged hills. Mary Gaunt was looking for an excuse to return to her native Ireland from England, so when Caragh Lodge, just across the lake from her holiday home, came up for sale, she saw its tremendous potential and made the decision to become a hotelier. Mary is a natural for the job—a caring hostess who has surrounded herself with a staff very much like herself. Nine lovely bedrooms with splendid lake views are found in the main house and an additional courtyard wing. Six less luxurious but very attractively decorated rooms are in two garden wings. Relax by the fire in one of the little lounges and enjoy an excellent meal in the dining room (Mary is the chef). More rigorous pursuits include a spin round the lake in the little boat (Mary encourages guests to fish for brown trout), a game of tennis (there's a court), or golf at one of the many local courses. Guests often make a day trip to Dingle, and Killarney is conveniently close at hand. *Directions:* From Killorglin take the N70 towards Cahersiveen for 5 km. Turn left at the sign for Caragh Lodge and Caragh Lake. Caragh Lodge is on the right after 1 km.

CARAGH LODGE
Owner: Mary & Graham Gaunt
Caragh Lake
Co Kerry, Ireland
Tel: (066) 9769115, Fax: (066) 9769316
Email: caraghl@iol.ie
15 rooms
Double: £125–£160, Suite: from £220
Dinner: £30
Open mid-Apr to mid-Oct
Credit cards: all major
Country house hotel
www.karenbrown.com/ireland/caraghlodge.html

Glencarne House is one of those welcoming places that guests love to return to, for Agnes Harrington is the most hospitable of hostesses. Agnes is particularly proud that her bed and breakfast has won three national awards. The perfume of flowers blends with that of the polish used to keep the lovely old furniture gleaming bright. All of the bedrooms have en-suite bathrooms—one, a family room, has two lovely old brass-and-iron beds and the large front bedroom has a beautiful brass-and-iron bed and a child's bed in the bathroom/dressing room. A hearty farmhouse dinner is served round the large dining-room table—the vegetables, fruits, lamb, and beef are fresh from the farm and carefully cooked by Agnes. The first thing you see as you cross the bridge into Carrick-on-Shannon is the flotilla of cabin cruisers for this is the premier cruising base on the River Shannon. You can hire a boat for a day or a week and meander along the River Shannon and her lakes, stopping off to visit the villages and their pubs along the way. The nearby Forest Park is found on the grounds of the former Rockingham House. The park's amenities include nature trails, a bog garden, and the relics of the former mansion. *Directions:* Glencarne House is on the N4, Dublin to Sligo road, between Carrick-on-Shannon and Boyle.

GLENCARNE HOUSE
Owners: Agnes & Pat Harrington
Carrick-on-Shannon
Co Leitrim, Ireland
Tel: (079) 67013, Fax: none
6 rooms
£25 per person B&B, Dinner: £20
Open Mar to Sep
Credit cards: none
Farmhouse B&B
www.karenbrown.com/ireland/glencarne.html

Hollywell is a lovely old house set in a large garden overlooking the River Shannon. It has a secluded riverside location, just a couple of minutes' walk to the heart of Carrick-on-Shannon, a lively riverside town which is a major terminus for weekly boat hire on the Shannon. For six generations, Tom Maher's family were the proprietors of the Bush Hotel and now Tom and Rosaleen keep up the family's tradition for outstanding hospitality as they welcome guests into their lovely home. Guests have a large sitting room with comfy sofas, books, games, and TV where they gather round the fire in the evening. Breakfast is the only meal served at the little tables arranged round the grand piano in the dining room, but there is no shortage of places to eat dinner in town. Three grandfather clocks grace the hallways and a sofa and books are grouped at the head of the stairs to take advantage of the view over a broad stretch of the river. The two very large front bedrooms share the same lovely view, while the back bedrooms are small only in comparison to those at the front. You can fish without ever leaving Hollywell's grounds. A few of the stately houses within reach are Strokestown House and gardens, Carriglass, Clonalis, King House, Florence Court, Castle Coole, Belvedre House and Gardens. *Directions*: From Dublin take the N4 (Sligo road) to Carrick. Cross the river, turn up the hill by Gings pub, and Hollywell is on the left.

HOLLYWELL
Owners: Rosaleen & Tom Maher
Liberty Hill, Carrick-on-Shannon
Co Leitrim, Ireland
Tel & fax: (078) 21124
Email: hollywell@esatbiz.com
4 rooms
£30–£39 per person B&B
Closed Christmas & New Year
Credit cards: all major
Country house
www.karenbrown.com/ireland/hollywell.html

The setting for Cashel House is spectacularly impressive: at the head of Cashel Bay with Cashel Hill standing guard behind, a solid white house nestles amongst acres and acres of woodland and gardens of exotic flowering shrubs. Kilometers of garden footpaths are yours to wander along, and the beautiful seashore is yours to explore. This is not the kind of hotel to spend just a night in—once you have settled into your lovely room and sampled the exquisite food in the splendid conservatory dining room, you will be glad that you have made Cashel House the base for your Connemara explorations. Graceful antiques, turf fires, and lovely arrangements of freshly picked flowers create a warm, country-house welcome. It feels particularly decadent to have breakfast served to you in bed on a prettily decorated tray. All the bedrooms are beautifully furnished and decorated, each accompanied by a sparkling bathroom. Thirteen exquisite suites occupy a more modern wing and enjoy comfortable sitting areas overlooking the garden. Tennis rackets are available so that keen tennis players can enjoy the court bordering the bay. Riding lessons and treks are a big feature for many guests. Beyond this sheltered spot Connemara is yours to explore. *Directions:* Take the N59 from Galway (towards Clifden) through Oughterard and turn left to the village of Cashel 2 km after Recess.

CASHEL HOUSE
Owners: Kay & Dermot McEvilly
Cashel
Connemara
Co Galway, Ireland
Tel: (095) 31001, Fax: (095) 31077
Email: info@cashel-house-hotel.com
32 rooms
Double: £170–£190*, Suite: £210*
Dinner: from £35*, *Plus 12½% service
Closed mid-Jan to mid-Feb
Credit cards: all major
Country house hotel
www.karenbrown.com/ireland/cashelhouse.html

A stupendous location, delectable food, and a warm welcome combine to make Legends Townhouse a real winner. The Rock of Cashel looms large behind the house and views of the rocky outcrop topped with its cluster of ancient buildings are relished from the restaurant, the guests' sitting area, and several of the bedrooms. The house was purpose-built by a former owner who was not concerned with architectural merit. However, once you are inside, lots of country pine, simple but pleasing décor, spectacular views, and superb food make up for architectural mediocrity. I enjoyed a heavenly Cashel blue cheese salad with greens, pears and walnuts; John Dory on a bed of spinach with a light lemon butter sauce; and, to finish, a perfect crème brulée with poached pear—all savored with a direct view of the floodlit Rock. After dinner we headed through the back garden and adjacent car park to the theater to enjoy a toe-tapping evening of traditional Irish dancing and music called Brú Ború. The town deserves a day for exploring and shopping, which gives you the excuse to come back for lunch. Legends tempts you to stay several days to visit Kilkenny, Waterford, and Cahir Castle, coming home each night in time for dinner. *Directions:* Arriving from Dublin on the N8, you see an Esso garage on the right on the outskirts of town. Twenty meters beyond, turn right and do a U-turn onto the R660 towards Holycross. Legends Townhouse is 20 meters down this road on the left.

LEGENDS TOWNHOUSE & RESTAURANT **New**
Owners: Rosemary & Michael O'Neill
The Kiln
Cashel
Co Tipperary, Ireland
Tel: (062) 61292, Fax: none
Email: info@legendsguesthouse.com
7 rooms
£30–£33 per person B&B, Dinner: £22–£26
Closed Christmas & mid-Feb to mid-Mar
Credit cards: MC, VS
Restaurant with rooms
www.karenbrown.com/ireland/legends.html

Ballyvolane House sits comfortably in a magnificent setting of gardens and wooded grounds—a grand old mansion, home to Merrie and Jeremy Green. Merrie is an ardent fisherwoman and takes every opportunity to go fishing, though Jeremy says that she usually just points guests in the right direction (she has 10 rods of salmon fishing). Jeremy also claims that their croquet lawn is the most challenging in Ireland—cheating to win is encouraged. Guests soon realize that Jeremy's unselfconscious humor and Merrie's straightforward sense of fun are applied to everything, which certainly means that guests to this gracious mansion do not walk around talking in hushed whispers: a cheerful camaraderie pervades the place. This is a friendly, happy house where guests wander in and out of the kitchen, which is in a vast, tall-ceilinged, drawing-type of room. After drinks in the drawing room guests gather for dinner round the long polished table watched over by a parade of benevolent ancestors. One of the lovely bedrooms has a bath so deep that you have to step up to get into it. Within a radius of a few kilometers there are no fewer than 16 golf courses and within an hour's drive are Blarney, with its famous castle, Cork city, Fota House with its paintings, and the bustling fishing and boating town of Kinsale. A self-catering cottage is also available. *Directions:* From Fermoy take the N8 towards Cork to Rathcormac where the 6-km drive to Ballyvolane House is signposted to your left.

BALLYVOLANE HOUSE
Owners: Merrie & Jeremy Green
Castlelyons Co Cork, Ireland
Tel: (025) 36349, Fax: (025) 36781
Email: ballyvol@iol.ie
6 rooms, 1 cottage
£40–£50 per person B&B, Dinner: £26
Open all year
Credit cards: all major
Country house & self-catering
www.karenbrown.com/ireland/ballyvolanehouse.html

Kathy and Paul Sheehy's Old Parochial House has been quite a few things during its time. The Earl of Shannon built it in 1784 for his land agent, though he used the house as a handy place to house a string of mistresses. Subsequently it became home to the Bishop of Cloyne and then the parish priest. The Sheehys have put its somewhat chequered past behind them and, after extensive renovations involving a lot of painstaking hard work, have created one of Castlemartyr's gems and a home for their young family. You can sit among the ancient grapevines in summer and toast your toes by the fire in the lovely sitting room in winter. Breakfast is the only meal served but there is no shortage of delectable restaurants to suit every price range in the area. Upstairs, the absolutely delightful bedrooms include four-posters and a big brass bed, sparkling modern bathrooms, and a sofa bed in some rooms to accommodate an extra person. Whether you enjoy playing golf, walking beaches, visiting craft shops, sailing, or walking, they are all nearby. Sightseers head for the Jameson distillery in nearby Midleton and the Cobh Experience in Cobh where the old railway station tells the story of this port, which was for many emigrants the departure point for a new life in America. *Directions:* From Cork take the N25 for 15 km towards Waterford to Castlemartyr. At the far end of the village go over the bridge and turn right, signposted Shanagarry. Keep immediately left and the Old Parochial House is the first house on the left.

OLD PAROCHIAL HOUSE   *New*
Owners: Kathy & Paul Sheehy
Castlemartyr, Midleton
Co Cork, Ireland
Tel: (021) 4667454, Fax: (021) 4667429
Email: oph@eastcork.net
3 rooms
£35–£40 per person B&B
Closed Christmas & New Year
Credit cards: MC, VS
Country house
www.karenbrown.com/ireland/parochial.html

With its close proximity to Shannon airport, Carnelly House makes an ideal first or last night's stay in Ireland. Dramatically set at the end of a long driveway, this grand Queen-Anne-style Georgian residence offers the most spacious, luxury accommodation at grand hotel prices. On arrival, guests are offered tea or coffee in the large drawing room where softly painted paneled walls and slipcovered chairs present an inviting picture. Guests sip pre-dinner drinks here under the ornate La Francini plasterwork ceiling. Apparently the Francini brothers labored for over a year on the delicate tracery and were paid for their efforts in Irish whiskey. Dinner is wonderful (parties of four plus) and the service personnel are charming and competent. Up the grand staircase are the very large bedrooms, with old paneled walls painted in soft pastels that coordinate with elegant drapes and fitted bedspreads. Each bedroom has a very large bathroom that is nothing short of splendid. Bunratty Folk Park is just down the road. The Burren, Ailwee caves, Cliffs of Moher, and Yeats's home, Thoor Ballylee, are also worth a visit. *Directions:* From Shannon airport take the N18 towards Ennis and Galway. Watch for Dromoland Castle on your right: Carnelly House is 4 km from Dromoland's gates on your left (after you go under the pylons watch for the entrance at the end of an old estate wall).

CARNELLY HOUSE
Owners: Rosemarie & Dermott Gleeson
Clarecastle
Co Clare, Ireland
Tel: (065) 6828442, Fax: (065) 6829222
Email: info@carnelly-house.com
5 rooms
Double: £180, Dinner: £35
Open: all year
Credit cards all major
Country house
www.karenbrown.com/ireland/carnelly.html

On a sunny day there is nowhere more magical than Dolphin Beach House, set on its own 35-acre headland at the head of Clifden Bay. The views across the water to Slyne Head and Ballconneely Bay are the best that wild, untamed places can supply. Billy and Barbara tell me that their headland offers views of dolphins, seals, otters, foxes, and all kinds of seabirds. The view changes by the minute with the vagaries of the Irish weather and you can sit for hours just watching the seascape unfold. Warm weather finds guest soaking up the sun on the most private of beaches. The house was built to give views not only from the dining room but also from several of the bedrooms—be sure to request one of these. I particularly enjoyed Bay View, a tall-ceilinged room with wooden floors, a king-sized sleigh bed, and French windows framing sea views. As well as telling exuberant tales about the area, Billy turns his hand to cooking and offers a set, three-course dinner. It's very much a family operation and when I visited, three of the Foyles' five children were working alongside their parents. *Directions:* Take the N59 from Galway to Clifden and follow the one-way system to the top of town where you take the upper fork at the first Y-junction (in front of the Alcock and Brown hotel) onto the Sky Road, which traces the peninsula. After 3 km take the first left, Lower Sky Road, a narrow lane, for 1 km to Dolphin Beach House.

DOLPHIN BEACH HOUSE   **New**
Owners: Barbara & Billy Foyle
Lower Sky Road
Clifden
Co Galway, Ireland
Tel: (095) 21204, Fax: (095) 22935
Email: dolphinbeach@iolfree.ie
8 rooms
£35–£45 per person B&B, Dinner: £23
Open Mar to Nov
Credit cards: MC, VS
B&B
www.karenbrown.com/ireland/dolphin.html

Mal Dua is not included because of its architectural merits (it's a stark modern building with flower-filled swans on the gateposts and concrete gnomes on the patio), but because it has most attractive, tastefully decorated bedrooms and welcoming owners in Peter and Aideen Byrne. The sunny lobby doubles as a sitting room with sofas and chairs in deep-pink velour which match the carpet and the balloon shades. An additional larger sitting room is decorated in shades of pink like the adjacent spacious dining room. All bedrooms except the tiny single are spacious and come with different combinations of double and single beds. All have a bath or shower, hairdryer, TV, phone, trouser press, excellent reading lights, and tea- and coffee-makings. The decor is very attractive, with pastel-painted walls and coordinating drapes and bedspreads. The bedrooms are no-smoking. Light meals are available between noon and 9 pm. There are also restaurants aplenty just up the road in the lively little town of Clifden. Rent a bicycle and explore the area (a courtesy bus is available for the less adventurous). During the third week in August, Clifden hosts the Connemara Pony Show and rooms are at a premium. *Directions:* Take the N59 from Galway to the outskirts of Clifden. Mal Dua is on your right as you enter the town.

MAL DUA
Owners: Peter & Aideen Byrne
Galway Road
Clifden
Co Galway, Ireland
Tel: (095) 21171, Fax: (095) 21739
Email: info@maldua.com
14 rooms
£35–£40 per person B&B, Meals: £10–£20
Open all year
Credit cards: all major
B&B
www.karenbrown.com/ireland/maldua.html

The harbormaster certainly picked a pretty site for his home on the quay, with its wide vista of the inlet of Ardbear Bay and the town of Clifden winding up the hillside. Since 1820, Quay House has served variously as the harbormaster's home, a convent, a monastery, and a hotel. Julia and Paddy bought the house and the adjacent cottages in almost derelict condition, giving them a new lease of life as a stylish hotel. They decorated the whole in a refreshingly eclectic style, blending old, modern, and unconventional in an idiosyncratic way with little jokes and quirks such as Vegetarian Alley, a corridor of hunting trophies. Breakfast is the only meal served in the conservatory. For dinner, a five-minute walk brings you into town where there are several good restaurants. There are seven spacious studios, of which six have small fitted kitchens and balconies, and seven bedrooms. All rooms have spacious bathrooms with separate showers and tubs. Several are "traditional country house" in their decor, others light, fresh, and more bohemian. Particular favorites are Napoleon, a tribute room to the famous Frenchman, Out of Africa, a safari-themed studio, and The Bird Room, a studio with a few wacky stuffed parrots and a couple of large pictures featuring parrots. *Directions:* Take the N59 from Galway to Clifden and follow the one-way system to the top of the town where you take the lower fork at the first Y-junction down onto the quay.

THE QUAY HOUSE
Owners: Julia & Paddy Foyle
Beach Road
Clifden
Co Galway, Ireland
Tel: (095) 21369, Fax: (095) 21608
Email: thequay@iol.ie
14 rooms
£45–£50 per person B&B
Open Easter to Nov
Credit cards: all major
Country house & self-catering
www.karenbrown.com/ireland/quayhouse.html

Rock Glen is a cozy hotel converted from an 18th-century hunting lodge with all the outdoor beauties of Connemara at its doorstep. Enjoy the delights of the area, safe in the certainty that a warm welcome, superlative food, and a snug retreat await you on your return to Rock Glen. John and Evangeline Roche and their daughter Siobhan are your personable hosts. An inviting grouping of plump chairs around a turf fire, the chatter of locals and guests, and the warmth of the adjacent sun lounge invite you to linger in the bar. The dining room, decked out in shades of gold and pink, its tables laid with silver, complements the fine country-house-style cuisine that is served here. The exceedingly comfortable bedrooms are by and large uniform in size and decorated in pastel shades, all well equipped with trouser press, hairdryer, and TV. Several have distant sea views. For families, request number 35, with two bedrooms and private balcony looking out to the sea. The hotel also has a full-sized snooker table and an all-weather tennis court. If you would like to rent a house on a weekly basis, enquire about Churchill House, a lovely four-bedroom, four-bath old schoolhouse in the heart of Clifden. Connemara's stunning scenery is on your doorstep. *Directions:* Take the N59 from Galway to Clifden, then just after passing the church, turn left towards Ballyconeely. Rock Glen is to your right about 1 km from town.

ROCK GLEN HOTEL
Owners: Evangeline, Siobhan, & John Roche
Clifden, Connemara
Co Galway, Ireland
Tel: (095) 21035, Fax: (095) 21737
Email: rockglen@iol.ie
27 rooms, 1 cottage
Double: £124*, Suite: from £208*, Dinner: £33*
*Plus 12½% service
Churchill House: £650–£950 weekly
Open mid-Mar to Nov, Credit cards: all major
Country house hotel & self-catering
www.karenbrown.com/ireland/rockglenhotel.html

If you long to visit a spot off the beaten track and enjoy wonderful hospitality and divine food, you can do no better than to stay with Lucy and Johnny Madden at Hilton Park. Lucy has such a reputation for her food that she makes TV appearances and Johnny's family home is so grand that it is hard to believe that it is a real home and not the kind where you pay a visitor's entrance fee. It's a beautiful house of lovely rooms where guestrooms range from vast, with grand floor-to-ceiling beds that you climb into (accompanied by huge bathrooms with claw-foot tubs), to more modest in size, with regular-sized bathrooms containing lovely old soaking tubs. Guests relax in the beautiful drawing room, enjoying pre-dinner drinks, conversation, and views across the terrace of formal gardens to the lake. The same enchanting view is enjoyed in the elegant dining room where guests dine at separate tables by the gentle flicker of candlelight. Breakfast is taken "below stairs" in the former servants' hall. Most of Hilton Park's sightseeing lies to the northwest and the most popular trips are to Belleek, with its pottery, Lough Erne, and the Enniskillen area to visit Castle Coole (a restored Palladian mansion) and Florence Court (a riot of rococo plasterwork). *Directions:* From Cavan take the Clones road. At the end of the speed limit turn right after the Statoil petrol station. Go through Ballyhaise and Scotshouse and the entrance to Hilton Park is on your left 1 km after the Clones Golf Club.

HILTON PARK
Owners: Lucy & Johnny Madden
Scotshouse, Clones
Co Monaghan, Ireland
Tel: (047) 56007, Fax: (047) 56033
Email: jm@hiltonpark.ie
6 rooms
Double: £128–£150
Dinner: £27–£50 (not Sun orMon)
Open Apr to Sep, Credit cards: MC, VS
Country house
www.karenbrown.com/ireland/hilton.html

Guests stopping at Rockwood House on their way north have been known to go no farther, contenting themselves with whiling away the hours in this peaceful spot and enjoying the warm hospitality that Susan and James McCauley offer. Susan and James returned here after living in Dublin for many years, acquired a derelict rectory with trees growing through the roof, and replaced it with a well-appointed replica—Rockwood House. Enjoy breakfast in the conservatory overlooking the garden and relax round the fire in the sitting room. Upstairs, the spacious, very nicely decorated bedrooms are each accompanied by a snug bathroom. Beds are double, twin, or king if you request that the twin beds be zipped together. County Cavan, delightfully off the hectic tourist route, is blessed with picture-postcard scenery—whichever way you turn you find waterways, rivers, and lakes set among gently rolling hills. Opportunities for fishing and walking abound. *Directions:* From Cavan follow signs for the N3 to Monaghan, then turn right at the sign for Monaghan/Butlersbridge (N54). Rockwood House is on your left, 3 km from the village of Butlersbridge.

ROCKWOOD HOUSE
Owners: Susan & James McCauley
Cloverhill
Belturbet
Co Cavan, Ireland
Tel: (047) 55351, Fax: (047) 55373
4 rooms
£20 per person B&B
Closed Christmas
Credit cards: MC, VS
B&B

The charm of Greenhill House is Elizabeth Hegarty, who is exceptionally sweet and helpful. I very much enjoyed the late-evening conversation around the drawing room fire with a cup of tea and cakes, while James and Elizabeth and fellow guests were "putting the world to rights." All this after a 6:30 pm dinner that included a groaning dessert trolley where Elizabeth encouraged guests to try a bit of everything. Wine is not served. The beautiful farmhouse is lovingly decorated with antiques, and bouquets of fresh garden flowers add the finishing touches. Our bedroom (overlooking an immaculate garden) had everything: sightseeing information; a tray set with teapot, kettle, tea bags, coffee, and chocolate; hairdryer; television; and even a little box of After Eight mints by the bedside. Plump comforters top the beds and fluffy towels hang on the old-fashioned towel rail, all coordinating in shades of pink with the curtains and the carpet. Bedrooms in the attic have bathrooms tucked neatly under the eaves while other rooms have snug shower rooms, in what at first appears to be large fitted closets. You should plan on staying here for several days. With Greenhill House as a base you can set off to explore the Antrim coast. *Directions:* From Co Donegal, take the N13 to Derry. Cross the Foyle Bridge and at Limavady take the A37 towards Coleraine, turn right on the A29 (Garvagh and Cookstown road) for 11 km, turning left on the B66 (Greenhill Road) and Greenhill House is on the right.

GREENHILL HOUSE
Owners: Elizabeth & James Hegarty
24 Greenhill Road
Aghadowey, Coleraine
Co Londonderry, BT51 4EU, Northern Ireland
Tel: (028) 7086 8241, Fax: (028) 7086 8365
Email: greenhill.house@btinternet.com
6 rooms
£25 per person B&B, Dinner: £17.50
Open Mar to Oct
Credit cards: MC, VS
Farmhouse B&B
www.karenbrown.com/ireland/greenhill.html

Markree Castle, Charles Cooper's ancestral family home, is a fine example of a castle built as an impressive family home complete with battlements and turrets rather than as a fortification. From the entrance broad stone steps lead you into the impressive reception hall with its grand staircase rising to an enormous stained-glass window portraying a fanciful depiction of the family tree with Henry VIII center stage. The reception hall opens up to the central hall, which rises through three stories to an elaborate wooden ceiling. This impressive room with its groupings of tables and chairs leads to several smaller sitting rooms and a bar. The elaborate plaster cherubs decorating the dining room all add to the castle-hotel ambiance. At the time of my visit (1996) the high-ceilinged principal bedrooms up the broad staircase were not as well decorated as they could have been but I appreciated their spaciousness. I much preferred the rooms at the top of the castle (lift access available). The castle is run in a more casual manner than the grander, more formal Irish castle hotels. Markree is in the heart of Yeats country with magnificent scenery all around. Golden sand beaches line the shore, while rugged mountains such as Knocknarea and Ben Bulben and placid lakes such as Lough Gill and Lough Arrow make for a marvelous variety of scenery. *Directions:* From Sligo take the N4 (Dublin road) for 11 km—Markree Castle is signposted to your left (1km).

MARKREE CASTLE
Owners: Mary & Charles Cooper Collooney
Co Sligo, Ireland
Tel: (071) 67800, Fax: (071) 67840
Email: markree@iol.ie
28 rooms
Double: £140–£170, Dinner: from £25.90
Closed Christmas
Credit cards: MC, VS
Country house hotel
www.karenbrown.com/ireland/markree.html

Ashford Castle was built over a period of 30 years by Lord Ardilaun in the 19th century. Incorporated into its castellated façade are the remains of the 13th-century de Burgo Castle and the original Ashford House, built in the style of a French château. However, I do not know of a château that has a setting comparable to Ashford Castle's—it is situated in spectacular parklike grounds on the shores of Lough Corrib, a vast, island-dotted lake. The views across the lake are stunning. It certainly was a sumptuous residence and in more recent years has been renovated and luxuriously appointed to create one of Europe's premier castle hotels. The decor of the public rooms is lavish and opulent—fit for a king and even a president. In fact, the billiard room was built for King George V (then Prince of Wales) when he came to stay in 1905, while a luxurious bed was commissioned for President Reagan's visit in 1984. No meals are included in the quoted tariff. After a splendid candlelit dinner in one of the castle's two restaurants (coat and tie required), you can enjoy Irish entertainment in the Dungeon Bar, take a stroll through the lakeside gardens, or saunter into the adjacent village of Cong. A nine-hole golf course and tennis courts are reserved for guests' use as is a health club with sauna, gym, and Jacuzzi. *Directions:* The castle is 43 km north of Galway on the shores of Lough Corrib.

ASHFORD CASTLE
Manager: Rory Murphy
Cong
Co Mayo, Ireland
Tel: (092) 46003, Fax: (092) 46260
83 rooms
Double: £264–£350*, Suite: £412–£675*
*Breakfast not included: £14.50**, Dinner: £40**
**15% service charge on food and beverages
Open all year
Credit cards: all major
Luxury resort

Cork has been up and coming for several years—its ancient buildings are receiving a face-lift, its stores are bustling, and, thanks to the new bypass, its streets are no longer clogged with traffic. Hayfield Manor, an oasis of calm just a mile from the heart of this lively metropolis, is a brand-new brick and yellow-painted hotel made to look like a dignified old *grande dame*, with much of the charm of an old building and none of the problems. The clubby bar has a no-smoking section and if you are not up for a formal country-house dinner in the gracious dining room, you can enjoy a light supper here. Relax in the library or the pretty residents' lounge or disport yourself at the leisure center with its swimming pool and well-stocked gym. Bedrooms are uniform in size and décor and have individually controlled air conditioning and heating. Walk into the city (20 minutes) for its wealth of shops but be sure not to miss the covered market with its stallholders selling everything from fish and vegetables to underwear and pots and pans. Farther afield lie Blarney, Kinsale, Midleton, and Cobh where you can take a spin around the vast expanse of Cork harbor. *Directions*: From the east go onto the one-way system following signs for city center, then university (brown sign) and Killarney. Pass Jury's Hotel, take the first left, trace the university grounds, go right, then immediately left and into Hayfield Manor's grounds. Best ask the hotel to send you a map.

HAYFIELD MANOR
Owners: Margaret & Joe Scally
Manager: Margaret Naughton
Perrott Avenue
Cork, Ireland
Tel: (021) 4315600, Fax: (021) 4316839
Email: enquiries@hayfieldmanor.ie
87 rooms
Double: £200–£220, Suite: £240–£350
Dinner: £35
Open all year, Credit cards: all major
Country house hotel
www.karenbrown.com/ireland/hayfield.html

Seven North Mall, a 1740s townhouse beside the River Lee, is a perfect location for exploring the up-and-coming historic town of Cork. Up the narrow stairs, bedrooms are spotless and simply decorated in pleasing colors—request a room with a view of the river or, if you prefer spaciousness over view, opt for the "best room" that faces the back of the house. A ground-floor room is wheelchair friendly and often requested by guests who have difficulty with stairs. Angela Hegarty prides herself on the excellence of her breakfasts, discussing with guests the array of cooked dishes available following the freshly squeezed juice, fruit, and cereal—her scrambled eggs deserve a special mention. There is no shortage of places to walk to for dinner, from atmospheric pubs to delightful restaurants. Cork is easily explored on foot and the medieval quarter is becoming more of a destination now it is receiving extensive restoration. The Cobh Experience, which traces the history of this historic port, is accessible by train. A short drive finds you at Blarney with its famous castle and woolen mill. *Directions:* Arriving in Cork, follow the one-way system beside the River Lee (lots of lane changing) past five bridges. Pull in between the large black gates beside Number Seven to the car park. The car park is locked at night.

SEVEN NORTH MALL
Owner: Angela Hegarty
7 North Mall
Cork City, Ireland
Tel: (021) 397191, Fax: (021) 300811
Email: sevennorthmall@tinet.ie
7 rooms
£35–£45 per person B&B
Closed Christmas
Credit cards: MC, VS
Guesthouse
www.karenbrown.com/ireland/seven.html

Fergus View is a perfect stepping-off place for those arriving at Shannon airport and heading north, but stretch your visit to several nights so that you can explore the area. Fergus View was built as a teacher's residence at the turn of the century and Declan's grandfather was its first occupant. Continuing in his grandfather's footsteps, Declan is the principal of Corofin's school. Mary has offered a welcome to the family home for many years and continues to find new ways to make it more appealing—recently she has added a spacious entryway and replaced all the windows with original-style Oregon pine. She cooks excellent farmhouse-style dinners incorporating salad and vegetables from the large garden. The fire is lit in the little parlor and guests browse through the books and information on the area. Declan and Mary take great pride in their heritage and have compiled a most intersting booklet on the area, which details its history and points of interest. Bedrooms are on the modest side when compared to many of this guide's listings and one has possibly the smallest of shower rooms. All are of the leave-large-cases-in-the-car variety—facilities are not designed for persons of large proportions. One bedroom has its large top-of-the-line bathroom across the hall. The Kellehers also have a lovely self-catering cottage for week-long stays. The nearby Burren is most interesting, and the magnificent Cliffs of Moher are close at hand. *Directions:* Shannon lies 37 km to the south. From the airport take the N18 to Ennis, the N85 towards Lisdoonvarna, turn first right to Corofin, pass through the village, and the house is on your left after 3 km.

FERGUS VIEW
Owners: Mary & Declan Kelleher
Kilnaboy, Corofin
Co Clare, Ireland
Tel: (065) 6837606, Fax: (065) 6837192
Email: deckell@indigo.ie
6 rooms, 1 cottage
£22–£24 per person B&B, Dinner: £17 (not Fri to Sun)
Open Apr to mid-Oct, Credit cards: none
B&B & self-catering
www.karenbrown.com/ireland/fergusview.html

St. Clerans has had an impressive list of Irish owners but came into the limelight when John Huston (film director extraordinaire) called it home for over 20 years and spent an absolute mint on the place. More recently this impressive home has prepared itself for the next millennium with another no-holds-barred facelift from chat-show host Merv Griffin and when he is not in residence you can enjoy a stay at his luxurious retreat. It's a treat to see an architectural gem coddled to the extent that this one is where everything is the absolute best that money can buy—the essence of pure indulgence. One of the most charming bedrooms is the octagonal little building that was once Angelica Houston's playhouse. She would not recognize it today with its stenciled walls and opulent bathroom. The other 11 bedrooms, all found in the main house, are boldly decorated in the most luxurious of country house styles. Local sightseeing is in short supply—guests usually spend the day lounging on the premises soaking up the ambiance and being totally spoiled by the attentive Irish staff; play golf at Athenry and Loughrea; or go horseriding or clay-pigeon shooting. *Directions*: From Galway take the N6 towards Dublin for 30 km to Craughwell. Go through the village and take the second left signposted St. Clerans and Athenry for the 8-km drive to St. Clerans.

ST. CLERANS   New
Owner: Merv Griffin
Manager: Seamus Dooley
Craughwell
Co Galway, Ireland
Tel: (091) 846555, Fax: (091) 846600
12 rooms
Double: £270–£380, Dinner: £45
Open all year when Merv's not there
Credit cards: all major
Country house hotel

Enniscoe House is the home of Susan Kellett—a descendant of the original family who settled this estate in the 1670s—her son, and their labrador Strider. Staying as her guest gives you a glimpse of what it was like to live in a grand country mansion—the old family furniture, portraits, books, and family memorabilia are yours to enjoy. The lofty rooms are decorated true to the Georgian period and all are in tiptop condition. The three front bedrooms, of enormous proportions, are reached by a grand elliptical staircase. Those in the older part of the house are less grand but just as lovely. I particularly enjoyed the old nursery with half-tester and twin beds, and comfortable chintz chairs drawn round the fireplace. Dinners by soft, flickering candlelight at little tables artfully arranged in the large dining room are a real treat. Tucked behind the house, the courtyard buildings house four delightful farmhouse-style self-catering apartments. The Victorian walled garden has been given a new lease of life and the barns display old farm machinery and local artifacts. Personable fishery manager Barry Segrave offers help to anglers fishing Lough Conn (*tel: 096-31853, fax: 096-31773*). Walk the trails that go through the woodlands past the forestry plantations and along the lake shore. There are great cliffs along the north coast, where the Stone-Age settlements at Céide Fields are being excavated. *Directions:* From Ballina take the N59 to Crossmolina, turn left in town for Castlebar, and the house is on the left after 3 km.

ENNISCOE HOUSE
Owner: Susan Kellett
Castlehill, Crossmolina
Co Mayo, Ireland
Tel: (096) 31112, Fax: (096) 31773
Email: mail@enniscoe.com
6 rooms, 4 apartments
Double: £120–£132, Dinner: £24
Apartments: £210–£360 weekly
Open Apr to mid-Oct, Credit cards: all major
Country house & self-catering
www.karenbrown.com/ireland/enniscoehouse.html

Cleevaun has the advantage not only of an exquisite position facing the mouth of Dingle Bay, but also of being purposely built as a bed and breakfast, so each of the bedrooms has a modern en-suite shower or bathroom, telephone, and television. The weather was blustery and cool when we stayed but, inside, efficient central heating kept the house toasty and we appreciated the abundance of hot water in the shower and the luxury of towels hot from the heated towel rail. The decor is tasteful and uncluttered and several rooms have exquisite views across the fields to the bay. Guests are encouraged to come into the sitting room for a cup of tea and a slice of porter cake and to browse through an extensive collection of books and pamphlets on Ireland and the Dingle Peninsula in particular, which help you appreciate the beauty and folklore of the area. Pine tables and chairs are arranged to capture the lovely view of Dingle Bay from the adjacent dining room and guests enjoy a hearty breakfast before setting out to explore. In 1994 Cleevaun won the Galtee Breakfast of the Year award. It would be a pity to come so far and not experience the peace and tranquillity that the unspoiled scenery of this area has to offer, so allow plenty of time for meandering down narrow country roads and walking along deserted beaches. The peninsula is rich in historical remains, particularly beehive huts that were used as individual cells by ascetic monks in the earliest monasteries. *Directions:* Cleevaun is 2 km beyond Dingle town on the road to Slea Head.

CLEEVAUN
Owners: Charlotte & Sean Cluskey
Lady's Cross, Dingle
Co Kerry, Ireland
Tel: (066) 9151108, Fax: (066) 9152228
Email: cleevaun@iol.ie
9 rooms
£25–£30.50 per person B&B
Open mid-Mar to mid-Nov
Credit cards: MC, VS
B&B
www.karenbrown.com/ireland/cleevaun.html

Doyle's Restaurant is famous the world over for the excellence of its seafood, fresh from the ocean. A small village shop and pub built in 1790 house the welcoming restaurant with its flagstone floor and cozy arrangements of tables and chairs while the house next door offers the most delightful accommodation in Dingle. The two houses are interconnected yet self-contained, so that guests can come and go to restaurant but will not have their peace disturbed when they are sleeping. You step from the street into the old-fashioned parlor with its pine floor, grandfather clock, and sofas drawn into seating areas—large umbrellas are close at hand to shelter you while bringing your luggage in, should it be raining. The eight spacious bedrooms here have good size bathrooms and are decorated in a most comfortable, traditional style with 20th-century amenities such as television and phone. The two ground-floor rooms are ideal for anyone who has difficulty with stairs. Just up the road a courtyard of four little townhouses offers complete privacy. Each has its own entrance, a snug downstairs sitting room, and a bedroom and bathroom upstairs. After dinner inquire at the bar which of the many little pubs has traditional music that night and stroll along to join in the merriment. *Directions:* Dingle is a 2½-hour drive from Limerick. Turn right at the roundabout, right into John Street, and Doyle's is on your left. Parking is on the street.

DOYLE'S
Owners: Sean & Charlotte Clusky
John Street
Dingle
Co Kerry, Ireland
Tel: (066) 9151174, Fax: (066) 9151816
Email: cdoyles@iol.ie
12 rooms
£39–£42 per person B&B, Dinner: £20–£32 (not Sun)
Closed Christmas & mid-Jan to mid-Feb
Credit cards: all major
Restaurant with rooms
www.karenbrown.com/ireland/doyles.html

Mary and John Curran built Greenmount House as a home for themselves and their small children then later expanded their moderately sized bungalow, adding a grand wing of eight luxurious rooms, a large sitting room, and additional accommodation for themselves and their family. Their top-of-the-line rooms are a delight: all have French windows opening onto a patio or balcony and are large enough to accommodate a spacious sitting area—the kind of rooms you want to spend time in. The considerably less expensive rooms, snug by comparison, are charmingly decorated. A conservatory breakfast room, prettily furnished with painted pine furniture, has a panoramic view across fields and Dingle's rooftops to the harbor. Mary prepares the most bountiful of breakfasts and tries to offer at least two fruit dishes, delicious mueslis, and yogurts as well as a cooked breakfast menu that includes not only the traditional breakfast but also fish and mushrooms in yogurt sauce. Breakfast is the only meal served. For dinner you can stroll down the hill into town where there are some particularly fine fish restaurants. Wander down to the harbor and watch the catch come in, window shop, and enjoy a pint in one of the many pubs. Explore the byways of the peninsula and if the weather is fine, take a trip to the Blasket Islands. *Directions:* Turn right at the roundabout in Dingle, next right into John Street, and continue up the hill to Greenmount House.

GREENMOUNT HOUSE
Owners: Mary & John Curran
Gortonora
Dingle
Co Kerry, Ireland
Tel: (066) 9151414, Fax: (066) 9151974
Email: greenmounthouse@tinet.ie
12 rooms
£25–£45 per person B&B
Closed Christmas
Credit cards: MC, VS
B&B
www.karenbrown.com/ireland/greenmounthouse.html

Heaton's, a purpose-built guesthouse, commands an enviable position at the head of Dingle Bay, with spectacular views across the water to Burnham Headlands and the mouth of this sheltered harbor, yet is just a five-minute walk from the heart of this lively town. Nuala and Cameron built the house a few years ago and while the style outside is modern, the inside is more traditional, with beechwood Shaker furniture and drapes and sofas in warm, cheerful colors. The bedrooms are smartly decorated in navy and beige, with beds coming in sizes from twin to king. Nuala is a stickler for quality when it comes to bedding and towels, so crisp white sheets adorn the beds and good-quality towels hang in the sparkling white bathrooms, which all have power showers over the tubs. Eight of the rooms have views to the bay and three are large enough to accommodate a second bed for a child. The four largest rooms have sitting areas with comfortable chairs. Daughter Jackie, the breakfast chef, makes certain breakfast is a full Irish spread of local produce with the fish and free-range egg omelets deserving a special mention. *Directions:* Arriving in Dingle, keep the harbor to your left and Heaton's is located 1 km beyond the marina on your right, overlooking the bay.

HEATON'S
Owners: Nuala, Jackie & Cameron Heaton
The Wood
Dingle
Co Kerry, Ireland
Tel: (066) 9152288, Fax: (066) 9152324
Email: heatons@iol.ie
16 rooms
£25–£40 per person B&B
Open all year
Credit cards: MC, VS
Guesthouse
www.karenbrown.com/ireland/heatons.html

Set on a wooded, tidal island in Donegal Bay and joined to the mainland by a narrow causeway, St. Ernan's house was built in 1826 by John Hamilton, a nephew of the Duke of Wellington, for his wife. Over lunch here one day, Brian and Carmel O'Dowd decided that St. Ernan's was the kind of hotel they would like to own, so several years later when it came on the market they took the plunge and forsook their careers in banking and teaching to become hoteliers. From almost every one of the rooms you are treated to marvelous views across a mirrorlike span of water. In the lounge, window seats offer views across the water to the mainland and chairs are artfully arranged to provide numerous nooks for intimate after-dinner conversation. A four-course candlelit dinner, with choices for each course, is served in the dining room. The attractive bedrooms come in all shapes and sizes, with the larger view rooms commanding the highest prices. Be sure to enjoy the walk around this delightful little island. The center of bustling Donegal town is The Diamond, a market place surrounded by shops (Magees sells the famous tweed), a hotel, and some pubs. Beyond Donegal town lies the wild, rugged landscape that has made this county famous. *Directions:* From Sligo take the N15 towards Donegal and St. Ernan's is signposted to your left 2 km before you reach Donegal town.

ST. ERNAN'S HOUSE HOTEL
Owners: Carmel & Brian O'Dowd
Donegal
Co Donegal, Ireland
Tel: (073) 21065, Fax: (073) 22098
Email: info@sainternans.com
12 rooms
Double: £166–£190, Suite: £250–£280
Dinner: £17–£35
Open mid-Apr to Oct
Credit cards: MC, VS
Country house hotel
www.karenbrown.com/ireland/sternans.html

"What a great place to have a party!" I exclaimed—and the thought had not escaped former owners, for there are tales in the town of grand parties long ago with guests dancing in the expansive drawing and dining rooms and a quartet in the back hallway, as well as more recent tales of more lowbrow entertainment. These aristocratic rooms have been restored to their former glory, with a wedding-cake icing of plasterwork ringing their lofty ceilings above sink-in sofas and chairs and a vast dining-room table. Upstairs has received the same sensitive treatment. The two premier rooms at the front of the house have vast bathrooms with large tubs and separate showers and enough room in the bedrooms to accommodate seating by the fire and a couple of beds. Between them stands an extra bedroom (without bath), ideal for an older child or traveling companion. The fourth bedroom overlooks the courtyard. For dinner, guests usually walk to the restaurant in town or, when that is closed, drive for five minutes to another restaurant. With advance notice Laura will prepare a simple supper. Michael and Laura find that many guests are interested in their restoration and often give a tour of "behind the scenes" portions of the property. *Directions*: From Mallow take the N20 towards Limerick for 6.5 km to New Twopothouse. Turn right for the 6.5-km drive to Doneraile where you find Creagh House on your left at the far end of the main street.

CREAGH HOUSE   ***New***
Owners: Laura O'Mahony & Michael O'Sullivan
Main Street
Doneraile
Co Cork, Ireland
Tel: (022) 24433, Fax: (022) 24715
Email: creaghhouse@eircom.ie
4 rooms, 3 en suite
£55 per person B&B
Open Feb to Nov, Credit cards: all major
Country house
www.karenbrown.com/ireland/creagh.html

Sylvan Hill House has that essential ingredient that ensures that guests return again and again—welcoming hosts, Elise and Jimmy Coburn. Elise and Jimmy began taking guests into their delightful home as a means of paying for the installation of a very expensive damp course and they discovered that they loved taking guests from all over the world and all walks of life. Staying here is to become part of the family—if there are two guests, Elise and Jimmy eat with them round the little pine table in the sitting room or if there are more, they join them for dinner in the dining room. The price of dinner includes wine. Dining with guests affords the Coburns the opportunity to help them plan sightseeing forays as far away as the Antrim coast and as close as the craft shops in the local villages. Upstairs, a spacious double-bedded room has an en-suite bathroom, while a snug twin-bedded room has its shower cubicle in the room and an adjacent loo. A third bedroom is available for families who wish to have children share the bathroom with them. *Directions:* Leave the A1 (Belfast to Dublin road) at Dromore (just south of Belfast) and at the mini-roundabout (a painted circle in the road) take the Lurgan road for 1 km where you turn right opposite the factory cottages for the 2-km drive up the hill to Sylvan Hill House.

SYLVAN HILL HOUSE
Owners: Elise & Jimmy Coburn
76 Kilntown Road
Dromore BT25 1HS
Co Down, Northern Ireland
Tel & fax: (028) 926 92321
3 rooms, 2 en suite
£25 per person B&B, Dinner: £16 (inc. wine)
Open all year
Credit cards: none
B&B
www.karenbrown.com/ireland/sylvanhill.html

"Beds and breakfast" are Mairead Power's watchwords—she makes sure that guests have a good bed to sleep in (good mattress, quality cotton sheets) and feeds them a hearty breakfast (bacon, egg, and the works along with homemade jams and breads). Surrender yourself to Mairead's care and enjoy her immaculate housekeeping and the natural friendliness of Dualla House. Seen from the road, the house looks very imposing, with a long driveway culminating in an impressive Georgian farmhouse. However, inside all is homey and charming as Mairead greets you and takes you into her care, brewing you a cup of tea and asking just what you have been up to and how you are liking your holiday. Stroll around the farm where the dogs work the sheep and the fields are full of grain. Relax in the spacious sitting room warmed by a turf fire in chilly weather and enjoy the morning repast in the breakfast room with its original pine boards. Recognize you deserve the best and request a front bedroom—you'll have masses of space and a grand view of the lovely Slievenamon, Comeragh, Knockmealdown, and Galtee mountain ranges. Five minutes' drive away, Cashel offers lots to see in the day and Brú Ború (folk dancing) and great places to eat in the evening. Other nearby attractions include Farney Castle, Tipperary Crystal, and Holycross Abbey. *Directions:* From Cashel take the R688 towards Clonmel, then take the first left (by the church) for the 4-km drive to Dualla where you see Dualla House on your left as you come down the hill.

DUALLA HOUSE   **New**
Owners: Mairead & Martin Power
Dualla, Cashel
Co Tipperary, Ireland
Tel & fax: (062) 61487
Email: duallahse@eircom.net
4 rooms
£22–£25 per person B&B
Open Mar to Nov, Credit cards: MC, VS
No-smoking house
Farmhouse B&B
www.karenbrown.com/ireland/dualla.html

The entrance to the Adams Trinity Hotel is off Dame Lane, a little lane that is hard to access though a maze of back streets in the heart of Dublin. I found it much easier to enter the hotel from the adjoining restaurant, The Mercantile, which fronts onto the main thoroughfare, Dame Street. The Mercantile is a lively bar and eating establishment where patrons sit on broad balconies tiered beneath an ornate plasterwork ceiling—a perfect place for people-watching. In contrast to the hubbub of the restaurant, all is serene in the hotel. A lift takes you from the paneled lobby to your room, which faces either Dame Lane or Dame Street—city views are the order of the day in this central Dublin location. I found the standard bedrooms to be small—just adequate for two people and their luggage. However, the superior rooms that I saw were much more appealing. I particularly enjoyed rooms 205, 208 (king-size bed), and 403. If you cannot afford to splurge on a larger room, request room 202, the largest of the standard rooms. The management and staff are young and friendly. *Directions:* Dame Street begins at the main gates of Trinity College and parallels the River Liffey. With Trinity College at your back the hotel is on your left before you reach Dublin Castle. See *Dublin Walking Tour* map for location.

ADAMS TRINITY HOTEL
Manager: Orla Crehan
28 Dame Lane
Dublin 2
Ireland
Tel: (01) 670 7100, Fax: (01) 670 7101
Email: adams@indigo.ie
28 rooms
Double: £120–£140, Dinner: £12.95
Open all year
Credit cards: all major
City hotel
www.karenbrown.com/ireland/adamstrinity.html

Isolated by acres of fields and gardens, Belcamp Hutchinson is an oasis of country house elegance just 15 minutes' drive from Dublin airport, making this the ideal first or last night's stop if you are flying to or from Dublin. However, it is such an outstanding home and Doreen is such a gracious hostess, that you will want to stay for several days. You'll doubtless be greeted by Digger, Lady, and Smiley who love to meet guests—especially Smiley who loves to talk to them. Up the elegant staircase, the bedrooms are decorated in strong, dark, Georgian colors, each beautifully coordinated with lovely fabrics. Burgundy can be a twin or a king room and has a sofa bed that can accommodate a child. Wedgwood has a romantic four-poster bed. Wicker and Pine are spacious king-sized rooms. Blue is a spacious double, while Terra Cotta and Green are smaller rooms. Doreen always has three or four perfumes on the dresser and a variety of interesting magazines by the bedside. While the heart of Dublin is just a half-hour's drive away, she also suggests that guests not overlook Newgrange, Malahide Castle, and the village of Howth. *Directions:* Belcamp Hutchinson is just off the Malahide Road in the Dublin suburb of Balgriffin. Doreen will fax or mail you detailed directions. See *Dublin Walking Tour* map for location.

BELCAMP HUTCHINSON
Owners: Doreen Gleson & Karl Waldburg
Carrs Lane
Malahide Road
Balgriffin, Dublin 17
Ireland
Tel: (01) 846 0843, Fax: (01) 848 5703
8 rooms
£44 per person B&B
Closed Christmas
Credit cards: MC, VS
Country house
www.karenbrown.com/ireland/belcamphutchinson.html

This delightful townhouse in the Victorian suburb of Ballsbridge has been meticulously restored to create the ambiance of an old country house, though the property has all the modern conveniences of modem points, individually controlled air conditioning (very handy on muggy summer days), and central heating. The house is decorated in a contemporary, airy, Victorian style and furnished in an attractive, uncluttered Victorian way, in keeping with the age of the building. Several of the bedrooms I saw were on the snug side but carefully thought out to provide plenty of room for luggage. Be sure to request the most spacious room available. Five high-ceilinged bedrooms accommodate four-poster beds (though I prefer the space offered by non-four-poster rooms). Tea and coffe are served on a complimentary basis 24 hours a day. You can enjoy a drink and a chat in the library sitting room before either going out to dinner or eating in, choosing from menus where food is delivered from local restaurants. Breakfast finds warm berries and cream and French toast with bacon and maple syrup on the menu as well as more traditional Irish fare. There is off-road parking to the front and rear of the house. It is an easy walk to the 6, 7, and 8 bus routes and a three-minute ride on DART (Dublin Area Rapid Transit) to the rear of Trinity College. *Directions*: Follow signs for South City till you come to Baggot Street, which continues south into Pembroke Street and Lansdowne Road (do not turn right in front of Jury's Hotel). Butlers Town House is on your left before you come to the stadium. See *Dublin Walking Tour* map for location.

BUTLERS TOWN HOUSE
Owner: Chris Vos
44 Lansdowne Road
Ballsbridge, Dublin 4, Ireland
Tel: (01) 667 4022, Fax: (01) 667 3960
Email: info@butlers-hotel.com
20 rooms
Double: £150, Dinner: from £15
Closed Christmas, Credit cards: all major
Guesthouse
www.karenbrown.com/ireland/butlers.html

Ballsbridge, just southeast of Dublin proper, is noted for its Victorian charm. Just across from the British Embassy, the pebbledash, Edwardian-style home of Mary and Gerard Doody offers guestrooms in a three-story extension overlooking their grassy garden. Guests are given a front-door key and come and go through Mary and Gerard's home where they have a hallway seating area with a blazing fire and a comfortable sitting room. Breakfast is the only meal served, but there is no shortage of delightful restaurants and pubs within walking distance. Bedrooms are spacious and splendidly kitted out with good reading lights, desk, phone, TV, and tea- and coffee-makings. Pastel-painted walls coordinate with attractive bedspreads and drapes and the rooms' uncluttered, tailored look is enhanced by fitted ash closets, bedheads, and bedside tables. Several more rooms are offered in the main house. While Merrion Road is a major thoroughfare, a quiet night's sleep is ensured by double-glazed windows. Two major attractions at the nearby Royal Dublin Society are the Agricultural Show in May and the Dublin Horse Show in August. A 15-minute bus ride brings you to the heart of Dublin. *Directions:* Follow signs for South City to Baggot Street, which becomes Pembroke Road. Turn right in front of Jury's Hotel into Merrion Road, continue past the Royal Dublin Society showgrounds, and Cedar Lodge is on your left opposite the British Embassy. See *Dublin Walking Tour* map for location.

CEDAR LODGE
Owners: Mary & Gerard Doody
Manager: Denise Finn
98 Merrion Road
Ballsbridge, Dublin 4, Ireland
Tel: (01) 668 4410, Fax: (01) 668 4533
Email: info@cedarlodge.ie
12 rooms
£35–£55 per person B&B
Closed Christmas, Credit cards: all major
Guesthouse
www.karenbrown.com/ireland/cedarlodge.html

The heart of Temple Bar with its trendy stores and vibrant nightlife is a most appropriate spot for Bono, of U2, and his business partners to open a luxury boutique hotel. Originally built in 1852, the hotel has been completely refurbished, keeping all the attractive architectural features such as oak paneling, wooden floors, and lovely old windows and adding a pleasing modern decor with uncluttered, simple lines. Relax in the peace and quiet of the study with its open fire, writing table, and wood-paneled walls or join the hubbub of the Octagon Bar with its crowded little alcoves. The Tea Room is one of the most lauded restaurants in the country. Bedrooms are decorated in natural tones and muted colors—all very serene—and double glazing ensures a quiet night's sleep. The handcrafted beds are king-sized and rooms are equipped with satellite TV and fax/PC points. In keeping with the hotel's desire to provide guests with all the technology expected by a leading city hotel, cellular phones are available for hire. The location, overlooking the River Liffey on Dublin's "left bank," is perfect for exploring Dublin on foot. The hotel does not have a garage but valet parking is available if needed. *Directions:* Wellington Quay is on the south bank of the River Liffey—see *Dublin Walking Tour* map for location.

THE CLARENCE
Manager: Robert Van Eerde
6–8 Wellington Quay
Dublin 2
Ireland
Tel: (01) 407 0800, Fax: (01) 407 0820
Email: reservations@theclarence.ie
50 rooms
Double: £210–£235*, Suite: £450–£1,500*
*Breakfast not included: £12–£15, Dinner: from £35
Open all year
Credit cards: all major
City hotel

Just steps from St. Stephen's Green in the heart of Georgian Dublin, Harrington Hall is ideally located for walking to all the city's attractions. The tranquillity of the spacious sitting room with its gold brocade sofas and comfortable armchairs drawn round a welcoming peat fire quickly convinced me that this was an enticing place to stay in central Dublin. Handsome Henry, who runs the hotel with his parents Monica and Joe, has taken great care with the design of the bedrooms—their size, amenities, and comfort—and the fitting out of the excellent marble bathrooms. The result is that you will enjoy a quiet night's repose with the aid of double glazing and ceiling fans in the most comfortable of attractively decorated rooms. Larger rooms can often accommodate an extra bed at a very reasonable price. A ground-floor room is wheelchair-friendly. The two suites, Kitty O'Shea and Charles Parnell, provide the most spacious accommodation in large rooms with ceilings so lofty that the bed occupies a mezzanine level above the bathroom. Breakfast is the only meal served in the sunny-yellow, below-stairs breakfast room but there is a "King family dining guide" for eating out. A short wine list is available. *Directions:* Harcourt Street leads from the southwestern corner of St. Stephen's Green and Harrington Hall is on your left. The hotel will fax driving directions. At the rear is a secure, off-road car park—let them know you are arriving by car as parking is limited. See *Dublin Walking Tour* map for location.

HARRINGTON HALL
Owner: Henry King
70 Harcourt Street
Dublin 2, Ireland
Tel: (01) 475 3497, Fax: (01) 475 4544
Email: harringtonhall@eircom.net
30 rooms
Double: £110–£130, Suite: £180–£220
Open all year
Credit cards: all major
Guesthouse
www.karenbrown.com/ireland/harringtonhall.html

The Hibernian Hotel, a grand, redbrick building, was constructed as a nurses' residence at the turn of the century and underwent a complete transformation to open as a congenial hotel. The staff is exceedingly gracious and helpul, which gives a particularly warm feeling to this city hotel. Decorated in a clubby, traditional style, the library and drawing room are full of luxuriously upholstered sofas and chairs arranged around fireplaces, and the sunny conservatory restaurant serves traditional country house fare. The bedrooms range from snug to spacious and are equipped with everything from a full range of toiletries in the sparkling bathrooms to fax/modem port, hairdryer, TV, candy bars, and tea- and coffee-makings. The Hibernian Hotel is located on a quiet side street in the Victorian suburb of Ballsbridge, just a ten-minute stroll from St. Stephen's Green, making it an ideal base for exploring the city. *Directions:* Follow signs for South City and cross the Baggot Street Bridge into Baggot Street. Pass a row of shops on your left, turn left at the AIB bank, and the Hibernian Hotel is on your left. The hotel has a small car park. See *Dublin Walking Tour* map for location.

HIBERNIAN HOTEL
Manager: Niall Coffey
Eastmoreland Place, Upper Baggot Street
Ballsbridge
Dublin 4
Ireland
Tel: (01) 668 7666, Fax: (01) 660 2655
Email: info@hibernianhotel.com
40 rooms
Double: £150–£170*, Suite: £190*, Dinner: £33*
*Breakfast not included: £12, plus 12.5% service
Closed Christmas
Credit cards: all major
City hotel
www.karenbrown.com/ireland/hibernian.html

For over 30 years Kilronan House has been offering visitors to Dublin a warm welcome. Rosemary and Terry are just the third owners of the place and they strive very hard to keep up Kilronan's reputation for cordial hospitality. Eight of the bedrooms are in the main house, all but two having snug en-suite shower rooms. However, my choice would be to stay in one of the four rooms in the "new wing" that stretches behind the house. These have no view (in fact, instead of windows you have an expanse of glass-block walls) but they have a little more space and larger bathrooms. Naturally, there is a full Irish breakfast on the menu but the most popular items are pancakes with syrup and scrambled eggs with smoked salmon. Terry recommends a variety of nearby restaurants that range from family establishments offering good value for money to ones providing a special night out on the town. A five-minute walk finds you at St. Stephen's Green, where you can stroll through the park to Grafton Street, the shopping heart of the town. *Directions*: From the east side of St. Stephen's Green (opposite The Shelbourne hotel) go straight into Earlscourt Terrace and take the second right into Adelaide Road where you find Kilronan House on your right after 100 meters. Double-park in front to unload and you will be directed to the bed and breakfast's off-street parking. See *Dublin Walking Tour* map for location.

KILRONAN HOUSE   **New**
Owners: Rosemary & Terry Masterson
70 Adelaide Road
Dublin 2
Ireland
Tel: (01) 475 5266, Fax: (01) 478 2841
Email: info@dublinn.com
12 rooms
£38–£48 per person B&B
Open all year, Credit cards: all major
No-smoking house
Guesthouse
www.karenbrown.com/ireland/kilronan.html

Places to Stay   161

Grand as life in Georgian Dublin may have been, it is surpassed at The Merrion, a dream of a hotel found in the heart of Georgian Dublin opposite Leinster House, home of Ireland's parliament. A few steps from bustling city streets and you are in vast drawing rooms enjoying traditional afternoon tea overlooking a tranquil expanse of garden watching the gardener manicure the box hedges. If you are in the mood for the most sophisticated of meals, adjourn to Restaurant Patrick Guilbaud (the only eatery in Ireland to command two Michelin stars) or enjoy more casual cuisine in Mornington's brasserie after letting your hair down over a few drinks in The Cellar Bar. The Tethra Spa is an aptly named spot to assist guests in recovering from the revelry of the night before—swimming in the pool, working out in the gym, or enjoying a massage. It costs a small fortune to stay in one of the elegant suites in the "old building," while more affordable accommodation is found in the deluxe garden wing whose most attractive rooms open up to views of the loveliest of gardens. A traditional hotel in the heart of this vibrant city—what more could you ask from a place to stay? Well worth a splurge! *Directions*: The Merrion is adjacent to Merrion Square, opposite Leinster House. Park in front of the hotel and the porter will take care of your car. See *Dublin Walking Tour* map for location.

THE MERRION
Manager: Peter MacCann
Upper Merrion Street
Dublin 2, Ireland
Tel: (01) 603 0600, Fax: (01) 603 0700
Email: info@merrionhotel.ie
145 rooms
Double: £220–£285*, Suite: £425–£750*
*Breakfast not included: £18, Dinner: from £23
Open all year
Credit cards: all major
City hotel
www.karenbrown.com/ireland/merrion.html

Modern hotels are not usually included in this guide but I was so taken with the value for money and excellent location offered by the Mespil Hotel that I decided to stay there—I was very pleased with the quality of the accommodation and the friendliness of the staff. Sitting on a quieter side street beside the Grand Canal with its grassy verges and leafy trees, the Mespil sports a pleasing modern exterior that complements its attractive contemporary interior. Dark-green leather sofas and stylish light-wood furniture deck the public rooms. The lunchtime carvery becomes the bar in the evening when the spacious restaurant offers a bistro-style menu. Bedrooms come in two varieties—front and back— and two colors—burgundy and green. Front rooms face the canal (opt for one of these as it's a treat to have a view room in Dublin), while back rooms have slightly larger bathrooms. All standard rooms offer one double and one single bed. *Directions:* Follow signs for South City to Baggot Street. Cross the canal, turn right, and the Mespil is on your left after 200 meters. The hotel has a private car park and there is plenty of off-road parking available. See *Dublin Walking Tour* map for location.

MESPIL HOTEL
Manager: Martin Holohan
Mespil Road
Ballsbridge, Dublin 4
Ireland
Tel: (01) 667 1222, Fax: (01) 667 1244
Email: mespil@leehotels.ie
262 rooms
Double: £90–£95*
*Breakfast not included: £9, Dinner: £16–£21
Open all year
Credit cards: all major
City hotel
www.karenbrown.com/ireland/mespilhotel.html

Temple Bar is Dublin's music and cultural hub, with restaurants, galleries, boutiques, and nightlife all within walking distance of this thoroughly modern hotel. All the noise and bustle of Dublin dims the moment you enter the hushed lobby. An elevator whisks you up to softly lit corridors where illuminated blue squares indicate the room numbers. Standard rooms are pleasurable, comfortable spaces with state-of-the-art minimalistic décor—either a ruby-red or royal-blue sculptured chair and a contrasting blue or red carpet, beechwood furniture, and a stack with CD player, TV with VCR (the hotel has a library of CDs and videos), and mini bar. If you can splurge, opt for one of the immaculate junior suites decked out in every shade of the softest of creams (how do they keep them so immaculately clean?) with the only splash of color being the bedhead designed by Pasquel Morgue. Continental breakfast, with, of course, state-of-the-art utensils, is served to you on a tray in your room. If you need a jolt from the soothing, hushed calm, try dining in the hotel's adjacent sports bar with its lights and razzle-dazzle. *Directions*: From O'Connell Bridge take Westmorland Street south for one block then turn right into Fleet Street and the hotel is on your right. Park in front of the hotel to unload then park in the public car park opposite.

THE MORGAN
Manager: Michelle McKenna
10 Fleet Street
Dublin 2
Ireland
Tel: (01) 679 3939, Fax: (01) 679 3946
61 rooms
Double: £130–£160*, Suite: £190–£375*
*Breakfast not included: £7
Closed Christmas
Credit cards: all major
City hotel

A tall, creeper-covered wall and a discreet plaque are the only indications that you have arrived at 31 Leeson Close. Ring the buzzer, open the tall doors, and you enter an oasis of tranquillity and greenery far from the clamor of the surrounding city. Number 31 was home to Ireland's most controversial modern architect, Sam Stephenson, who fashioned it from two coach houses and Noel and Deirdre Comer, the present owners, have kept the cool, clean lines of this modern home. A bright, contemporary painting hangs above the fireplace in the living room where the leather sofa, the only piece of furniture, hugs the wall of the conversation pit and stark, whitewashed brick walls contrast texturally with the mosaic tiled floor strewn with Oriental rugs. A great variety of bedrooms is spread over two buildings. The main house has grand, high-ceilinged rooms (I loved the spaciousness and décor of room 21, which faces onto Fitzwilliam Street), while the coach house naturally has lower-ceilinged rooms, several of which have their own private patio. Noel, Deirdre, and Homer (the Labrador) work hard to give a gracious welcome and (Homer excluded) provide you with all the information you need on what to see and where to go in Dublin. *Directions:* Lower Leeson Street runs off the southern end of St. Stephen's Green. Leeson Close is opposite 41 Lower Leeson Street. A secure, off-road car park is adjacent to Number 31.

NUMBER 31
Owners: Deirdre & Noel Comer
31 Leeson Close
Dublin 2
Ireland
Tel: (01) 676 5011, Fax: (01) 676 2929
Email: number31@iol.ie
18 rooms
Double: £94–£150
Open all year
Credit cards: all major
Guesthouse
www.karenbrown.com/ireland/number31.html

The city of Dublin stretches inland through the vast acres of Phoenix Park and beyond to the prosperous, peaceful suburb of Castleknock. Here, on a quiet crescent of contemporary detached homes, you find Park Lodge, distinguished by its Tudor façade and, in summer, a garden ablaze with flowers. Surprisingly, inside you find a lovely Regency-style decor designed to complement Eileen's enviable collection of antiques. Starched white linen cloths and napkins grace the breakfast table where tea is served in a silver pot. The sumptuous breakfast menu includes dishes such as baked trout and Irish smoked salmon with eggs as well as the traditional Irish breakfast. Choose from three delightful bedrooms: William Butlers Yeats in soft creams and whites is spacious with a queen bed and bathroom with both shower and bath; James Joyce has a queen brass-and-wrought-iron bed with a snug shower room; Oscar Wilde is sleek and modern in silver and blue and has a very large shower room. For trips into the city the bus stop is a three-minute walk away. Being just 14 kilometers from Dublin airport (most of it motorway), Park Lodge is ideal for your first or last night in Ireland but you may regret that you did not stay longer. *Directions*: Take the N3 exit off the M50 motorway. Turn towards the city center and at the roundabout first right, signposted Castleknock (Auburn Avenue). Turn left at the T-junction, first left on Deerpark Road, and third right on Deerpark Drive. Park Lodge is on your right. See *Dublin Walking Tour* map for location.

PARK LODGE
Owners: Eileen & Patrick Kehoe
19 Deerpark Drive
Castleknock, Dublin 15, Ireland
Email: prklodge@gofree.indigo.ie
Tel & fax: (01) 821 2887
3 rooms
£45–£50 per person B&B
Open Mar to Oct
Credit cards: none
B&B
www.karenbrown.com/ireland/parklodge.html

Dublin's residential areas were built during the 1860s and Ballsbridge emerged as a well planned suburb of wide, tree-lined streets with smart redbrick houses fronted by impressive gardens. More recent times have seen this fashionable suburb come to house diplomatic missions and commercial institutions, but fortunately the aura of a sedate residential area has been retained. On one of Ballsbridge's most attractive streets, Raglan Lodge offers visitors a quiet respite from the hustle and bustle of the city. This splendid, three-story Victorian is Helen's home. The large traditional sitting room with its stripped-pine floor has the feeling of a comfortable Victorian parlor. Downstairs is a cozy breakfast room with groupings of little tables and chairs. Breakfast is the only meal served but Helen has local restaurant menus on the hall table for guests' convenience. Room 1 is a large ground-floor room with long, flowing drapes and tall ceilings with pretty cornices recalling the elegance of the Victorian era. Like the other rooms, it has a snug shower room tucked into the corner. An August 2000 visit found the décor to be tired and in need of a freshen up—hopefully Helen will soon have everything put to rights. Just round the corner is Jury's Hotel with its many restaurants and popular cabaret show. A long walk or a short stroll and a bus ride bring you into the heart of Dublin. *Directions:* Follow signs for South City to Baggot Street which becomes Pembroke Street, turn right on Raglan Road, and Raglan Lodge is on your left. There is plenty of off-road parking available. See *Dublin Walking Tour* map for location.

RAGLAN LODGE
Owner: Helen Moran
10 Raglan Road
Dublin 4, Ireland
Tel: (01) 660 6697, Fax: (01) 660 6781
7 rooms
£55 per person B&B
Closed Christmas & New Year
Credit cards: all major
Guesthouse

Irish nobility and country gentlemen needed to spend time in Dublin, so in 1824 the Shelbourne opened its doors to the gentry who did not have a residence in the city. Since then, the Shelbourne has been "the" place to stay and today it remains as Dublin's deluxe hotel, suffused with the elegance of other eras, living up to its motto as "the most distinguished address in Ireland." The comings and goings of Dublin are reflected in the enormous gilt mirrors of the Lord Mayor's Lounge where people gather to enjoy afternoon tea. Traditional decor, good conversation, and the presence of Dublin characters combine to make the Horseshoe Bar a most convivial place. The very elegant dining room, No.27 The Green, provides equally elegant food, while the adjacent Shelbourne Bar provides a friendly atmosphere for a relaxed drink. Just off the bar is a jazzy, bistro-style restaurant, The Side Door. Bedrooms are lovely and beautifully appointed, though Standard rooms are not large. The premier room is the Princess Grace Suite, a two-bedroom suite that the princess occupied on her trips to Dublin. No premium is charged for rooms with a view of St. Stephens Green, but remember that these are the not the quietest rooms. While you are there be sure to visit the Constitution Room where the Irish Constitution was drafted in 1922. There is a full health and fitness center, which includes a swimming pool. *Directions:* The Shelbourne is on the north side of St. Stephen's Green. Park in front of the hotel. See *Dublin Walking Tour* map for location.

THE SHELBOURNE
Manager: Jean Ricoux
27 St. Stephen's Green
Dublin 2, Ireland
Tel: (01) 663 4500, Fax: (01) 661 6006
Email: shelbournereservations@forte-hotels.com
190 rooms
Double: £200–£308*, Suite: £364–£1,073*
*Breakfast not included: £16.50, plus 15% service
Open all year, Credit cards: all major
City hotel
www.karenbrown.com/ireland/shelbourne.html

If you yearn for a home away from home in Dublin, you should stay at Simmonstown House, a most attractive, solid, Victorian end-of terrace townhouse where Jim and Finola Curry welcome you as guests and make certain you leave as friends. The house itself is comfortable, formal, and restful and Finola and Jim find that having only four bedrooms means that they have plenty of time for their guests. On arrival coffee or tea is proffered, then comes a chat about what to see and do, maps come out, dinner plans are discussed, and so it goes. The Curries show a genuine interest in their guests. Upstairs, the bedrooms range from a small double (usually used as a single room) to the spacious front room all decked out in shades of raspberry where two commodious armchairs occupy the window bay. All have snug shower rooms. Guests breakfast together round the dining room table and for other meals can choose from top-quality restaurants just a five-minute walk away. A fifteen-minute bus ride finds you in the heart of the city. *Directions:* Follow signs for South City to Baggot Street, which becomes Pembroke Road. Turn right in front of Jury's Hotel into Merrion Road. With the Royal Dublin Society showgrounds (RDS) on your right, turn left into Sydenham Road and Simmonstown is the first house on the left. Off-road parking is available behind the house or on a quiet cul-de-sac in front. See *Dublin Walking Tour* map for location.

SIMMONSTOWN HOUSE
Owners: Finola & Jim Curry
Sydenham Road
Ballsbridge, Dublin 4
Ireland
Tel: (01) 660 7260, Fax: (01) 660 7341
Email: info@simmonstownhouse.com
4 rooms
£50–£70 per person B&B
Closed Christmas
Credit cards: all major
Guesthouse
www.karenbrown.com/ireland/simmonstown.html

"You should have this in your book—it's just the kind of place you are looking for," wrote a reader. And that is how we discovered Waterloo House, two tall Georgian townhouses cleverly combined to become a delightful guesthouse. Just a 15-minute walk to St. Stephen's Green and Trinity College, it looks out over a quiet street (a peaceful night's sleep is guaranteed) and has parking in front. Evelyn Corcoran and her friendly staff really look after guests well. Soft strains of classical music play in the lobby sitting room and there's an elevator for luggage and for those who do not want to climb up to four flights of stairs. Whether your bedroom is on the garden level or at the top of the house, you'll be pleased with its smart décor. Breakfast is taken downstairs in a spacious, perky, raspberry-painted room with French windows leading to a sunny conservatory and gardens. Key-cards give you access to the front door as well as your room so that you can come and go on your own timetable. There are lots of restaurants and bars within easy walking distance. *Directions:* Follow signs for South City. Cross the Baggot Street bridge into Baggot Street. Pass a row of shops on your left and turn right into Waterloo Road—Waterloo House is on your left with a car park in front. See *Dublin Walking Tour* map for location.

WATERLOO HOUSE   *New*
Owner: Evelyn Corcoran
8–10 Waterloo Road
Ballsbridge, Dublin
Ireland
Tel: (01) 660 1888, Fax: (01) 667 1955
Email: waterloohouse@tinet.ie
19 rooms
£45 per person B&B
Open all year, Credit cards: MC, VS
No-smoking house
Guesthouse
www.karenbrown.com/ireland/waterloo.html

Norah Brown so loves to cook that she not only provides dinners for her resident guests but will also open her dining room to larger groups looking for that special dinner party. Norah's imaginative dishes using fresh local ingredients have won her an award-winning reputation as a talented cook and her eye for detail is demonstrated in the fine glassware, crisp linen, and wildflowers that decorate the plates. To avoid being disappointed it is best to pre-book dinner when you make your room reservation. Norah and Ralph are inveterate collectors, filling every nook and cranny with collections of old china, pewter, stoneware, and fascinating bygones. Upstairs are the very comfortable, individually decorated bedrooms, all with their own pretty bathrooms full of little extras. You can tour the nearby Tyrone crystal factory and try your own hand at cutting the hand-blown sparkling crystal. The National Trust has two properties close at hand: Ardress House, a 17th-century manor, and The Argory, an 1820s house with a lot of original furniture set in 300 acres of woodland. Being very centrally situated, Grange Lodge is within easy reach of many of Northern Ireland's other major attractions. *Directions:* Take the M1 from Belfast to junction 15 where you take the A29 towards Armagh for 2 km to the left-hand turn to Grange. Turn immediately right and Grange Lodge is the first white-walled entrance on the right.

GRANGE LODGE
Owners: Norah & Ralph Brown
7 Grange Road
Dungannon
Co Tyrone, Northern Ireland
Tel: (02887) 784212, Fax: (02887) 784313
Email: grangelodge@nireland.com
5 rooms
£39 per person B&B, Dinner: from £25 (not Sun)
Open Feb to mid-Dec
Credit cards: MC, VS
Country house
www.karenbrown.com/ireland/grange.html

Killaghtee House offers you spacious accommodation and the chance to enjoy your breakfast in an art gallery. Jackie and Robin came to County Donegal so that Robin could paint and they could have a gallery in their home. The thought of doing bed and breakfast never entered their heads until a local restaurateur asked them if they could take his overflow guests for a couple of nights. Jackie discovered she loved being a hostess so Robin was moved to a studio in an outbuilding and they relocated their living quarters to the attics. Displays of Robin's watercolors and oil paintings hang in the ground-floor gallery where guests enjoy breakfast amongst the art. Up the open-tread pine staircase guests have an airy sitting room with comfortable sofas drawn round the fire. There are books and pamphlets on the area and Jackie is always on hand to direct guests to her favorite places such as the Slieve League Mountains and the beautiful countryside that surrounds the little harbor of Port. Two of the bedrooms are very large and enjoy lovely sea views across the road and the fields. A smaller double room at the back of the house faces Robin's studio. As breakfast is the only meal served, guests usually dine at the nearby Castle Murray restaurant or the Bay View restaurant in Killybegs. In addition to the gallery, Robin and Jackie have opened a Heritage Center that includes a tearoom and a museum. *Directions:* From Donegal take the N56 toward Killybegs. Killaghtee House is on your right just beyond Dunkineely.

KILLAGHTEE HOUSE
Owners: Jackie & Robin Atkinson
Dunkineely, Co Donegal, Ireland
Tel: (073) 37453, Fax: (073) 37499
Email: atkin@iol.ie
3 rooms
£30 per person B&B
Open all year
Credit cards: MC, VS
B&B
www.karenbrown.com/ireland/killaghtee.html

Joe and Kay O'Flynn bought Rathsallagh House, a converted Queen Anne stables with 530 acres of farmland, in 1978. Encouraged by the spaciousness of the house, Kay opened three rooms for bed and breakfast guests and thus began a venture that has evolved into the country house hotel and golf and country club that you see today. Tractor sheds and barns are gone, replaced by a parade of bedrooms, and fields that lined the driveway are now the groomed fairways of the championship golf course. The indoor pool, billiard room, tennis court, and capacious gardens encourage total relaxation. While the size of the operation makes it all seem rather grand, Rathsallagh manages to keep the bonhomie of a friendly, relaxed country house hotel complete with homey touches like Joe still paying his bills at the old pine table in the breakfast room. Begin the day with a lavish breakfast, choosing from an array of savory dishes on the sideboard. Relax with a drink before dinner and enjoy the comfortable country house style of the place. Golf is a great attraction and ardent fans often play here and at the nearby "K Club." From Rathsallagh House you can easily visit the Wicklow Mountains, ancient Glendalough, the Japanese Gardens, and the National Stud, and Dublin is about an hour's drive away. *Directions:* From Dublin airport take the M50 to exit 9 for the N7, which you exit for the M8/N9 towards Carlow. After 9.5 km pass the Priory Inn on the left and just over 3 km later turn left for Rathsallagh.

RATHSALLAGH HOUSE   *New*
Owners: The O'Flynn family
Dunlavin
Co Wicklow, Ireland
Tel: (045) 403343, Fax: (045) 403343
Email: info@rathsallagh.com
29 rooms
Double: £110–£210, Dinner: £35–£45
Closed Christmas
Credit cards: all major
Country house hotel
www.karenbrown.com/ireland/rathsallagh.html

The scenery on the Inishowen Peninsula is breathtaking, the historic villages are small and attractive, and you won't find much in the way of crowds unless you choose to go to a late-night music session in one of the pubs. It really is a world apart. You can preview the beauty of Inishowen as you dine in the conservatory of St. John's, just at the edge of Fahan village, looking across Lough Swilly to Inch Island. Phil McAfee and Reg Ryan have been restauranteurs for many years so food takes pride of place and Phil always ensures that she has local lamb and seafood on the menu. Relax before dinner in the cozy bar with its turf fire. Upstairs, the five bedrooms are a more recent addition and range in size from smaller (with a view to the back of the house) to huge (overlooking the lough), with the former going for half the price of the latter. No matter if you cannot see the view from your bed, provided the weather behaves, you'll have no shortage of spectacular views as you explore the peninsula. Drive over the Pinch or the Gap of Malmore on your way to Malin Head (the most northerly spot on the Irish mainland) and the only traffic you are likely to meet is a sheep or two. For those who decide to leave the peninsula, the historic city of Derry lies 13 km away, and the Giant's Causeway is an hour-and-a-half's drive. *Directions:* St. John's is situated in the village of Fahan on the R238 Derry to Buncrana road.

ST. JOHN'S COUNTRY HOUSE
Owners: Phil McAfee & Reg Ryan
Fahan, Inishowen
Co Donegal, Ireland
Tel: (077) 60289, Fax: (077) 60612
Email: stjohnsrestaurant@eircom.net
5 rooms
£35–£75 per person B&B*, Dinner: £28*
*Plus 10% service
Closed Christmas & mid-Feb to mid-Mar
Credit cards: all major
Restaurant with rooms
www.karenbrown.com/ireland/stjohns.html

Grim determination led me to Farran House—how could I get so lost?—but my endeavors paled into insignificance when I saw the amount of work it took, over a seven-year period, for Patricia and John to rescue this splendid Italianate house from ruin. They now live in a wing while guests can rent the main house on a self-catering basis or choose dinner, bed, and breakfast country house style. Relax round the fire in the sitting room, enjoy a game of billiards in the former music room, and chat with fellow guests round the dining-room table. Upstairs, you find four lovely, spacious bedrooms all enjoying south-facing views across the valley. Room one is extra special because of its bathroom—a super-sized affair with a claw-foot tub sitting center stage in front of a fireplace. If renting an estate is not within range of your pocketbook, Patricia and John also have a three-bedroom cottage available at a more modest rate. Your hosts have collected a picture library of all things Ireland—they go hither and yon the length and breadth of the country taking photos, which gives them an intimate knowledge of every scenic spot in the country—very handy for advising guests where to go and what to see. Blarney is 16 kilometers away, Kinsale and the coast about 40 kilometers. *Directions*: From Cork take the N22 towards Killarney for 15 km. Go through Ballincollig to Farran and after Dan Sheanhan's pub, on your right, take the second right. Take the next right up the hill and the entrance to Farran House is on your left.

*FARRAN HOUSE   **New***
Owners: Patricia Wiese & John Kehely
Farran
Co Cork, Ireland
Tel & fax: (021) 7331215
Email: info@farranhouse.com
4 rooms
£50 per person B&B, Dinner: £25
Open Apr to Oct
Credit cards: all major
Country house & self-catering
www.karenbrown.com/ireland/farran.html

Valerie and Lorcan Sinnott had long admired The Old Deanery, the grandest house in Ferns, built in 1735, so when it came up for auction they took the plunge and bid on it, furniture and all. They decided to put the property to work for them, so Lorcan and sons Fiachra and Seamus set to work to add 20th-century amenities to the house, while Valerie used her creative skills to decorate and daughter Sinead opened a garden center by the gatelodge. The result is absolutely charming—a warm and welcoming family home filled with lovely furniture. Valerie has chosen bold Georgian colors, with buttercup-yellow walls mellowed by champagne slip covers and drapes in the sitting room, a vibrant red for the hallway, and mellow navy blue for the dining room. Bedrooms are absolutely delightful, with Tiger Lily and Delphinium being enormous. Breakfast is the only meal served though there is no shortage of restaurants in the area. The adjacent stables in the courtyard have been converted to exquisite holiday cottages for two to eight people. Now the cottages are complete the Sinnotts will embark on restoring the gardens according to the 1841 plans that have been unearthed. Ferns is a most interesting historical town and an ideal touring base, being less than 75 km from Kilkenny, Waterford, and the Wicklow Mountains. *Directions:* Take the N11 south from Dublin towards Wexford. As you enter Ferns (just before the speed limit sign) turn right for The Old Deanery.

THE OLD DEANERY
Owners: Valerie & Lorcan Sinnott
Ferns
Co Wexford, Ireland
Tel: (054) 66474, Fax: (054) 66123
4 rooms, cottages
£40 per person B&B
Open Mar to Nov (cottages all year)
Credit cards: all major
Country house & self-catering

Grace and Padraig's families have farmed around Fivealley for as long as anyone can remember. After remodeling their Georgian farmhouse, keeping all the lovely old aspects and adding all the modern conveniences, Grace set about filling it with a melange of antiques: gilt Napoleonic furniture with raspberry taffeta upholstery in the sitting room; painted Austrian country furniture in one bedroom; Victorian in another; and an antique pine famine hutch in the country kitchen. From crisp white cotton sheets to authentic Victorian bathrooms, Grace believes in giving her guests quality. Another added bonus is her delicious home-baking and -cooking. The land hereabouts is known as Ely O'Carroll Country, a diverse landscape that goes from the River Shannon to the Slieve Bloom Mountains through gently undulating farmland. At its center lies the nearby town of Birr with its Georgian homes and grand castle. The ruins of the monastic settlement of Clonmacnois cast their spell on all who visit—an ideal day out is to combine the monastic ruins with a ride on the West Offaly Railway which takes visitors to the heart of a peat bog to see how Ireland's "brown gold" is harvested. The Slieve Bloom Mountains offer walks in wooded valleys of singular beauty. *Directions*: From Birr take the N52 toward Tullamore for 8 km (sadly, Fivealley is not signposted though it appears on maps) where you turn right (signposted Rath)—Parkmore Farmhouse is on your left after 1km.

PARKMORE FARMHOUSE
Owners: Grace & Padraig Grennan
Fivealley
Birr
Co Offaly, Ireland
Tel: (0509) 33014, Fax: (0509) 333054
3 rooms
£30 per person B&B, Dinner: £25
Closed Christmas
Credit cards: none
Farmhouse B&B
www.karenbrown.com/ireland/parkmore.html

Olive and Paddy O'Gorman have a relaxed, easy-going attitude to life. They welcome guests to the newly converted wing of their commodious farmhouse nestled in the pretty Nire Valley, an off-the-beaten-tourist-path area of Ireland noted for its beautiful scenery. Knowing that you deserve the best, request one of Olive's premier rooms with Jacuzzi tub and shower. Olive takes such pride in her bedrooms that the hospitality tray in each room has cups and saucers that match the room's decor. Olive finds it no problem at all to juggle her family and a houseful of guests, chatting to them over a cup of tea and homemade cake, feeding them copious breakfasts, packing tempting lunches, and arranging for them to go walking with a knowledgeable local guide. Guests come to this quiet corner of County Waterford to walk the Comeragh Mountains and experience the very best of Irish farmhouse hospitality. If the outdoor pursuits of fishing, pony-trekking, and walking are not your cup of tea, you can drive to Lismore, Cashel, or over The Vee, returning in time for a visit to one of the nearby pubs for a drink and a chat with locals or perhaps (more often in the summer months) a late-night Irish music session. Bedrooms are as neat as new pins, attractively decorated, and each sporting a bathroom with a Jacuzzi tub. *Directions*: From Clonmel or Dungarven follow the R672 to Ballymacarbry. The little village of Four-Mile Water is signposted to your right just before you reach Ballymacarbry if you are coming from Clonmel or just after to your left if you are coming from Dungarven.

GLASHA
Owners: Olive & Paddy O'Gorman
Four-Mile Water, Via Clonmel
Co Waterford, Ireland
Tel & fax: (052) 36108
Email: glasha@eircom.net
8 rooms
£25–£30 per person B&B
Closed Christmas, Credit cards: MC, VS
Farmhouse B&B
www.karenbrown.com/ireland/glasha.html

Richard's family received the Kilrush estate as a land grant from Charles II in 1660 and until this grand home was built in the 1820s his forbears occupied the tower house, the small castle that stands in the garden. This is a home of vast rooms which Sally, Richard, and Bramble and Teal, the welcoming Springer Spaniels, make feel remarkably homey. Up a grand sweep of staircase, guests can choose from the Yellow Room, a vast twin-bedded room overlooking the castle (my favorite), the very spacious Pink Room with its large white wrought-iron bed, or the coziness of Uncle Arthur's Room, named because to Richard it will always be Uncle Arthur's room. The wallpaper in the drawing room has celebrated its centenary, while that in the dining room went up when the house was built—just about the time the dining-room furniture was moved in. Richard is happy to discuss the colorful family history and his love for this rural part of Ireland. Guests enjoy walking out to see the thoroughbred mares and their foals on the St. Georges' farm. Sally is happy with advanced notice to prepare dinner with main course and dessert or cheese. The delightful town of Freshford is a half-hour drive from Kilkenny, with its castle and many fine old buildings, and Cashel, with its famous rock. Cahir Castle and the Swiss Cottage make a popular day trip while garden lovers are directed to the peaceful Lutyens garden in nearby Balinakill. *Directions*: From the N8, Cork to Dublin road, turn left in Johnstown towards Freshford and Kilkenny and Kilrush is on your right after 10 km.

KILRUSH HOUSE
Owners: Sally & Richard St. George
Freshford
Co Kilkenny, Ireland
Tel: (056) 32236, Fax: (056) 32588
Email: stgeorge@gofree.indigo.ie
3 rooms
£45 per person B&B, Dinner: £20–£25
Open Apr to Oct
Credit cards: all major
Country house
www.karenbrown.com/ireland/kilrush.html

Stay awhile with Dee and Mark Keogh at Norman Villa, their tall Victorian townhouse just a 15-minute walk from the center of Galway city. Norman, as he is fondly referred to, is a delightful fellow, decorated in sunny colors and full of antiques, his walls hung with contemporary Irish art, and with broad plank-and-slate floors underfoot. Each very attractive bedroom sports a lovely antique bed—the most spacious, room 4, is large enough to accommodate two double beds. Each bedroom offers interesting artwork, antiques, books, and snug shower facilities unobtrusively disguised as cupboards, giving the maximum amount of space to the bedroom. Breakfast is the only meal served round the long pine tables in the dining room but there is no shortage of places to walk to for dinner. The evening often concludes with a nightcap at the adjacent pub. Dee and Mark highlight maps for exploring the sea coast and Burren of County Clare, the wonderful wilds of Connemara, or for taking a day trip to the Aran Islands. Leave your car in the secure car park and explore Galway on foot. *Directions*: Follow signs for Salthill and then Lower Salthill. Norman Villa is next to P.J. Flaherty's pub. Avoid getting lost by having one of the Keoghs' maps with you.

NORMAN VILLA
Owners: Dee & Mark Keogh
86 Lower Salthill
Galway
Ireland
Tel & fax: (091) 521131
Email: normanvilla@oceanfree.net
5 rooms
£35–£37.50 per person B&B
Open all year
Credit cards: MC, VS
Guesthouse
www.karenbrown.com/ireland/norman.html

Look no further—this is **it**: an idyllic Irish pub off the beaten tourist path with country-cozy bedrooms, good chat with locals in the old-world bar, and wonderful food in the intimate little restaurant. You'll be so captivated by the place that you'll want to base your Irish holiday here—the challenge is how far can you tour in a day and be back in time for Ken's delicious dinner? (Waterford of crystal fame, Cashel with its castle, and the coastal villages of Dungarven, Ardmore, and Ballycotton are all realistic possibilities.) Lovely, well-kitted-out little bedrooms lie upstairs (leave your large suitcases in the car). Soak in the claw-foot tubs, admire the country antiques, and relax in the little guest sitting room or over a drink in the bar. The pub's snugness, its plethora of country memorabilia, and its proximity to the road make it unsuitable for young children. Ken and Kathleen are extremely patient and welcoming—given a few years, I feel confident that their hospitality and the old-world Irishness of what they offer in this little country pub will put this quiet part of Ireland on the map. Go before it gets too crowded! *Directions*: Take the N25 (Waterford to Cork road) to Lismore, pass the castle, and as you leave the town bear right at the Toyota dealership for the 4-km drive to Glencairn where Buggy's Glencairn Inn, fronted by a cottage garden, is on the right.

BUGGY'S GLENCAIRN INN
Owners: Kathleen & Ken Buggy
Glencairn
Tallow
Co Waterford, Ireland
Tel & fax: (058) 56232
Email: buggysglencairninn@eircom.net
5 rooms
£36–£40 per person B&B, Dinner: £24
Closed Nov & 2 weeks in Feb
Credit cards: MC, VS
Inn
www.karenbrown.com/ireland/buggy.html

Desmond, the 29th Knight of Glin's demesne is a 400-acre farm and late-18th-century castle stretching along the banks of the River Shannon. Staying here affords you the opportunity to live luxuriously—the house is a real beauty, full of exquisite furniture, family portraits, and beautiful artifacts. It is all very grand but not at all stuffy, for your host is Bob Duff, a gregarious New Zealander who ensures that you are well taken care of and well fed. He will give you a tour of the house with lots of suitably embellished stories. If you are passionate about art, literature, furniture, or books, be sure to ask if the Knight is in residence, for Desmond is happy to meet with guests when he is at home. Sip tea in the grand drawing room or curl up with a good book in the oh-so-comfortable sitting room. Bedrooms range from large and luxurious with extra-large bathrooms and dressing rooms to small and ordinary. Ballybunion golf course is close at hand. For something different, Bob can arrange for a helicopter to wing you to the Cliffs of Moher for a picnic (he packs a champagne lunch). *Directions:* From Limerick take the N69 towards Tralee for 50 km to Glin. At the end of the village turn left following the estate's wall to the castle entrance.

GLIN CASTLE
Owners: Olda & Desmond FitzGerald, Knight of Glin
Manager: Bob Duff
Glin, Co Limerick, Ireland
Tel: (068) 34173, Fax: (068) 34364
Email: knight@iol.ie
15 rooms
Double: £190–£300, Dinner: £32
Closed Nov to Mar
Credit cards: all major
Country house hotel
www.karenbrown.com/ireland/glin.html

This dazzling, three-story Regency house, formerly the dower house of the Courtown estate, has an atmosphere of refined elegance created by vivacious hostess Mary Bowe and her delightful daughter Margaret. Mary has great charm and energy—during our stay she chatted with guests before dinner, made the rounds during dinner, and was back again at breakfast checking up to make certain that everything was perfect. The house is full of antiques, classic pieces that transport you back to the days of gracious living in grand houses. While we especially enjoyed our large, twin-bedded room with impressive, well-polished furniture, elegant decor, and a grand bathroom, I found the other bedrooms equally attractive. Six prized units are the ultra-luxurious, gorgeously decorated, extravagantly priced, State Rooms tucked away in a separate ground-floor wing: request the Print Suite, Stopford, Georgian, or French. Dinner is served in the ornate Gothic conservatory dining room—all greenery and mirrors. The food is a delight—superb French and Irish dishes. This is one of the few hotels in Ireland where it is appropriate to dress for dinner. An atmosphere of formal extravagance prevails. *Directions:* Marlfield House is 88 km from Dublin. Take the N11 south to Gorey and as you enter the town turn left, before going under the railway bridge, onto the Courtown Road, straight across the roundabout, and the house is on your right after 2 km.

MARLFIELD HOUSE
Owners: Mary, Ray, & Margaret Bowe
Courtown Road, Gorey
Co Wexford, Ireland
Tel: (055) 21124, Fax: (055) 21572
Email: info@marlfieldhouse.com
20 rooms
Double: £165–£189, Suite: £270–£490
Dinner: £39
Closed Dec & Jan
Credit cards: all major
Country house hotel
www.karenbrown.com/ireland/marlfield.html

Virginia creeper, wisteria, and roses cover the exterior of Berryhill, a small-scale manor house perched high on the side of the valley overlooking the River Nore. Built by George's ancestors in the 1780s, the house received a much-needed face-lift a few years ago when George and Belinda moved into the family home, adding modern plumbing and wiring along with a light-hearted sense of fun in the decorating. The bedrooms—Frog, Pig, and Elephant—are subtly themed. My problem was to decide which one to choose: Pig with its claw-foot tub gracing the bathroom and grandfather clock in the sitting nook; Frog with its spacious bedroom, terrace overlooking the garden, and cozy sitting room overlooking the valley; or Elephant with the opportunity to sink into a bubble bath by the flicker of firelight. Make yourself at home in the beautiful drawing room and enjoy a drink from the honesty bar before going out to dinner in one of the nearby restaurants— there is such a wonderful selection of places to eat that you have to stay for a week to sample the best. Staying a week is certainly not a problem—it would take several days to explore all the quality craft shops (William Mosse Pottery is nearby at Bennetsbridge). Kilkenny is just up the road and Waterford just down. Dog lovers will be happy to know that the Dyers have six adorable dogs of various breeds and sizes. *Directions*: From Thomastown take the R700 for 8 km to Inistoge. Go through the village, cross the bridge, bearing right, take the next left (Graignamanagh Rd), first right, then second left.

BERRYHILL
Owners: Belinda & George Dyer
Inistoge
Co Kilkenny, Ireland
Tel & fax: (056) 58434
Email: info@berryhillhouse.com
3 rooms
£45 per person B&B
Open May to Oct
Credit cards: MC, VS
Country house
www.karenbrown.com/ireland/inistoge.html

Glenlohane is a lovely Georgian home of spacious but not overly grand rooms, sitting in beautiful, parklike grounds. It is a comfortable house, full of attractive things—lovely antiques, furnishings, fires, and rooms in cheerful colors. Hosts Desmond, Melanie—the tenth generation of the family who built the house—are most welcoming as are their dogs (Melaine is very involved in greyhound rescue). Enjoy tea by the fire in the drawing room, play a tune on the grand piano, and immerse yourself in the charm of it all. Return at night to this lovely haven to recount your adventures to Desmond over dinner—Melanie prepares the delicious food and Desmond often eats with guests, hosting them Irish-house-party style. The entire house is available on a weekly, self-catering basis. Garden lovers are directed to Anne's Grove gardens at Castletownroche and Garinish Island with its grand Italianate gardens. Glenlohane is also a working farm of 300 acres with cattle, sheep, horses, and hens, as well as barley, wheat, and oats. Outdoor activites are very much a part of life, including riding, fishing, horse shows, carriage driving, rough shooting, and agricultural shows. *Directions*: From Kanturk take the R576 toward Mallow. Very soon, bear left at the religious monument towards Buttevant on the R580. Take the first right at Sally's Cross towards Ballyclough. Glenlohane is the first residential entrance on the left after 2½ kilometers—the house does not have a sign.

GLENLOHANE
Owners: Melanie & Desmond Sharp Bolster
Kanturk
Co Cork, Ireland
Tel: (029) 50014, Fax: (029) 51100
Email: msb@iol.ie
4 rooms
£55–£65 per person B&B, Dinner: £25
Closed Christmas
Credit cards: all major
Country house & self-catering
www.karenbrown.com/ireland/glenlohane.html

Eighteenth-century Boltown House, the much-loved home of Jean Wilson and her daughter Susan, is a charming farmhouse set in 200 acres of rolling farmland. If you were to fly into Dublin, pick up your car, head northwest for just over an hour, and stay at Boltown, you could enjoy an excellent dinner and a quiet night's sleep, and start your vacation with an excellent example of Irish hospitality and Irish home cooking. The house speaks of times past with its creaking floorboards, wooden window shutters, and antique furniture. Two of the spacious bedrooms have en-suite bathrooms while the third has its private bathroom next door. Nearby Kells is one of the most historical towns in Ireland, known worldwide for its famous illuminated manuscript, which now resides in the library of Trinity College in Dublin. Today it is an old-style town of small dwellings and business premises where you can take a walk back in time to the era of the early Christian settlements—the high crosses in the churchyard are particularly impressive. The megalithic tombs of Newgrange, Knowth, and Dowth should not be missed. Many guests visit Trim castle (where *Braveheart* was filmed) and enjoy the wonderful gardens at Butterstream, Ballinlough Castle, and The Grove. Boltown is an ideal place to stay if you are en route to Donegal or Northern Ireland. *Directions:* From Kells take the Oldcastle/Castlepollard road. After 6½ km take the second left after the petrol station, signposted Kilskyre. Boltown House is on the right after 1 km.

BOLTOWN HOUSE
Owners: Jean & Susan Wilson
Kells
Co Meath, Ireland
Tel: (046) 43605, Fax: (046) 43036
3 rooms, 3 en suite
£35 per person B&B, Dinner: £24
Closed Christmas
Credit cards: all major
Country house

The Irish name for Kenmare, *An Neidin*, means "the little nest," which is a good description of this attractive town nestling beside the River Kenmare at the foot of some of Ireland's most spectacular scenery. On the Cork road, out of the main bustle of town, The Lodge (purpose-built as a guesthouse and a substantial family home for the Quills and their three young sons) sits back from the road in 2 acres of grassy garden. Finbar works in the family's woollen shop in town, which has the largest selection of sweaters in the town, if not all of Kerry, while Rosemary runs the bed and breakfast. She is exceedingly personable as is her staff of local ladies. Not a thing in the place (with the possible exception of two gigantic vases) is older than the house from the traditional furniture to the portraits that line the staircase. Bedrooms are spacious and have large, top-of-the-line bathrooms. All have queen-size beds and nine are large enough to accommodate an additional single bed. One ground-floor bedroom is specially equipped for the handicapped. Kenmare is ideally placed for touring the Ring of Kerry and the prettier Beara Peninsula, as well as for visiting several historic houses and gardens including Muckross House and Derrynane House, home of Daniel O'Connell. *Directions:* Kenmare is about a three-hour drive from Shannon on the N71 between Killarney and Bantry. The Lodge is on the R569 (Cork road) opposite the golf club.

THE LODGE   New
Owners: Rosemary & Finbar Quill
Killowen Road
Kenmare
Co Kerry, Ireland
Tel: (064) 41512, Fax: (064) 42724
Email: thelodgekenmare@eircom.net
11 rooms
£30–£40 per person B&B
Open Mar to Nov, Credit cards: MC, VS
No-smoking house
Guesthouse
www.karenbrown.com/ireland/lodge.html

The Park Hotel began life in 1897 as the Great Southern Hotel Kenmare to provide a convenient overnight stop for railway travelers en route to or from the Ring of Kerry. The furnishings are those of a hotel of the late Victorian or Edwardian age—almost every piece of furniture is antique, some of it massive, but somehow in keeping and much of it very valuable. Owner Francis Brennan's charm, humor, and dedicated professionalism all infect his young staff. Guests are greeted by a blazing coal fire which casts its glow towards the cozy bar and lounge, and you sit down at a partners' desk to register before being shown to your room. Such touches give a small-hotel feeling to this larger establishment. Exquisite accommodations are provided in nine very luxurious suites with splendid views out over Kenmare Bay. Just as lovely are the superior bedrooms in the old house, many of which have bedrooms and an arch to the seating area—these also all have wonderful views of the bay. Rooms in the "newer" wing have balconies, or patios to capture sideways bay views. The restaurant produces some of the finest food that you will find in Ireland. The Park provides programs for the Christmas and New Year holidays. Adjacent to the hotel is an 18-hole golf course and the hotel also arranges golfing programs at Killarney, Ballybunion, and Waterville. *Directions:* Kenmare is about a 3-hour drive from Shannon on the N71 between Killarney and Bantry.

THE PARK HOTEL KENMARE
Owner: Francis Brennan
Manager: John Brennan
Kenmare, Co Kerry, Ireland
Tel: (064) 41200, Fax: (064) 41402
Email: info@parkkenmare.com
49 rooms
Double: £264–£378, Suite: £450–£524
Dinner: £44
Open Apr to Oct & Christmas
Credit cards: all major
Luxury resort
www.karenbrown.com/ireland/parkhotel.html

Kenmare is one of my favorite Irish towns, and how appropriate that several of my favorite bed and breakfasts are located here, amongst them Sallyport House. Janie Arthur returned home after working for 15 years in California to help her brother, John, convert the family home into a luxurious bed and breakfast, decorating it in an uncluttered, sophisticated style. Return in the evening to chat round the fire in the drawing room or curl up in one of the comfortable chairs in the less formal sitting area with its exposed stone wall and photographs of Kenmare at the turn of the century. Breakfast is the only meal served—for dinner, it's a two-minute walk into town. The bedrooms are delightful, each furnished with antiques and accompanied by a large luxurious bathroom. Muxnaw has views of Muxnaw mountain and deep window seats; Ring View looks out to the Kenmare river; Reen a Gross has an American king-sized four-poster bed; The Falls has a view of the pretty garden. It's delightful to stroll along the riverbank, through the park, and back through the town. You can spend several days exploring the Beara Peninsula, Ring of Kerry, and lakes of Killarney. *Directions:* Kenmare is about a three-hour drive from Shannon on the N71 between Killarney and Bantry. From Bantry, Sallyport House is on your right just after you cross the bridge. From Killarney, follow Bantry signposts through Kenmare and Sallyport House is on your left before you come to the bridge.

SALLYPORT HOUSE
Owners: Janie & John Arthur
Kenmare
Co Kerry, Ireland
Tel: (064) 42066, Fax: (064) 42067
Email: port@iol.ie
5 rooms
£35–£50 per person B&B
Open Apr to Oct
Credit cards: none
B&B
www.karenbrown.com/ireland/sallyport.html

When Owen O'Sullivan retired, his wife Mary Patricia persuaded him to move "home" to her parents' farm overlooking a grand sweep of the Kenmare river estuary and expand the house into a comfortable home for themselves and top-quality accommodation for guests. They welcome you, brew tea, get the biscuits, ask you how you have been doing, and tell you of all the things that there are to do in and around Kenmare—just the kind of spontaneous, genuine Irish hospitality that we love. All of the bedrooms look over the fields across the River Kenmare to the mountains of the Beara Peninsula. A downstairs room has a handicap shower and room 3 enjoys two views: the estuary and upriver to the Caha Mountains. It's a blissfully quiet and rural place to stay yet also just a five-minute drive or twenty-minute walk from Kenmare with its excellent restaurants, pubs, and shops. You are just off the Ring of Kerry where hopefully, if the weather is fine, you'll see views like those out of your bedroom window. Mary Patricia advises guests who do not want to deal with coaches and lots of other traffic to forsake the Ring in favor of driving round the Beara Peninsula where you get quieter roads and spectacular mountain and water views. *Directions*: From Kenmare take the Killarney road (N71) for 300 meters. Pass the Esso petrol station on your right and take the next left onto the Ring of Kerry. Sea Shore Farm Guesthouse is signposted to your left after 300 meters.

SEA SHORE FARM GUESTHOUSE   *New*
Owners: Mary Patricia & Owen O'Sullivan
Tubrid, Kenmare
Co Kerry, Ireland
Tel & fax: (064) 41270
Email: seashore@eircom.net
6 rooms
£40 per person B&B
Open Mar to Nov, Credit cards: MC, VS
No-smoking house
Guesthouse
www.karenbrown.com/ireland/seashore.html

After visiting Shelburne Lodge, I can understand why I was showered with readers' letters urging me to visit and praising not only the high quality of the decor but also the delicious breakfasts. The building, a Georgian farmhouse, is lovely and the grounds with their lawns, herb garden, and tennis court are very attractive but it is the interior that is outstanding. The polished wooden floors gleam and lovely antiques grace the sitting room and hallway. Admire Maura's enviable art collection—all by local artists. Each lovely bedroom is accompanied by a luxurious bathroom, each with a different color scheme. Of course, the towel rails are heated and you'll find books of just the sort you want to read and browse through in your room. The same attention to detail goes into the scrumptious breakfast she prepares—even the compote of fresh fruits is artfully garnished. Husband Tom is helpful and friendly, always there with a map and pointing guests in the right direction. Kenmare has some excellent restaurants (look out, Kinsale!) and Packies (named for Uncle Packie who used to run a grocery business here) is one of the best—it offers a lively, informal atmosphere and your hostess Maura as chef (advance reservations are a must). Maura also helps her sister Grainne at The Purple Heather, a great venue for lunch or snacks. After dinner wander into one of Kenmare's many pubs—there's entertainment and music to suit all tastes. *Directions:* Kenmare is about a three-hour drive from Shannon on the N71 between Killarney and Bantry. Shelburne Lodge is on the R569 (Cork road) opposite the golf club.

SHELBURNE LODGE
Owners: Maura & Tom Foley
Kenmare
Co Kerry, Ireland
Tel: (064) 41013, Fax: (064) 42135
9 rooms
£40–£50 per person B&B
Open Mar to Nov
Credit cards: MC, VS
B&B
www.karenbrown.com/ireland/shelburnelodge.html

Apparently Dunromin's former owner was an insurance agent who had traveled all over Ireland, so when he bought this house, he changed its name from Whittington Cottage to reflect his circumstances, "done roaming." Just a narrow strip of garden separates the house from the busy main road so there's lots of traffic noise, but Dunromin is one of the few listings in this book that is within easy walking distance of bus and rail transportation. Guests have a snug sitting room where Valerie provides a carefully compiled book detailing the many attractions of the town and leaflets for guests to take. She discusses the merits of the various restaurants and pubs and has sample menus on hand. Traditional Irish music is a feature of the local pubs, but as it does not start until very late in the evening, guests often ask Tom for a couple of tunes on his accordion and he is always happy to oblige. Upstairs, Tom has done an excellent job of fitting small shower rooms into the bedrooms and Valerie has made the little rooms very pretty with attractive wallpaper, drapes, and bedcovers. A ten-minute walk brings you to the picturesque heart of town with its many fine old buildings, including beautifully painted shops and pubs with hand-crafted signs. Kilkenny Castle is definitely worth a visit. *Directions:* From Carlow take the N10 to Kilkenny. At the first roundabout follow signs for the city center and you will find Dunromin on your right after 1 km.

DUNROMIN
Owners: Valerie & Tom Rothwell
Dublin Road
Kilkenny
Co Kilkenny, Ireland
Tel: (056) 61387, Fax: (056) 70736
Email: valtom@oceanfree.net
4 rooms
£20–£25 per person B&B
Closed Christmas
Credit cards: MC, VS
B&B
www.karenbrown.com/ireland/dunromin.html

Behind a traditional downtown Kilkenny shopfront sits Zuni (the name of a native American tribe adopted on a whim by twin sisters and owners Sandra and Paula), a swish complex of bar, restaurant, and accommodation where ornamentation is kept to a minimum. The narrow bar—the kind where you sip martinis rather than gargle pints of bitter—opens up to the restaurant where vermilion-red walls contrast with black-and-cream décor and swathes of stainless steel can be seen in the adjacent kitchen. Of course, the food is modern and fun—more Mediterranean than Irish (restaurant closed Mondays). You find the same modern, minimalist look in the bedrooms, all identically decorated in soft cream with a vermillion-red wall adding a splash of color behind the bed. Beds are heavenly, with crisp white cotton linens and plump duvets. Rooms are by and large snug in size so ask for 101 to 104 or 201 to 204, the larger rooms, or 300, the largest with a queen and two single beds and a big bathroom. Zuni's excellent central location allows you to walk to everything in town. *Directions:* Arriving in Kilkenny from Dublin on the N10, follow signs for City Centre, which bring you down John's Street. Cross the River Nore and you see the castle on your left. Go straight at the traffic lights (signposted N10 Waterford) into Patrick Street and Zuni is on your right after 200 meters. Park in front and collect a map that directs you to parking behind the building or in the nearby multi-story car park.

ZUNI   New
Owners: Sandra & Alan McDonald, Paula & Paul Byrne
26 Patrick Street
Kilkenny
Co Kilkenny, Ireland
Tel: (056) 23999, Fax: (056) 56400
Email: info@zuni.ie
5 rooms, 4 en suite
£35–£55 per person B&B, Dinner: £20–£30 (not Mon)
Open all year, Credit cards: all major
Restaurant with rooms
www.karenbrown.com/ireland/zuni.html

Killarney is a pleasant town to visit after the crowds of daytime visitors have departed. Staying at Earls Court gives you the opportunity to go sightseeing out of town during the day, return in the evening for a cup of tea, and then walk into town for dinner. Emer and Ray built the house a few years ago and while the style outside is very modern, the inside is very traditional, for Emer is a great collector of lovely English and Irish antiques—guests sign in at a writing desk once owned by President Cearbhaill O'Dalaigh. Many of the delightful bedrooms have balconies with views of the distant mountains across the trees. The larger, non-view rooms have the advantage of spacious sitting areas and bigger bathrooms. All have lovely antique furniture, queen-sized beds (one is a four-poster and one an exquisite brass bed), excellent bathrooms with power showers, satellite TV, and phones. Several also have an extra single bed and two bedrooms have an interconnecting door, making them ideal for families. Earls Court makes an excellent base for exploring this popular part of Kerry and there's enough sightseeing to keep you busy for a week. Golfers are spoiled for choice, with Killarney, Waterville, Dooks, Tralee, and Ballybunion being the most popular courses—there's a golf room for clubs. *Directions*: Arriving from Cork on the N22, take a left-hand turn 1km before the first roundabout in Killarney (or go to the roundabout and retrace your steps, taking the first right). Proceed for 2 km past a slew of bed and breakfasts and Earls Court is on your right.

EARLS COURT
Owners: Emer & Ray Moynihan
Woodlawn Junction
Killarney
Co Kerry, Ireland
Tel: (064) 34009, Fax: (064) 34366
Email: earls@tinet.ie
18 rooms
£35–£55 per person B&B
Open Mar to mid-Nov, Credit cards: MC, VS
Guesthouse
www.karenbrown.com/ireland/earlscourt.html

This traditional farmhouse in the rich farmlands of County Cork is run by Margaret Browne, a cookbook writer and one of the area's leading chefs. Margaret's culinary endeavors had so taken over the family home that Michael retired from farming to help her and they built a restaurant just down the road. Margaret now combines cooking at the restaurant in the evening with making sure that her guests are well taken care of back at home. Relax in the sunny conservatory or on the Victorian sofas in the cozy sitting room all decked out in shades of green. Bedrooms are named after local rivers and are all attractively decorated with well-chosen antique furniture, wallpaper, and fabrics—two have six-foot beds. An excellent breakfast is served at the house and in the evening rides are arranged down to the restaurant to save guests driving. The same care that goes into looking after houseguests goes into her cooking—Margaret uses only the finest local meats, fish, and vegetables and there are lots of choices on the à-la-carte menu. Next to the restaurant is the Brownes' equestrian center, catering to both experienced and novice riders. There are masses of things to do in the area: Youghal (pronounced "yawl") is famous for its delightful old buildings and medieval streets; the Midleton Jamestown Centre tells the history of Irish whiskey production; and Cobh has an interesting maritime museum. *Directions:* Killeagh is on the N25 between Youghal and Cork. Turn at The Old Thatch Tavern, then after 1 km turn right: Ballymakeigh House is on your right after 1 km.

BALLYMAKEIGH HOUSE
Owners: Margaret & Michael Browne
Killeagh
Co Cork, Ireland
Tel: (024) 95184, Fax: (024) 95370
Email: ballymakeigh@tinet.ie
6 rooms
£30–£35 per person B&B, Dinner: £24
Open Feb to Nov
Credit cards: MC, VS
Farmhouse B&B
www.karenbrown.com/ireland/ballymakeighhouse.html

As newlyweds, Philomena and her husband John put in an exceedingly low bid on a very tumbledown Woodlands Farmhouse and it was many years before she found out why their offer had been accepted. To hear why and enjoy intriguing tales of gold sovereigns, cursed families, and arranged marriages, you will have to go and stay and ask Philomena for an after-dinner story session. What started out as a simple bed and breakfast has now grown into a very professional guesthouse business. Guests have a cozily cluttered parlor with an eclectic assortment of chairs, from stately Victorian to modern leather. The parlor opens up to an expansive dining room lit by two grand crystal chandeliers, which overlooks the lovely back garden. The front garden is even more impressive: a grand sweep of lawn with shrubs and trees going down to the river and the tennis court. All the smartly decorated bedrooms enjoy garden views and range in size from large family rooms to snug twins—all have electric blankets and small en-suite shower or bathrooms with hairdryers. The nearby beaches are particularly attractive. In Wexford you can visit Wexford Heritage Park or Johnstown Castle Agricultural Museum. To the north lies the Vale of Avoca where you can visit the hand-weavers, and see where the television series *Ballykissangel* is filmed. *Directions:* Woodlands House is signposted on the N11 between Arklow (10 km) and Gorey (6 km). Woodlands is just before the village of Killinierin, 2 km west of the N11.

WOODLANDS HOUSE
Owner: Philomena O'Sullivan
Killinierin, Gorey
Co Wexford, Ireland
Tel: (0402) 37125, Fax: (0402) 37133
Email: woodlnds@iol.ie
6 rooms
£25–£30 per person B&B
Dinner: £25 (groups only)
Open Apr to Oct, Credit cards: MC, VS
Guesthouse
www.karenbrown.com/ireland/woodlands.html

Flemingstown House, an 18th-century farmhouse, is just an hour's drive south of Limerick and Shannon airport, a quiet countryside world away from the hustle and bustle of the cosmopolitan area. Walk round the farm, watch the cows being milked, and chat with Imelda as she works in her spacious kitchen, for the two things that Imelda loves are cooking and taking care of her guests. It would be a shame to stay and not eat, for Imelda prepares tempting meals in which, following the starter and soup, there is a choice of meat or fish as a main course and always three or four desserts and farm cheeses made by her sister and her husband. The intricate stained-glass windows of the conservatory-style dining room were made by the same artist as those in the local church. Upstairs, the low-ceilinged bedrooms are very nicely kitted out and come with a variety of twin and king-size combinations that can accommodate families of all sizes. The decor is spotless, unfussy, and most attractive, with painted and wallpapered walls and matching bedcovers and drapes. Each bedroom has a small shower room. Nearby Kilmallock has the ruins of two friaries and the remains of its fortified wall weaving through the town. Imelda's guests often use her home as a base for touring counties Limerick, Tipperary, Kerry, and Cork. *Directions:* From Limerick take the N20 (Cork road) for 40 km and turn left to Kilmallock (10 km). From Kilmallock take the Kilfinane road (R512) for 3 km and the house is on your left.

FLEMINGSTOWN HOUSE
Owner: Imelda Sheedy-King
Kilmallock
Co Limerick, Ireland
Tel: (063) 98093, Fax: (063) 98546
Email: flemingstown@keltec.ie
5 rooms
£25 per person B&B, Dinner: £20
Open Feb to Nov
Credit cards: MC, VS
Farmhouse B&B
www.karenbrown.com/ireland/flemingstownhouse.html

Desmond House, a quiet walk to everything in Kinsale, was built by Spanish merchants in 1780 and more recently served as the home of the parish priest. John and Liam are very make-yourself-at-home people and have been great friends for over two decades, much of it working together in the Hong Kong police force. Liam lives at the top of the house while John lives just up the road with his wife and young family. You'll always find one of them about the place ready with advice on what to see and do and where to eat. Where to eat is an important topic of conversation in Kinsale for the town offers a veritable plethora of tempting little restaurants and, I might add, some very tempting shopping opportunities. Equip yourself for a busy day with an excellent breakfast (fresh-squeezed juice, lots of home baking and jams) served in a sunny yellow front room where the individual tables are laid with crisp blue-and-white cloths. Upstairs, the bedrooms are uncluttered and inviting and large enough for king- (can also be twins) or queen-size beds. Bathrooms (all with shower) are spacious. The two largest bedrooms also have an additional single bed, making them ideal for families. If you wish to have a separate bedroom for your children, one is sometimes available at the top of the house. *Directions:* Go straight up the main street in Kinsale (Pearse Street) to the end, turn left, first right, and first right, and Desmond House is on your right. Parking is opposite.

DESMOND HOUSE   New
Owners: John Carroll & Liam Scally
42 Cork Street
Kinsale
Co Cork, Ireland
Tel & fax: (021) 4773575
Email: desmondhouse@compuserve.com
4 rooms
£45 per person B&B
Closed Christmas, Credit cards: MC, VS
No-smoking house
B&B
www.karenbrown.com/ireland/desmond.html

Sitting beside the harbor, The Old Bank House occupies a prime waterfront location in this busy town. At one time these two Georgian townhouses served as a bank and the post office for the community but now they have achieved a new lease of life as premier accommodation opposite the sailboat-filled harbor. Here you are at the heart of town, having finally managed to obtain secure a spot for your car in the car park across the street. On the ground floor guests have a little sitting area perfect for browsing through the menus from nearby restaurants and toasting their toes on a chilly evening. In the morning enjoy a lavish breakfast cooked by owner, Michael Riese, a master chef. Bedrooms at the front enjoy superb harbor views and the higher you go, the better the view—fortunately there is an elevator. The largest room is the Postmaster's Suite, with a spacious sitting area and fireplace. Beds are twin or king-sized if you request that the twin beds be zipped together. All the rooms have phone, TV, bath with shower over the tub, and Egyptian-cotton towels and bathrobes. The location at the very heart of this most attractive harbor town is ideal: you can stroll round the shops perusing the restaurant menus as you go. *Directions:* Follow the main road into Kinsale (Pearse Street)—the Old Bank House is on the right as you come to the harbor. Parking is on the street, which is well lit.

OLD BANK HOUSE
Owners: Marie & Michael Riese
Pearse Street
Kinsale
Co Cork, Ireland
Tel: (021) 4774075, Fax: (021) 4774296
Email: oldbank@indigo.ie
17 rooms
Double £120–£180
Closed Christmas
Credit cards: all major
B&B
www.karenbrown.com/ireland/oldbank.html

Beyond the yacht-filled harbor, the narrow streets of Kinsale terrace upwards to high ground. Here you find The Old Presbytery, the home of Noreen and Philip McEvoy who offer a choice of bed-and-breakfast or self-catering accommodation. The three-bedroom, three-bathroom self-catering apartments offer a sitting room with cheery gas fire in an antique grate and an extra bed that can be pulled down from a wall cupboard, and a kitchenette equipped with a washer/dryer combination and light cooking facilities. The Penthouse has a narrow circular staircase going from the living room to the bedrooms where you have views across the rooftops to the harbor (an excellent choice for a party of four). Bed-and-breakfast guests can choose accommodation that ranges in size from cozy to spacious (a family room with a double and two single beds), with all but one of the rooms found up a narrow staircase—leave your large cases in the car. Another attractive larger room has its own private entrance up a steep iron stairway. Philip, who used to be a seafood chef, now concentrates his culinary efforts on breakfast, offering everything from traditional Irish fare to crepes filled with fruit in the breakfast room where an antique Irish pine credenza takes pride of place. *Directions:* Go straight up the main street in Kinsale (Pearse Street) to the end, turn left, first right, and first right, and The Old Presbytery is on the right. The Old Presbytery has a large yard for off-road parking.

THE OLD PRESBYTERY
Owners: Noreen & Philip McEvoy
43 Cork Street
Kinsale, Co Cork, Ireland
Tel: (021) 477 2027, Fax: (021) 477 2166
Email: info@oldpres.com
6 rooms, 3 apartments
£30–£45 per person B&B, Apartment: £100–£200
Closed Christmas
Credit cards: MC, VS
B&B & self-catering
www.karenbrown.com/ireland/oldpresbytery.html

Laura and Andrew Corcoran have given a new lease of life to this grandiose Victorian edifice overlooking the harbor in Kinsale and they even have a grandiose plan of their own to add a tower of luxurious rooms with one suite on each floor. Previous owners have executed their visions of grandeur and it is a tribute to the Corcorans' skills that they have pulled all the additions to the property together to form a unified whole. A perky fire radiates a welcome in the vast reception hall (plenty of room for all guests to arrive at once) while the sitting and drawing rooms are large enough to provide a seating spot for every guest. Non-public rooms, however, are of more normal proportions. Bedrooms come in all shapes and sizes, from spacious junior suites to snug double rooms. All are attractively decorated in a traditional vein and priced according to their location—how wonderful if they all had harbor views! No matter—you step out the front door onto the harbor and into the heart of this lively town. A buffet breakfast is included in the tariff and there is no shortage of restaurants nearby for dinner. *Directions:* Follow the main road into Kinsale (Long Quay)—Perryville House is on the right just as you come to the harbor. The hotel has several parking spaces opposite the hotel, on the harbor.

PERRYVILLE HOUSE
Owners: Laura & Andrew Corcoran
Long Quay
Kinsale
Co Cork, Ireland
Tel: (021) 4772731, Fax: (021) 4772298
Email: sales@perryville.iol.ie
22 rooms
Double: £140–£180*, Full breakfast: £8 per person
*Buffet breakfast included in tariff
Open Apr to Oct
Credit cards: all major
No-smoking house
B&B
www.karenbrown.com/ireland/perryville.html

Facing the Cliffs of Moher across Lahinch Bay, Moy House is a scrumptious boutique hotel caressed by wispy breezes rising off the sea, with waves almost lapping at the bottom of the garden. Built as a stylish holiday home in the early 1800s, the property has undergone a complete transformation from one to two stories, with all but two bedrooms having sea views. Relax with a drink from the honesty bar in the chic drawing room and contemplate the delectable offerings on the menu before going down the narrow spiral staircase to the dining room. Downstairs bedrooms Kilmaheen and Kilfarboy are particularly spacious and have large bathrooms, with separate bathtubs and showers with dinner-plate-sized showerheads. Upstairs, Moymore is a favorite with lots of room and a window seat in its bay window. For the most spectacular view, clamber up the narrow stairs that take you to the top of the tower. At low tide wander along the quiet beach and round the headland to the bustling little holiday town of Lahinch. While golfers head for the popular Lahinch golf course, sightseers drive along the coast and enjoy spectacular seascapes. Visit the Cliffs of Moher and the unusual, almost lunar landscape of the Burren. *Directions*: From Ennis take the N85 through Ennistymon to Lahinch. Go up the main street and take the first left, then turn left again following signposts for Miltown Malbay. After 2 km the entrance to Moy House is on the right.

MOY HOUSE   **New**
Manager: Bernie Merry
Lahinch
Co Clare, Ireland
Tel: (065) 7082800, Fax: (065) 7082500
Email: moyhouse@eircom.net
8 rooms
Double: £170, Dinner: £30
Closed Christmas to mid-Jan
Credit cards: all major
Country house hotel
www.karenbrown.com/ireland/moy.html

Delphi Lodge with its surrounding estate was for centuries the sporting estate of the Marquis of Sligo. This wild, unspoilt, and beautiful valley with its towering mountains, tumbling rivers, and crystal-clear loughs was acquired in 1986 by Jane and Peter Mantle. Fortunately for those who have a love of wild, beautiful places, they have restored the Marquis's fishing lodge and opened their home to guests who come to walk, fish for salmon, relax, and enjoy the camaraderie of the house-party atmosphere. In the evening Peter often presides at the head of the very long dinner table (guests who catch a salmon take the place of honor) and guests enjoy a leisurely meal and lively conversation. A snug library and an attractive drawing room are at hand and guests often spend late-night hours in the billiard room. Bedrooms are all furnished in antique and contemporary pine, several having large comfortable armchairs and views to the peaceful lake. Such is the popularity of the place that it is advisable to make reservations well in advance to secure a summer booking. Five deluxe, self-catering cottages are also available on the estate. *Directions:* Leenane is between Wesport and Clifden on the N59. From Leenane go east towards Westport for 5 km, turn left and continue along the north shore of Killary harbor towards Louisburgh for 10 km. Delphi Lodge is in the woods, on the left after the adventure center.

DELPHI LODGE
Owners: Jane & Peter Mantle
Leenane
Co Galway, Ireland
Tel: (095) 42222, Fax: (095) 42296
Email: delfish@iol.ie
12 rooms
£40–£80 per person B&B, Dinner: £27
Open mid-Jan to mid-Dec
Credit cards: MC, VS
Country house & self-catering
www.karenbrown.com/ireland/delphi.html

Rosleague Manor is a lovely Irish hotel—a comfortable country house hotel overlooking Ballinakill Bay and an ever-changing panorama of wild Connemara countryside. This is a quiet, sparsely populated land of steep hills, tranquil lakes, and grazing sheep, where narrow country lanes lead to little hamlets. Manager Mark Foyle is much in evidence, making certain that guests are well taken care of. The hotel is beautifully furnished with lovely old furniture, and the sitting rooms are cozy with their turf fires and comfortable chairs. The garden-style conservatory is a popular place for before- or after-dinner drinks. Bedrooms are most attractive. I prefer those with views across the gardens to the loch and distant hills. The dining room is my favorite room in the house: tall windows frame the view and lovely old tables and chairs are arranged in groupings on the polished floor. There is an à-la-carte menu as well as the fixed-price menu which offers four or five choices for each course. Dishes vary with the seasons and include a wide selection of locally caught fish and Connemara lamb. This is a peaceful place to hide away and a well located base for exploring the ruggedly beautiful countryside of Connemara. *Directions:* Take the N59 from Galway to Clifden then turn right at the church for the 10-km drive to Rosleague Manor.

ROSLEAGUE MANOR
Owner: Edmund Foyle
Letterfrack, Connemara
Co Galway, Ireland
Tel: (095) 41101, Fax: (095) 41168
Email: rosleaguemanor@eircom.net
20 rooms
Double: £100–£150, Suite: £120–£170
Dinner: £32
Open Easter to Nov
Credit cards: all major
Country house hotel
www.karenbrown.com/ireland/rosleague.html

Golf and contented cows typify Listowel, which lies just 16 kilometers from Ballybunion golf course and is the home of Kerry Dairies, which produces vast quantity of butter and cheese. It's a prosperous, traditional town with lots of life and there's no better place to experience a taste of Ireland than by staying with Helen and Armel at their bar and bistro, which occupies two shopfronts and the houses above. A traditional "snug" sits just inside the main door of the bar, which opens up to an informal restaurant. The other shopfront is a guests' entrance with access to the more formal restaurant (the same food is served in both places and you can choose from either the supper or the dinner menu). Above the restaurant are three bedrooms, one on each floor. Two are queens, with spacious bathrooms with claw-foot tubs and separate showers, while the third, a twin with shower, is tucked under the eaves. There's a real buzz to the place and while the town is not busy at night, this is not a place to consider if you are looking for countryside peace and quiet. Golfers head for Ballybunion while scenery-watchers head for the Dingle Peninsula and the Lakes of Killarney. *Directions*: From Tralee take the N69 to Listowel for 27 km. Follow the one-way system through the town going back towards Tralee and you will find Allo's Bar & Bistro on your left in Church Street. Park outside to unload and you will be directed to off-road parking round the back.

ALLO'S BAR & BISTRO   New
Owners: Helen & Armel White
41 Church Street
Listowel
Co Kerry, Ireland
Tel: (068) 22880, Fax: (068) 22803
Email: allosbistro@eircom.net
3 rooms
£45–£65 per person B&B, Dinner: £23–£25
Open all year
Credit cards: MC, VS
Restaurant with rooms
www.karenbrown.com/ireland/allos.html

Standing on the shores of Lough Eske, a 20-minute drive from Donegal and overlooking some of Ireland's prettiest scenery, Ardnamona House is the place to visit if you have an interest in rhododendrons and azaleas. Without a doubt, Amabel and Kieran Clarke's 40 acres of grounds contain some magnificent specimens from giant trees (many over 100 years old) to small bushes. Until Kieran (a piano tuner by profession) gave me a short tour of their property, I was unaware that there were so many varieties of rhododendrons and azaleas. Upon arrival I was greeted by an effusive Amabel and Debbie the donkey, who wanders the grounds and searches out guests, hoping for a pat and a treat. Guests enjoy a cozy sitting room and a little conservatory overlooking the lough. In the evening guests dine together round the long dining-room table at 8:30 pm to a set three-course meal. Upstairs the very attractively decorated bedrooms are priced according to size and whether their little bathroom is en suite or down the hall. The rhododendrons are at their peak during April and May, the azaleas at their peak in May. Donegal town bustles and parking can be a problem but the effort of finding a space is worth it. The scenery is rugged and beautiful, the roads quiet and narrow. *Directions:* From Donegal town take the N15 towards Letterkenny for 5 km to a small signpost that indicates a left turn to Harvey Point Hotel. Follow this road for 11 km and Ardnamona's driveway in on your right.

ARDNAMONA HOUSE
Owners: Amabel & Kieran Clarke
Lough Eske
Co Donegal, Ireland
Tel: (073) 22650, Fax: (073) 22819
5 rooms
£45–£50 per person B&B
Dinner: £25 (not Sun)
Open all year
Credit cards: all major
Country house

Kilkenny is a most attractive, historic town, and there is no more perfect a base for exploring its many charms than Blanchville House, a 15-minute drive away. Acres of farmland give this handsome Georgian home seclusion. You'll know you've arrived when you see a tall square church-tower-like folly—in days gone by it was equipped with clocks and bells. Inside Blanchville House, tall-ceilinged, generously proportioned rooms are the order of the day, and Monica is particularly proud of having several pieces of furniture that were made for the house. One of these is the glorious half-tester bed that graces the principal bedroom. Apparently Sir James Kearny, a great eccentric, was fond of waxing and singeing his mustache, an operation he performed in his bed. One day, while practicing this routine, he set fire to the bedding and narrowly escaped burning the house down. There's a portrait of Sir James in the drawing room, which has the lovely wallpaper hung in 1823: guests enjoy a drink here before going in to dine together round the long polished table. Three lovely self-catering cottages (one handicap-friendly) are found in the old stables and gardener's cottage (sleep three to six). County Kilkenny is particularly lovely and Monica can give you a tourist map that directs you to a great many craft shops. *Directions:* Leave Kilkenny on the N10 in the direction of Dublin and Blanchville House is signposted to your right after The Pike pub, 5 km out. Pass over the railway crossing, go 2 km and turn left at Connly's pub, and the house is on your left after 1 km. (There is no village of Maddoxtown and Dunbell is Connly's pub.)

BLANCHVILLE HOUSE
Owners: Monica & Tim Phelan
Dunbell, Maddoxtown
Co Kilkenny, Ireland
Tel (056) 27197, Fax: (056) 27636
Email: info@blanchville.ie
6 rooms, 5 en suite, 3 cottages
£35–£37.50 per person B&B, Dinner: £25 (not Sun)
Open Mar to Oct, Credit cards: all major
Country house & self-catering
www.karenbrown.com/ireland/blanchville.html

If you are seeking a romantic interlude on a gracious country estate, you can do no better than to choose Longueville House, whose size takes your breath away. Set on a hill overlooking the River Blackwater, this elegant country house offers you the very best of Irish hospitality. It was built by Richard Longfield, who was spurred on to grander things by a sum of money he received for supporting the British Act of Union. The house is back with the O'Callaghan family whose forebears had it taken from them by Cromwell in 1650. The O'Callaghans take great pains to make sure that you enjoy your stay: Aisling makes certain you are well cared for and made to feel completely at home while William ensures that you are well fed. William is blessed with the fact that Longueville is almost completely self-sufficient. Vegetables, salmon, lamb, and herbs—even a few bottles of wine—come from the estate. The dining room in soft shades of pink is a picture, while the adjacent library provides a snug place to dine. Each and every bedroom is beautifully decorated and accompanied by a splendid modern bathroom. Below stairs is a new conference center. The nearby River Blackwater offers salmon and trout fishing for guests. There are several 18-hole golf courses within easy reach of Longueville—Mallow, Killarney, Cork, and Tralee and the links at Ballybunion. *Directions:* The hotel is located on the N72, 5 km west of Mallow on the Killarney road. Shannon airport is 85 km away.

LONGUEVILLE HOUSE
Owners: Aisling & William O'Callaghan
Mallow
Co Cork, Ireland
Tel: (022) 47156, Fax: (022) 47459
Email: info@longuevillehouse.ie
21 rooms
Double: £135–£180, Suite: £190–£250, Dinner: £32
Open mid-Feb to mid-Dec
Credit cards: all major
Country house hotel
www.karenbrown.com/ireland/longuevillehouse.html

Joan laments that she had the 15th-century stone turret staircase taken out to make way for two shower rooms. That was many years ago when living in an old keep held no appeal at all and Joan's concern was to get some 20th-century amenities into the place. She has certainly succeeded and along the way kept several other "older" features—the 5-foot-thick wall in the dining room, the stone arch that leads to the kitchen, and the ancient defense wall in the garden. The "modern wing" is a mere 300 years old, with a couple of bits and bobs added on in later years. Joan is the most welcoming and attentive of hostesses, though on matters of history she refers you to her husband Emmett. Joan strongly believes in keeping you well fed: breakfasts have to be seen to be believed—a vast array of fruit dishes alongside fresh scones and a variety of hot dishes. Scones and a pot of tea (sometimes homemade pie) are served in the afternoon to keep you going between lunch and dinner. My favorite bedrooms were room 1 with its big bay window looking across the garden wall to miles of countryside and room 5, a spacious room at the back. There are some lovely drives in this area (The Vee and Nire Valley to Clonmel) and several castles (Cahir and Lismore), and the sea with Dungarven and Youghal is just over the hills. *Directions:* From Dungarven take the N72 towards Cork for 9.5 km (just through Cappagh) and turn right on the R761 signposted Clonmel. After 5 km you arrive in Millstreet where you turn right, then cross the bridge and Castle Farm is on your right.

CASTLE FARM   New
Owners: Joan & Emmett Newgent
Millstreet, Cappagh
Co Waterford, Ireland
Tel: (058) 68049, Fax: (058) 68099
Email: castlefarm@iol.ie
5 rooms
£25–£30 per person B&B
Open Mar to Nov, Credit cards: MC, VS
No-smoking house
Farmhouse B&B
www.karenbrown.com/ireland/castlefarm.html

Amongst the scattered modern holiday cottages and retirement homes surrounding the village of Miltown Malbay, a popular Irish holiday destination, you find a traditional Irish farmhouse that is now a welcoming guesthouse, restaurant, and cookery school operated by Rita Meade. Rita offers cookery courses for adults, teenagers, and children and the heart of the house is the kitchen with its large central island designed for day-long cooking classes. Two small rooms have been combined and extended with a conservatory to serve as a guest sitting and dining room filled with pine tables and chairs and decorated with an old pine dresser. The country theme is continued in the bedrooms with their pine furniture and old iron beds topped with colorful quilts. All bedrooms have televisions and compact shower rooms and three rooms have a double and a single bed. There is a small ground-floor double-bedded room for those who have difficulty with stairs. The nearby Cliffs of Moher are a great attraction but one guest used Berry Lodge as a base for visiting Bunratty Folk Park, Craggaunowen Megalithic Centre, the Aran Islands, exploring the Burren, and sailing to Scattery Island. *Directions:* From Ennis (on the Limerick to Galway road) take the N85 to Inagh then the R460 to Miltown Malbay (32 km total). Take the N67 Spanish Point Road in the center of the village, pass the caravan park, cross the bridge, take the second left, and Berry Lodge is first on the right.

BERRY LODGE
Owner: Rita Meade
Annagh
Miltown Malbay
Co Clare, Ireland
Tel: (065) 7087022, Fax: (065) 7087011
Email: rita.meade@esatclear.ie
5 rooms
£25 per person B&B, Dinner: £25
Closed mid-Jan to mid-Feb
Credit cards: MC, VS
B&B
www.karenbrown.com/ireland/berry.html

Temple takes its name from the medieval monastery that once stood on the site. The present home is more than 250 years old and John and Charles Wesley, founders of Methodism, visited and preached here in 1748–49. Converts, few and far between, would have been invigorated by the facilites available to today's guest—sauna, steamroom and hydrotherapy bath (no pool), aromatherapy massage, reflexology, and Yon-Ka beauty treatments—not to mention the guided country walks, yoga, relaxation classes, and golf. (Please book treatments in advance.) With its location less than a two-hour drive from Dublin airport, it's just the place to spend a couple of days at either end of your holiday. Daytime finds guest relaxing with a cup of herbal tea in the sunroom while at night they congregate by the fire in the little parlor and sitting room after sampling one of Bernie's delicious dinners. Three lovely bedrooms are found in the main house—one is a family room with a single bed and a grand draped metal-and-brass bed. Smaller, more contemporary rooms are found across the courtyard above the spa. Local attractions include a miniature train that steams you through a vast bogland while a guide explains its history and management. Just down the road in Killbeggan is Locke's whiskey distillery, while the Clonmacnois monastic ruins and round tower are a half-hour's drive away. *Directions:* Temple is about 1 km off the N6 midway between Dublin and Galway, between Horseleap and Moate. The house is well signposted.

TEMPLE COUNTRY HOUSE AND SPA
Owners: Bernadette & Declan Fagan
Horseleap, Moate
Co Westmeath, Ireland
Tel: (0506) 35118, Fax: (0506) 35008
Email: templespa@spiders.ie
8 rooms
£40–£60 per person B&B*, Dinner: £20 (not Sun or Mon)
*3-, 5-, and 7-day packages available
Open mid-Jan to Nov, Credit cards: all major
Country house
www.karenbrown.com/ireland/temple.html

A crooked little lane winds you up the hill to Crookedwood House, a 200-year-old rectory that sits at the crest of the hill overlooking Lough Derragh (the lake of the oaks) where mythology has it that the children of Lir were turned into swans. It's a lovely spot almost in the center of Ireland—a delightful place to unwind and enjoy good food and a warm welcome. Noel is one of Ireland's noted chefs and the recent addition of guestrooms means that diners now also have an agreeable place to lay their heads. Gather by the fire in the reception sitting room and study the menu before going below stairs to the restaurant, which is divided into intimate nooks in several whitewashed cellars. The bedrooms each have identical decor with matching drapes and bedspreads, reproduction furniture, and an immaculate modern bathroom: more Hilton than Irish county house. The center of Ireland with its quiet roads, low hills, and warren of lakes is a delight to explore (see other Mullingar listings). *Directions:* From Dublin take the Sligo Road (N4). When you are on the Mullingar bypass, exit for Castlepollard, following this road for 10 km to Crookedwood where you turn right by The Wood pub. Crookedwood House is on your right after 2 km.

CROOKEDWOOD HOUSE
Owners: Julie & Noel Kenny
Crookedwood, Mullingar
Co Westmeath, Ireland
Tel: (044) 72165, Fax: (044) 72166
Email: cwoodhse@iol.ie
8 rooms
Double: £100–£110, Dinner: £26 (not Mon)
Closed Christmas
Credit cards: all major
Restaurant with rooms
www.karenbrown.com/ireland/crookedwood.html

Lough Owel Lodge is a modern house set between Lough Owel and a quiet country road that runs into Mullingar. While the house has no architectural distinction, this is a tranquil country spot where you can cycle down quiet roads, stroll the shores of Lough Owel, and generally enjoy the peace and quiet of the center of Ireland. Aideen and Martin Ginnell find that the house works really well for raising a family of four children and providing bed and breakfast, for it is divided into two parts, the front being for guests and the back for their family. I particularly appreciated the large car port which sheltered me from the rain as I arrived. A large sitting room with comfortable sofas and floor-to-ceiling windows offering views of the garden and lake leads into the dining room with its lovely old table and chairs. Upstairs, the most spacious room has an enormous, almost 2-meter-square bed. A family suite consists of a small double bedroom leading to a small twin-bedded room and a large bathroom. A smaller double room has a lovely family-heirloom half-tester bed and small bathroom. Guests often wander down to the lough, enjoy a game of tennis, and make use of the children's game room. Tullynally Castle, Carrickglass Manor, Belvedere House, Fore Abbey, and Athlone Castle are within an hour's drive. *Directions:* Take the N4 from Dublin towards Sligo. After passing the third exit for Mullingar, Lough Owel Lodge is signposted to your left after 1 km.

LOUGH OWEL LODGE
Owners: Aideen & Martin Ginnell
Cullion
Mullingar
Co Westmeath, Ireland
Tel: (044) 48714, Fax: (044) 48771
Email: aideen.ginnell@ireland.com
5 rooms
£20–£25 per person B&B
Open Mar to Dec
Credit cards: MC, VS
B&B
www.karenbrown.com/ireland/loughowel.html

Readers' letters praise the warmth of welcome, the delectable food, the quality and utter charm of this country house, and the fact that Mornington is an hour and a half's drive from Dublin Airport making it an ideal first or last destination in Ireland. I totally concur, for a stay at Mornington House with Anne and Warwick, the fifth generation of his family to call this home, is also something I find completely delightful. The O'Haras have an easy way of making guests feel at home. They chat with them in the drawing room after dinner and put a lot of trouble into helping them with their activites and sightseeing in this unspoiled region with its lakes, canals, and gently undulating countryside. Anne is a talented cook, producing delicious dinners and outstanding breakfasts. Families are welcome and children can be served an early tea. The two front bedrooms are enormous: one has a large brass bed sitting center stage which requires a climb to get into it, while the other has a Victorian double bed and shares the view across the peaceful grounds. The third bedroom, a twin-bedded room, looks out to the side garden and the woods. The oldest wing of the house contains two smaller bedrooms overlooking the kitchen garden. *Directions:* From Dublin take the Sligo Road (N4) to the Mullingar bypass. Exit for Castlepollard and go 10 km to Crookedwood where you turn left by The Wood pub. After 2 km turn right and Mornington House is on your right after 1 km.

MORNINGTON HOUSE
Owners: Anne & Warwick O'Hara
Mornington, Multyfarnham, Mullingar
Co Westmeath, Ireland
Tel: (044) 72191, Fax: (044) 72338
Email: info@mornington.ie
5 rooms, 4 en suite
£40 per person B&B, Dinner: £25
Open Apr to Oct
Credit cards: all major
Country house
www.karenbrown.com/ireland/morningtonhouse.html

Margaret's mother grew up down the road and remembered Ashley Park as the premier house in the town, renowned for its formal gardens and elegant interior, so when it came up for auction almost 20 years ago mum and dad bought the place—it has been the family restoration project ever since. The house is a real beauty, with lots of in-character big furniture and sofas drawn round the fire. Upstairs, the two rooms at either end of the house are enormous suites: red has twin four-poster brass beds and a huge sitting alcove while green has a double and a single bed, again with a lovely big sitting alcove. Presidents is a most attractive bedroom named for President Mary McAleese who came to lunch—she was considering several places to dine in the area but when Margaret let her know that her dad, Sean, was one of her greatest supporters it tipped her decision. Sean still bursts with pride at the memory and among an array of family photos you'll see several commemorating the event. Margaret juggles her young family and guests in a seemingly effortless fashion and has a local chef come in to cook dinner. Wander the grounds and admire their restoration or row out to the island with its little ruined building or across the lake to the copse, which contains a fairy castle. Farther afield lie Bunratty Castle and Folk Park, and Clonmacnois, the 6th-century monastic settlement on the River Shannon. *Directions:* From Nenagh town take the Borrisokane road for 5 km and the house is on your right (there is an arched stone entry to the driveway).

ASHLEY PARK HOUSE   **New**
Owners: Margaret & P.J. Mounsey
Ardcroney, Nenagh
Co Tipperary, Ireland
Tel & fax: (067) 38223, Fax: (067) 38013
Email: margaret@ashleypark.com
6 rooms, 5 en suite
£28–£30 per person B&B, Dinner: from £23
Open all year, Credit cards: none
Country house
www.karenbrown.com/ireland/ashleypark.html

Isolated by a tall hedge of cypress trees, Creacon Lodge and its exquisite rose garden look for all the world like a little bit of England transported to Ireland. Josephine Flood, your stylish hostess, is often there to greet you. Enjoy a drink in the bar and a meal in the handsome dining room or listen to music in the sitting room with its comfy sofas and chairs arranged around the fire. Up a narrow flight of stairs, the little bedrooms with their sloping ceilings are tucked under the roof and their tiny, floor-level windows offer glimpses of the garden. Each bedroom is equipped with TV and direct-dial phone. On the ground floor is Peach, named for its color scheme, where you have to be prepared to tolerate the muffled noise of late-night festivities in the adjacent bar. Across the courtyard are three bedrooms in the cottage and two in a little gatehouse. On my last visit I found the decor in the bedrooms to be rather tired-looking but Josephine reassured me that decorational changes were scheduled, and I feel certain that by the time I visit again everything will be in decorator-perfect order. The staff is especially friendly and helpful. Ten minutes away is the John F. Kennedy Park. The nearby Hook Peninsula with its secluded coves has the oldest lighthouse in Europe. Creacon Lodge is only a 40-km drive from Rosslare harbor. *Directions:* From Wexford take the N25 New Ross to Cork road. Just before reaching New Ross turn left on the R733 signposted John F. Kennedy Park (do not take the first left for JFK Park). After 5 km turn left for Creacon Lodge.

CREACON LODGE HOTEL
Owner: Josephine Flood
Creacon Lower, New Ross
Co Wexford, Ireland
Tel: (051) 421897, Fax: (051) 422560
Email: creacon@indigo.ie
10 rooms
£30–£40 per person B&B, Dinner: £17.50
Open all year
Credit cards: MC, VS
Family hotel
www.karenbrown.com/ireland/creacon.html

Kevin is a madly keen gardener and Bernadette says he is in danger of landscaping the entire farm! He is presently constructing a wild garden with duck pond and has made pathways down and along the riverbanks so that guests can go for a stroll or a fish—trout fishing is a great draw. Walkers head for the hills—Kilmaneen is surrounded by the Comeraghs, Knockmealdowns, and Galtee Mountains, ideal for day hikes. Kevin can either take you out for the day in a group or supply you with maps that guide you on your rambles. Guests have their own wing of the trim little farmhouse. Upstairs you find three very nice bedrooms: a double, a twin, and a very snug double, which is rented as a single, while downstairs is a small sitting room, though guests usually gravitate to the comfortable chairs round the map of the locale that is set under glass on the coffee table in the sunny bay window in the hallway. If you want more private space or have a family, enquire about renting the adjacent little two-bedroom cottage, either for bed and breakfast or on a self-catering basis. Fishing, walking, and music in the pubs at night are big attractions, though sightseers have lots to keep them busy with driving The Vee and visiting Lismore, Cahir, Cappoquin, and Swiss Cottage, all within a 16-kilometer radius. *Directions:* Newcastle is signposted from the R671 Clonmel to Dungarven road. Go through the village of Newcastle, towards Cloheen, at the first junction (a Y), bear right down a narrow, winding lane, and Kilmaneen is on your right after 2 km.

KILMANEEN FARMHOUSE   **New**
Owners: Bernadette & Kevin O'Donnell
Newcastle, Clonmel
Co Tipperary, Ireland
Tel & fax: (052) 36231
Email: kilmaneen@eircom.net
3 rooms
£20–£22.50 per person B&B, Dinner £17.50
Open Apr to Dec, Credit cards: MC, VS
No-smoking house
Farmhouse B&B & self-catering
www.karenbrown.com/ireland/kilmaneen.html

Dromoland Castle is a spectacular, albeit very expensive, place to spend either your first or last night if you are flying into or out of Shannon airport. Before it became a luxury hotel in 1963, Dromoland Castle saw almost 400 years as the ancestral home of the O'Brien clan. Now it is the luxurious sister hotel of the prestigious Ashford Castle. Jacket and tie for gentlemen are required after 7 pm in the elegant, formal dining room and the book-lined bar where guests often settle after dinner to join in the singing of popular Irish ballads. The sumptuous, ornate drawing room is an ideal haven for morning coffee and afternoon tea. Up the grand staircase are found the hotel's premier rooms and luxurious suites and a portrait gallery of past incumbents of the estate. The Moriarty wing has 24 deluxe rooms. Smaller, cozy rooms are located round a courtyard in the castle's oldest part (1736) and have the same lavish amenities: robes, slippers, masses of toiletries, fruit bowl, and a decanter of Irish Mist. Treat yourself to a leisurely breakfast in bed or order dinner from the extensive room service menu. Various massages and treatments are available at the health spa. Tennis courts and Dromoland's golf course are here for you to use and fishing, horse riding, and bird shooting can be arranged nearby. Just down the road Bunratty Castle and Folk Park are well worth a visit. *Directions:* The Dromoland estate is on the N18, Ennis to Limerick road, 13 km north of Shannon airport.

DROMOLAND CASTLE
Manager: Mark Nolan
Dromoland, Newmarket-on-Fergus
Co Clare, Ireland
Tel: (061) 368144, Fax: (061) 363355
100 rooms
Double: £264–£328*, Suite: £386–£850*
*Breakfast not included: £14, Dinner: £42
Open all year
Credit cards: all major
Luxury resort

When Lord Inchiquin sold Dromoland Castle in 1963, he moved five minutes up the hill to Thomond House, a large Georgian-style mansion. Now it is home to his nephew Conor O'Brien (the present Lord Inchiquin and head of the O'Brien chieftancy) and his family—and what a delightful home it is, with its high-ceilinged rooms looking out through tall windows to the surrounding countryside. The Inchiquins and their staff are not effusive hosts, and an air of quiet formality is the order of the day. Guests enjoy a comfortable drawing room, take breakfast in the dining room, and watch television in the library. A sweeping staircase leads to the upper gallery and bedrooms, which are all nicely kitted out and offer views of the parkland or the adjacent castle. Additional bedrooms are found on the ground floor. Dinner, incorporating farm-fresh ingredients, is served every evening except Sundays. Alternatively, you might want to walk down to Dromoland Castle for a superb formal meal or drive a few kilometers to Durty Nelly's and enjoy casual fare in this traditional Irish pub. Guests often play golf on the neighboring Dromoland course or roam over the estate, while farther afield lie the dramatic Cliffs of Moher and the Burren with its rocky landscapes. *Directions:* The Dromoland estate is on the N18, Ennis to Limerick road, 13 km north of Shannon airport. The entrance to Thomond House is south of Dromoland Castle.

THOMOND HOUSE
Owners: Helen & Conor Inchiquin
Manager: Martin Duffy
Dromoland
Newmarket-on-Fergus
Co Clare, Ireland
Tel: (061) 368304, Fax: (061) 368285
Email: info@thomondhouse.com
8 rooms
Double: £140–£180, Dinner: £40
Closed Christmas, Credit cards: all major
Country house
www.karenbrown.com/ireland/thomand.html

A cottage, a church, and Hanora's Cottage nestle beside the tumbling River Nire in this delightfully wild and isolated spot on the edge of the Comeragh Mountains. Seamus's great-grandparents would not recognize their little cottage with its parade of sitting rooms, spacious restaurant, hot tub for eight in the conservatory, and array of spacious bedrooms. Small wonder that Hanora's was awarded Guesthouse of the Year in 1999. Nine of the eleven bedrooms have Jacuzzi bathtubs—just for fun, reserve one of the three most spacious rooms whose bathrooms come equipped with Jacuzzi tubs for two. Try to plan your stay to include a Saturday so you can accompany Seamus and Victor, the family dog, on their ramble and hear stories of the folklore and history of the rocky, heather-clad Comeraghs. Whenever you come to stay, you can be sure of being well fed—Mary lays out a feast of a breakfast for which Seamus gets up early to bake a variety of breads. In the evening son Eoin (pronounced "Owen") and his wife Judith offer a set, four-course dinner with lots of choices for starters and main courses. Packed lunches, maps, and directions are available for walks that range from leisurely woodland rambles to challenging hill hikes. If you're not worn out by walking, visit the local pubs for music and dancing. *Directions:* From Clonmel or Dungarvan, follow the R672 as far as Ballymacarbry village where you turn left into the Nire Valley at Melody's Lounge Bar. Travel 5.6 km and Hanora's is beside the church just before the stone bridge.

HANORA'S COTTAGE GUESTHOUSE
Owners: Mary & Seamus Wall
Nire Valley
Via Clonmel
Co Waterford, Ireland
Tel: (052) 36134, Fax: (052) 36540
Email: hanorascottage@eircom.net
11 rooms
£45–£65 per person B&B, Dinner: £30
Closed Christmas, Credit cards: MC, VS
Guesthouse
www.karenbrown.com/ireland/hanoras.html

Guests at Currarevagh House (pronounced "Curra-reeva") find themselves entering a world reminiscent of the turn of the century. Tranquillity reigns supreme and things are done the good old-fashioned way at Currarevagh House. However, do not be afraid that you will be deprived of central heating and private bathrooms, for this is not the case. Bedrooms are all priced the same. If you book well in advance, you may be able to secure room 1, 2, or 3 in the old house or room 16 in the new wing with its lake views. Try to arrive by 4:30 pm when tea and cakes are served—you will then have enough time for a brisk walk to make room for a delicious dinner at 8 pm. A gong announces dinner and while there are no choices, the helpings are of generous proportions. A tempting breakfast buffet of cold meats, cheeses, and traditional cooked breakfast dishes is spread on the sideboard and the hotel is happy to pack you a picnic lunch for your day's excursion. It's all very old-fashioned and un-decorator-perfect, but I must admit that I thoroughly enjoyed it—the Hodgsons really do manage to create the illusion of being back in Victorian times. Harry can arrange for fishing on the adjacent Lough Corrib, the second-largest lake in Ireland, a haven for fishermen. *Directions:* From Galway take the N59 to Oughterard, turn right in the center of the village, and follow the lake shore for the 6-km drive to the house.

CURRAREVAGH HOUSE
Owners: June & Harry Hodgson
Oughterard, Connemara
Co Galway, Ireland
Tel: (091) 552312, Fax: (091) 552731
15 rooms
Double: £100–£125*, Dinner: £24*
*Plus 10% service
Open Apr to mid-Oct
Credit cards: MC, VS
Country house hotel
www.karenbrown.com/ireland/currarevaghhouse.html

The Narrows, named for the narrow body of water it overlooks, sits on the sea front in the small port of Portaferry with its traditional shops, pubs, and market square. Brothers Will and James Brown were brought up in one of the tall townhouses that makes up their guesthouse and when the adjacent house came up for sale, they decided to purchase it, amalgamating the two buildings into a guesthouse and restaurant. While the building is traditional, the decor is fresh and modern, with country-pine furniture throughout. All the bedrooms have water views and similar decor, with twin or double beds topped with plump duvets, coir (coconut matting) covering the floors, and attractive watercolors decorating the walls. The Browns have built their guesthouse to be wheelchair friendly, so all of the modern shower rooms have level-deck showers and there is a ramp into the herb and flower garden found on a high terrace off the back verandah. The restaurant has been rated very highly and makes good use of fresh local produce whenever possible. Mount Stewart, a fascinating 18th-century house, and its beautiful gardens are a big attraction as is Castle Ward, a 280-acre country estate on the banks of Strangford Lough. *Directions:* From Belfast take the A20 through Newtownards to Portaferry and turn left along Shore Road when you reach the water.

THE NARROWS
Owners: Will & James Brown
8 Shore Road
Portaferry BT22 1JY
Co Down, Northern Ireland
Tel: (028) 4272 8148, Fax: (028) 4272 8105
13 rooms
£42.50 per person B&B, Dinner: £15–£20
Open all year
Credit cards: all major
Family hotel

On John's retirement the Deanes demolished the holiday cottage they owned on this site and in its place built Croaghross, a stylishly modern building that captures the stunning views of Ballymastocker Strand, one of Donegal's loveliest beaches. While the house is of modern design, the interior is very traditional and furnished with antiques. In the evenings a fire burns a welcome to the parlor where guests often gather for a drink before enjoying one of Kay's absolutely excellent dinners. We were treated to mushroom paté, fresh cod with tiny new potaotes and fresh vegetables, and apple tart with homemade ice cream—followed by a walk to the little pub on the pier. Three bedrooms capture the view (a double, a twin-bedded, and a family room) and each has French windows opening up to private patios. Another very spacious twin-bedded room is specially equipped for wheelchair access. (I have not quoted rates for the additional small double-bedded room.) For longer stays there is a three-bedroomed cottage at the far end of the garden. Guests often play golf on Portsalon golf course, which runs beside the beach. Enjoy spectacular ocean views as you drive round the Fanad Peninsula or traveling farther afield to visit the beautiful gardens and castle in Glenveagh National Park. *Directions:* From Donegal, take the N56 to Letterkenny and on the outskirts of the town look for the T72, signposted for Ramelton and Rathmullen. Cross the bridge in Ramelton and turn left for Portsalon (25 km from Letterkenny). At the crossroads in Portsalon take the Fanad road for 1 km and just before the golf club (right) take a left-hand turn up a narrow lane to Croaghross.

CROAGHROSS
Owners: Kay & John Deane
Portsalon
Co Donegal, Ireland
Tel & fax: (074) 59548
Email: jkdeane@croaghross.com
5 rooms, 1 cottage
£20–£35 per person B&B, Dinner: £17.50
Open mid-Mar to Oct, Credit cards: MC, VS
B&B & self-catering
www.karenbrown.com/ireland/croaghross.html

Ardeen was an especially welcome haven after we explored the Donegal coast on a particularly gloomy, wet summer's day. This attractive Victorian house was once the town doctor's home. Anne Campbell and her husband had always admired Ardeen's airy rooms and large riverside garden, so when it came up for sale, they jumped at the opportunity to call it home. Breakfast around the large dining-room table is the only meal that Anne prepares, though she is happy to offer advice on where to eat in Ramelton. Guests can plan their sightseeing from the warmth of the sitting room. Upstairs, a sunny yellow double room faces the water. It has a lovely en-suite shower room, as does the pretty peach double next door. A twin room enjoys a large private bathroom. The adjacent stable has been converted to a snug holiday cottage with an exposed stone living room, attractive kitchen, and two attic bedrooms. Ardeen is an ideal base for exploring the Donegal coastline and visiting Glenveagh National Park and the Glebe Art Gallery with its fine collection of Irish paintings. *Directions:* If you are arriving from Donegal, take the N56 to Letterkenny and on the outskirts of the town look for the T72, signposted for Rathmullen. It's an 11-km drive to Ramelton. When you reach the river turn right, following the bank, and Ardeen is on your right.

ARDEEN
Owner: Anne Campbell
Ramelton
Co Donegal, Ireland
Tel & fax: (074) 51243
Email: ardeenbandb@eircom.net
3rooms
£20–£25 per person B&B
Open Easter to Oct
Credit cards: MC, VS
B&B & self-catering
www.karenbrown.com/ireland/ardeen.html

Rathmullan House has a perfect setting amidst acres of lovingly tended gardens that slope down to a sandy beach, with views of the mountains across Lough Swilly. It's a rambling kind of house with three large sitting rooms (one decorated in an Indian Raj style) leading to a Bedouin-style dining pavilion where vast meters of fabric have been gathered across the ceiling to give a tentlike appearance. A three- or four-course dinner is offered with enough selections in each course to satisfy the most discerning diner. Less sumptuous fare is offered in the convivial cellar bistro. Accommodation comes in three categories: view, large room with no view, and standard. Lough views are the prerogative of all the deluxe accommodation. The newer wing offers spacious rooms, terraces or balconies, and large state-of-the-art bathrooms. Main house deluxe guestrooms are spacious bay-windowed view rooms with more dated bathrooms. Treat yourself to a massage, a walk on the beach, a game of tennis, or a swim in the pool. A 10% service charge is added to your bill. Adjacent to the hotel is a complex of holiday cottages. Rathmullan is a particularly attractive village and there are some spectacular drives round the Fanad Peninsula. Inland lie Glenveagh National Park and the Glebe Art Gallery. *Directions*: From Donegal town take the N15 to Ballybofey, then the N56 to the outskirts of Letterkenny, through Ramelton, and follow the shores of Lough Swilly through Rathmullan. The house is on your right as you leave the village.

RATHMULLAN HOUSE
Owners: Robin & Bob Wheeler
Rathmullan, Letterkenny
Co Donegal, Ireland
Tel: (074) 58188, Fax: (074) 58200
Email: rathhse@iol.ie
24 rooms
Double: £130–£150, Dinner: £30
Open Mar to Nov
Credit cards: all major
Country house hotel
www.karenbrown.com/ireland/rathmullan.html

"There is nothing which has yet been contrived by man by which so much happiness is produced as by a good inn"—Hunters Hotel has adopted Samuel Johnson's words as a creed and they certainly describe it. Dating back to the 1720s, the hotel retains its old-world charm with creaking wooden floorboards, polished tile floors, old prints, beams, ancient sofas covered in old-fashioned chintz, and antique furniture. The Gelletlie family has owned the inn since 1820, and now Tom and Richard Gelletlie (the fifth generation) ably assist their mother, Maureen. There is a delightful feeling of another age which endures in the tradition of vast, Sunday roast lunches (1 pm prompt: book ahead) and afternoon teas of oven-fresh scones and strawberry jam—a particularly delightful feast when enjoyed in the garden on a warm summer's afternoon. You can sleep in bedrooms that kings have slept in—the king of Sweden has paid several visits. I loved my room 12a with its pretty double iron-and-brass bedstead and light, airy decor. Be sure to request a room with a view of the flower-filled gardens stretching beside the hotel down to the River Vartry. Some of the country's most interesting gardens and houses are a short drive away: Powerscourt with its grand gardens, Mount Usher with its informal gardens, and Avondale House, the home of Charles Stewart Parnell with its wooded parklands. *Directions*: Take the N11 from Dublin to Rathnew and turn left in the village for the 1-km drive to Hunters Hotel.

HUNTERS HOTEL
Owners: The Gelletlie family
Rathnew
Co Wicklow, Ireland
Tel: (0404) 40106, Fax: (0404) 40338
Email: reception@hunters.ie
16 rooms
Double: £110–£130, Dinner: £27.50
Closed Christmas
Credit cards: all major
Inn
www.karenbrown.com/ireland/hunters.html

Tinakilly House maintains the purpose for which it was designed—gracious living. The house was built in the 1870s by Captain Robert Halpin, the commander of the ship *Great Eastern*, which laid the first telegraph cable connecting Europe to America. Tinakilly House's ornate staircase is reputed to be a copy of the one on this ship. Whether or not this is true is a matter of conjecture, but the Captain certainly spared no expense when he built this classical house with its fine, pitch-pine doors and shutters and ornate plasterwork ceilings. Bee and William Power bought the house as a family home before deciding to open it as a luxurious country house hotel. They have done a splendid job, extending the home and adding rooms that fit in perfectly, furnishing the house with appropriate Victorian furniture, and adding a welcoming charm to the place. Five of the bedrooms have four-poster beds, while all twenty-five junior suites and the two admiral's suites have breathtaking sea views. Rooms tucked into the original attics are snug and country-cozy and proportionately less expensive. Dining is a delight—there is a table d'hote menu, which changes daily. Tinakilly is an ideal countryside base for exploring Dublin, Glendalough, and the Wicklow Mountains. *Directions:* From Dublin take the N11 (Wexford road) to Rathnew village. Turn left, towards Wicklow, and the entrance to the hotel is on your left as you leave the village.

TINAKILLY HOUSE
Owners: Josephine & Raymond Power
Rathnew
Co Wicklow, Ireland
Tel: (0404) 69274, Fax: (0404) 67806
Email: reservations@tinakilly.ie
52 rooms
Double: £148–£280
Dinner: from £39
Open all year
Credit cards: all major
Country house hotel
www.karenbrown.com/ireland/tinakillyhouse.html

Coopershill, built in 1774, has always been home to the O'Hara family and offers the best of both worlds—the luxury of a country house hotel and the warmth of a home. Continuing a tradition begun by Joan O'Hara, Lindy and Brian welcome guests to their lovely home through the massive front door into the stove-warmed hall whose flagged floor is topped by an Oriental rug, and where rain gear hangs at the ready. Beyond lies a parade of lovely rooms tastefully decorated and beautifully furnished with grand, antique furniture, much of which is as old as the house itself. All but three of the bedrooms have the original four-poster or half-tester beds, but, of course, with modern mattresses. All the bedrooms are large and have private bathrooms, though one is across the hall. Ancestors' portraits gaze down upon you in the dining room, set with tables to accommodate individual parties. After an excellent dinner, guests chat round the fire over coffee. Secluded by 500 acres of farm and woodland, there are many delightful walks, and since no shooting is allowed, wildlife is abundant. There's a tennis court, and boating and trout and coarse fishing are available on the River Arrow, which flows through the property. There is enough sightseeing beyond the estate to justify spending a whole week here. *Directions:* From Dublin take the N4 to Drumfin (18 km south of Sligo). Turn right towards Riverstown and Coopershill is on your left 1 km before the village.

COOPERSHILL
Owners: Lindy & Brian O'Hara
Riverstown
Co Sligo, Ireland
Tel: (071) 65108, Fax: (071) 65466
Email: ohara@coopershill.com
8 rooms, 7 en suite
£59–£63 per person B&B, Dinner: £30–£32
Open Apr to Oct
Credit cards: all major
Country house
www.karenbrown.com/ireland/coopershill.html

Margaret and Dick Johnson have been used to a house full of children, for between them they have nine. Dick has retired as the local vet and now that their family is grown, Margaret has redecorated bedrooms, added shower rooms, and opened their delightful old home to guests. Creaking polished pine floors are topped with rugs, rooms are furnished with antiques, and guests are welcomed as friends. Guests have a comfortable sitting room where they can chat round the fire, watch TV, and relax after dinner. You can opt to dine either with your fellow guests or more privately at separate tables. Dinner might be a mackerel soufflé, beef bourguignon with salad and new potatoes, and, for dessert, cheese or profiteroles with raspberry sauce. All bedrooms except the small single (bathroom down the hall) have snug en-suite shower rooms. The front bedrooms, a twin and a double, offer the most spacious quarters with lots of room for suitcases and a writing table and chair. Ballyteigue House is about an hour-and-a-half drive from Shannon airport. Margaret finds that guests often use this countryside base for taking day trips to Cashel and Killarney, an hour and a half away. Closer at hand lie Adare (the prettiest village in Ireland) and Bunratty with its interesting folk park. *Directions:* Traveling south on the N20, go through Croom, through a crossroads 7 miles on called O'Rourke's Cross, and take the next right, signposted for Ballyteigue House. Pass Rockhill church and Ballyteigue House is on your right after 500 meters.

BALLYTEIGUE HOUSE
Owners: Margaret & Dick Johnson
Rockhill, Bruree
Co Limerick, Ireland
Tel & fax: (063) 90575
Email: ballyteigue@eircom.net
5 rooms, 4 en suite
£26 per person B&B, Dinner: £20
Closed Christmas & New Year
Credit cards: MC, VS
Farmhouse B&B
www.karenbrown.com/ireland/ballyteigue.html

In summer, the driveway of Rosturk Woods is lined with wild red fuchsias that lead you to the low white house hugging a vast expanse of firm, sandy beach on the shores of Clew Bay. Home to Louisa and Alan Stoney and their young family (Alan grew up in the imposing castle next door, while Louisa's parents live up the road), the house has the feel of an old cottage, though it is only a few years old. Bedrooms have stripped-pine doors and several have pine-paneled, sloping ceilings. There's a lot of old pine furniture, antique pieces, and attractive prints and fabrics. The house cleverly divides so that a wing of two or three large bedrooms, a living room, and a kitchen can be closed off and used as self-catering accommodation (with the option of dinner being served). Dinner is available with 24 hours advance notice. A delightful self-catering cottage is equipped for handicapped guests. Louisa can sometimes direct you to nearby places where traditional Irish music is played. You can play tennis on the Stoneys' court, or hire a boat for a full- or half-day trip on Clew Bay. In contrast to the lush green fields and long sandy beaches that hug Clew Bay, a short drive brings you to the wilder, more rugged scenery of Achill Island. To the south lie Newport and Westport. *Directions:* From Westport take the N59 through Newport towards Achill Island. Before you arrive in Mulrany, cross the Owengarve river and after 500 meters turn left into the woodland to Rosturk Woods.

ROSTURK WOODS
Owners: Louisa & Alan Stoney
Rosturk, Mulrany
Co Mayo, Ireland
Tel & fax: (098) 36264
Email: stoney@iol.ie
3 rooms, 1 cottage
£30–£35 per person B&B
Dinner: £25
Open Feb to Nov, Credit cards: none
B&B & self-catering,
www.karenbrown.com/ireland/rosturk.html

Ballymaloe House is a rambling, 17th-century manor house built onto an old Norman keep surrounded by lawns, a small golf course kept cropped by grazing sheep, and 400 acres of farmland. Run by members of the extended Allen family, Ballymaloe has established a reputation for outstanding hospitality and superb food, yet everything is decidedly simple and homey. Guests gather before dinner in the lounge to make their selections from the set menu, which offers four or five choices for each course. The bedrooms in the main house come in all shapes and sizes, from large and airy to cozy and paneled. Several ground-floor rooms have been designed to take wheelchairs. Surrounding a courtyard, the smaller stable bedrooms offer country-cottage charm, sprigged-flowered wallpaper, and beamed ceilings for those on the upper floor. Most unusual accommodations are in the doll-sized gatekeeper's cottage has a bathroom on the ground floor and a ladder to the twin-bedded room above. Perhaps the most famous of the Allen clan is Darina Allen who came here to learn cooking, married son Tim, then founded Ballymaloe Cookery School in the courtyard of her nearby home. Her brother Rory O'Connell is head chef at Ballymaloe. *Directions:* Ballymaloe is signposted from the N25 (Cork to Waterford road). Ballymaloe is 3 km beyond Cloyne on the Ballycotton Road.

BALLYMALOE HOUSE
Owners: The Allen family
Manager: Hazel Allen
Shanagarry
Midleton
Co Cork, Ireland
Tel: (021) 4652531, Fax: (021) 4652021
32 rooms
Double: £150–£190, Dinner: £37.50
Open all year
Credit cards: all major
Country house hotel

The K Club began life as The Kildare Hotel & Country Club but as everyone shortened the name, they changed it. The K Club is immensely proud that it will be the venue for the prestigious Ryder Cup golf tournament in 2005. Stay here and you get preference for tee times on the championship golf course designed by Arnold Palmer. If you do intend to play, enquire about the golf packages that include accommodation and green fees. Even if you are not a golfer, this is the most sumptuous of places to stay—the grandest of houses with a parade of luxurious, beautiful rooms. The artwork is exquisite, with an entire room devoted to Jack Yeats' paintings; Orpen's beautiful *Mrs. St. George* presiding in the lobby sitting room; and, taking pride of place in the magnificent dining room, *The Byerly Turk*, a massive 17th-century portrait of one of the three stallions that sired every thoroughbred in the world. Fine cooking is an essential ingredient here and the menu includes Irish classics such as roast Wicklow lamb as well as more Nirvana-like fare. Pamper yourself in the state-of-the-art health spa, splash in the pool, or just stroll through the acres of gardens and revel in the sheer luxury of the place. Exquisite self-catering apartments are available. It is easy to understand why this lovely hotel, just an hour's drive from Dublin, though astonishingly expensive, represents an ideal of luxury for so many people. *Directions*: Take the N7 (Kildare road) out of Dublin to Kill where you turn right for the 5-km drive to The K Club, on your left just before the village of Straffan.

THE K CLUB   *New*
Manager: Ray Carroll
Straffan
Co Kildare, Ireland
Tel: (01) 6017200, Fax: (01) 6017299
69 rooms
Double: £320–£395, Suite: £450–£2,500
Dinner: £60
Open all year
Credit cards: all major
Luxury resort & self-catering

Built in 1867 by John Langham's great-great-grandfather, Tempo Manor is as interesting inside as it is out. Ancient armaments and hunting trophies line the paneled walls of the entrance halls, while overhead hang John's great-grandfather's World War I airplane's wooden propeller. Much of the furniture was made for the house, and a redoubtable collection of ancestors' portraits occupies a great deal of wall space. This is home to Sarah and John Langham, their young children Tyrone and Phoebe, and five very friendly dogs. John and Sarah are young and enthusiastic, and have put a great deal of work into the restoration of this interesting home. A below-stairs bedroom has a lovely four-poster bed and en-suite bathroom with courtyard view. Upstairs, two bedrooms have four-poster beds while the other one has twin beds. Bathrooms are just down the hall and thick toweling robes are provided. Lovely gardens sweep down to the lake and acres of woodlands provide the opportunity for peaceful walks. Breakfast is the only meal served so guests are directed to local pubs and restaurants for dinner. Within an hour's drive are three National Trust houses: Florence Court, Castle Coole, and Crom Castle. *Directions:* From Belfast take the M1 motorway west and at Fivemiletown turn right for Tempo. In Tempo turn left at the Spar supermarket (signposted Brookeborough). Tempo Manor is the first gate on the left, with a "Private Road" sign.

TEMPO MANOR   New
Owners: Sarah & John Langham
Tempo
Co Fermanagh BT94 3PA, Northern Ireland
Tel: (028895) 41953, Fax: (028895) 41202
Email: info@tempomanor.com
4 rooms, 1 en suite
£65 per person B&B
Open Apr to Oct
Credit cards: MC, VS
Country house
www.karenbrown.com/ireland/tempo.html

Tir Na Fiúise offers you a perfect base for experiencing rural Ireland and exploring the mid-west and Shannon region. Inez and Niall Heenan have converted the barns just down the lane from their farmhouse to self-catering accommodation available by the week. The cottages, restored in the vernacular style using environmentally friendly products, are decorated with a simple, fresh country look. The kitchen/living areas feature solid-fuel stoves and modern appliances, such as dishwashers and microwaves, designed to make your stay as trouble-free as possible. The Granary is a one-bedroomed cottage just perfect for a couple getting away from it all to a cozy little nook, while The Stables has two bedrooms, making it more suitable for a family or larger group. The area has some excellent restaurants and local pubs, which also serve great food if you don't want to cook. Inez and Niall encourage guests to explore their organic farm and adjacent bog land. You can cycle along the quiet lanes, try your hand at fishing in the nearby lough, visit the Sunday market, and join in village activities. If you must rush off to tourist spots, Bunratty Folk Park is an hour-and-a-half's drive away (as is Shannon airport). Closer at hand is the ancient monastic settlement of Clonmacnois and Birr Castle with its gardens and science park. *Directions*: Nenagh is on the N7, Limerick to Dublin road. Leave the main road in Nenagh and travel through Borrisokane and Ballinderry to Terryglass. The lane that leads to Tir Na Fiúise (1 km on your left) is opposite the bridge in the village.

TIR NA FIÚISE
Owners: Inez & Niall Heenan
Terryglass, Nenagh
Co Tipperary, Ireland
Tel & fax: (067) 22041
E-mail: nheenan@eircom.net
2 cottages
Granary: £130–£185 per week
Stables: £190–£310 per week
Open all year, Credit cards: MC, VS
Self-catering
www.karenbrown.com/ireland/tirnafuise.html

As you enter the Mount Juliet estate, you may catch glimpses of pheasants feeding along the driveway or see riders enjoying a trek through the 1,500-acre walled estate. A narrow, mellow-stone bridge takes you across the River Nore to the heart of Ireland's premier luxury resort. Guests need not travel beyond the estate's boundaries, for here you can enjoy swimming, relaxing at the spa and leisure centre, tennis, croquet, archery, clay-pigeon shooting, fishing for salmon and trout along the Nore, and riding along kilometers of idyllic park and woodland trails. Golfers can sharpen up their shots on the 18-hole putting course before taking on the magnificent Jack-Nicklaus-designed championship golf course. With lawns tumbling down to the river and overlooking fenced pastures and vast woodlands, Mount Juliet was built as a grand home for the Earls of Carrick in the 1760s. Its numerous rooms have received a complete and elegant revamping to provide quiet lounges, distinguished dining, clubby bars, a parade of deluxe bedrooms, and two superlative suites. More casual accommodation and dining is available in Hunters Yard, a stableyard-like complex beside the golf clubhouse. The new Kendals Restaurant in Hunters Yard is establishing a reputation for excellent Irish contemporary cuisine. Self-catering apartments are available. *Directions:* Thomastown is on the Kilkenny to Waterford road. The 5-km drive to the hotel is signposted from the center of town.

MOUNT JULIET
Manager: Richard Hudson
Thomastown
Co Kilkenny, Ireland
Tel: (056) 73000, Fax: (056) 73019
59 rooms
Double: £140–£300*, Suite: £240–£400*
*Breakfast not included: £8.50–£12.50
Dinner: from £25
Open all year
Credit cards: all major
Luxury resort & self-catering

Only in Ireland can you have a village that does not exist. Inch House is the only building in Inch while the nearest village, Bouladuff, is known and signposted only as "The Ragg," in spite of being marked as Bouladuff on maps—hence we list Inch House under Thurles! Follow the directions and you'll reach this stately Georgian home surrounded by miles of farmland. The house was built in 1720 by the Catholic Ryan family who mysteriously flourished in an area where the British routinely rid themselves of troublesome papists. Nora and John Egan came here to farm with their eight children (most are now grown, though chances are you'll meet one or two around the place), rescuing the house from near ruin. The restoration is now complete, resulting in just the kind of place to relax and make yourself at home, for Inch House is homey and convivial in spite of having ballroom-sized drawing and dining rooms resplendent with 15-foot-high ceilings. Michael Doyle is in charge of the kitchen and his set dinner menu (with plenty of choices for each course) focuses on fine local produce. A grand sweep of staircase leads up to the bedrooms where room 21 has a stupendous half-tester bed and room 27 offers a four-poster. Cashel with its famous rock is a half-hour drive away. An hour's drive brings you to Cahir Castle and the scenic drive across The Vee. *Directions:* From the N8 (Dublin to Cork road) take the turnoff to Thurles. Go to the town square and take the Nenagh road for 6 km past "The Ragg" and the driveway to the house is on your left.

INCH HOUSE   **New**
Owners: Nora & John Egan
Inch, Thurles
Co Tipperary, Ireland
Tel: (0504) 51348, Fax: (0504) 51754
Email: inchhse@iol.ie
5 rooms
£35 per person B&B, Dinner: £27
Closed Christmas
Credit cards: MC, VS
Country house
www.karenbrown.com/ireland/inch.html

Waterford Crystal is the reason that tourists come to Waterford and a grand place to stay is with Barbara, Leslie, and Charlie Brown at their delightful guesthouse on a peaceful side street just a few minutes' walk from the heart of this busy city. Leslie has a quiet, welcoming way also found in Charlie, his faithful golden Labrador. Charlie must be the most photographed dog in Ireland—Leslie just has to say, "photograph" and Charlie poses on cue. He'll be happy to take you for a walk around town and has been known, when he senses that he has won a guest's heart, to curl up on the sofa with him in the TV room. Upstairs are six bedrooms. The most spacious quarters are at the top of the house—with a large pine-paneled room with extra beds for children. The suite has a separate sitting room but is rather dark as the only window is in the sitting room. Leslie often directs guests in the evening to an excellent show of Irish dancing, music, and singing held in the lovely old City Hall (Thursdays, Saturdays, and Sundays May to October). Stay for several days: venture along the pretty coastal road to Dungarven and take the little ferry across Waterford harbor to explore the Hook Peninsula. *Directions*: Arriving in Waterford from the north, cross the river, follow the road along the quay, pass the Tower Hotel on your left, and at the second set of traffic lights turn left into South Parade. Brown's is on your right after 700 meters.

BROWN'S
Owners: Barbara & Leslie Brown
29 South Parade
Waterford
Co Waterford, Ireland
Tel: (051) 870594, Fax: (051) 871923
Email: info@brownstownhouse.com
6 rooms
£30–£35 per person B&B
Closed Christmas
Credit cards: MC, VS
Guesthouse
www.karenbrown.com/ireland/browns.html

Foxmount Farm is the sort of house that feels like home from the moment you walk in the front door. Margaret has been taking guests for many years now and she still looks for new ways to make the house more comfortable. Such is the popularity of the place that people who came as children now return with their children. Whenever David Kent is not occupied with farm matters, he loves to talk to visitors and discuss the farm and what to do and see in the area—the Waterford crystal factory is a big draw. Margaret is one of those people who shows her appreciation of her guests by feeding them lavishly. She delights in the preparation of dishes using meat from the farm and homegrown fruits (strawberries, raspberries, gooseberries, apples, and rhubarb, to name but a few) and vegetables—her specialty is her homemade ice cream. Her bountiful breakfasts have won her national awards. Guests are served after-dinner coffee in the lounge and often linger for discussions around the fireside. Upstairs, the comfortable bedrooms are delightfully decorated and have sparkling, modern bathrooms. Three have extra beds, making them ideal for family accommodation. *Directions:* To find the house, take the road from Waterford toward Dunmore East. Three km after passing the regional hospital, take the left fork toward Passage East. Foxmount Farm is signposted on the right 500 meters from the Maxol garage.

FOXMOUNT FARM
Owners: Margaret & David Kent
Passage East Road
Waterford
Co Waterford, Ireland
Tel: (051) 874308, Fax: (051) 854906
Email: foxmount@iol.ie
6 rooms, 4 en suite
£35 per person B&B, Dinner: £20
Open Mar to Oct
Credit cards: none
Farmhouse B&B
www.karenbrown.com/ireland/foxmountfarm.html

The owner's plans for Clonard House, begun in 1783, showed a grand three-story structure, but skirmishes with the British continually interrupted construction and depleted funds so he got no farther than the second floor, leaving the grand central staircase to curve into the ceiling. The massive front door opens to a smiling welcome from Kathleen Hayes who takes a great interest in her guests and pride in her home. I particularly admired her traditional, high-ceilinged sitting room with its peach-colored walls and traditional chairs covered in soft colors that coordinate with the draperies and carpet. Crisp white tablecloths top the little tables in the attractive breakfast room. Guests are often directed for dinner to fish restaurants in the nearby fishing villages. The bedrooms are all appealingly decorated and have TVs, en-suite showers, and hairdryers. The five bedrooms that face the front of the house, while smaller in size, offer lovely views across farmland to the distant sea. Being just a short drive from Rosslare, Clonard House is ideal for your first or last nights in Ireland if you are arriving by ferry. Sightseeing attractions nearby include the Irish National Heritage Park, Wexford, and Johnstown Castle garden and agricultural museum. *Directions:* From Rosslare travel 13 km towards Wexford, make a left at the first roundabout (N25), left at the second roundabout on to the R733, and immediately left to Clonard House.

CLONARD HOUSE
Owners: Kathleen & John Hayes
Clonard Great
Wexford
Co Wexford, Ireland
Tel & fax: (053) 43141
Email: clonardhouse@indigo.ie
9 rooms
£22.50–£25 per person B&B
Open Mar to mid-Nov
Credit cards: MC, VS
Farmhouse B&B
www.karenbrown.com/ireland/clonard.html

Youghal (pronounced "you all" with an American southern drawl), a workaday fishing port, is beginning to flaunt its historic past: drab, gray buildings are being restored, empty shopfronts are coming to life, and, standing amongst them, Aherne's old-world pub exterior is decked out in shiny new paint. Aherne's pub, in the Fitzgibbon family since 1923, includes a seafood restaurant and bedrooms. There's an old-world, traditional atmosphere in the bars where you can enjoy a pint with the locals and an array of tempting bar food. The restaurant specializes in locally caught seafood and the menu changes daily, depending on what is fresh and available. In the guests' sitting room, a cozy fire is flanked by comfortable sofas and a coffee table stacked with books on all things Irish. Three ground-floor bedrooms offer easy access, with one specially equipped for wheelchairs. I particularly enjoyed the upstairs rooms, which have little balconies facing the courtyard. If you want privacy, request one of the suites in the adjacent townhouse. All guestrooms have attractive decor, antique furniture, and large firm beds, each accompanied by an immaculate bathroom. For a stay of longer than a couple of nights the Fitzgibbons have a luxurious two-bedroom penthouse apartment with breathtaking views of the harbor. *Directions:* Youghal is between Waterford and Cork on the N25. Aherne's is on the main street in town.

AHERNE'S
Owners: Gaye, Kate, John, & David Fitzgibbon
163 North Main Street
Youghal
Co Cork, Ireland
Tel: (024) 92424, Fax: (024) 93633
Email: ahernes@eircom.net
12 rooms, 1 apartment
Double: £120–£160, Dinner: £30
Apartment: £600 per week
Closed Christmas, Credit cards: all major
Restaurant with rooms & self-catering
www.karenbrown.com/ireland/ahernes.html

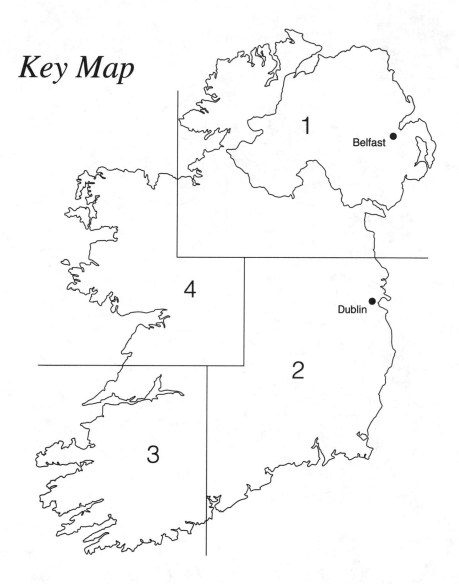

Key Map

1

Belfast

Dublin

4

2

3

Map 1

Map 2

243

Map 3

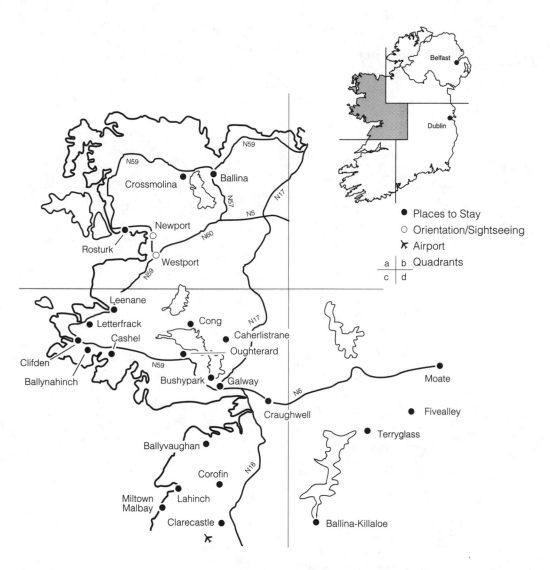

Map 4

Ireland's Counties

ATLANTIC
OCEAN

Donegal

Londonderry

Antrim

Tyrone

Down

Fermanagh

Armagh

Sligo

Monaghan

Mayo

Leitrim

Cavan

Louth

Roscommon

Longford

Meath

Westmeath

Galway

Dublin

Offaly

Kildare

Clare

Laois

Wicklow

IRISH SEA

Carlow

Tipperary

Kilkenny

Limerick

Wexford

Kerry

Waterford

Cork

Places to Stay by County

County Antrim
Belfast, Ash-Rowan
    The Crescent Townhouse
    McCausland Hotel
Broughshane, Dunaird House
Bushmills, The Bushmills Inn

County Carlow
Bagenalstown, Kilgraney House
Borris, Lorum Old Rectory

County Cavan
Cloverhill, Rockwood House

County Clare
Ballina Killaloe, Waterman's Lodge
Ballyvaughan, Drumcreehy House
    Gregans Castle
Clarecastle, Carnelly House
Corofin, Fergus View
Lahinch, Moy House
Miltown Malbay, Berry Lodge
Newmarket-on-Fergus, Dromoland Castle
    Thomond House

County Cork
Ballinacurra, Rathcoursey House
Ballydehob, Lynwood
Ballylickey, Sea View House Hotel
Bantry, Bantry House

Bantry, Dunauley
Butlerstown, Butlerstown House
Castlelyons, Ballyvolane House
Castlemartyr, Old Parochial House
Cork, Hayfield Manor
    Seven North Mall
Doneraile, Creagh House
Farran, Farran House
Kanturk, Glenlohane
Killeagh, Ballymakeigh House
Kinsale, Desmond House
    Old Bank House
    The Old Presbytery
    Perryville House
Mallow, Longueville House
Shanagarry, Ballymaloe House
Youghal, Aherne's

County Donegal
Donegal, St. Ernan's House Hotel
Dunkineely, Killaghtee House
Fahan, St. John's Country House
Lough Eske, Ardnamona House
Portsalon, Croaghross
Ramelton, Ardeen
Rathmullan, Rathmullan House

County Down
Dromore, Sylvan Hill House

County Down (cont.)
Portaferry, The Narrows

County Dublin
Dublin, Adams Trinity Hotel
      Belcamp Hutchinson
      Butlers Town House
      Cedar Lodge
      The Clarence
      Harrington Hall
      Hibernian Hotel
      Kilronan House
      The Merrion
      Mespil Hotel
      The Morgan
      Number 31
      Park Lodge
      Raglan Lodge
      The Shelbourne
      Simmonstown House
      Waterloo House

County Fermanagh
Tempo, Tempo Manor

County Galway
Ballynahinch, Ballynahinch Castle
Bushypark, Killeen House
Caherlistrane, Lisdonagh House
Cashel, Cashel House
Clifden, Dolphin Beach House
      Mal Dua

Clifden, The Quay House
      Rock Glen Hotel
Craughwell, St Clerrans
Galway, Norman Villa
Leenane, Delphi Lodge
Letterfrack, Rosleague Manor
Oughterard, Currarevagh House

County Kerry
Beaufort, Beaufort House
Caherdaniel, Iskeroon
Caragh Lake, Caragh Lodge
Dingle, Cleevaun
      Doyle's
      Greenmount House
      Heaton's
Kenmare, The Lodge
      The Park Hotel Kenmare
      Sallyport House
      Sea Shore Farm Guesthouse
      Shelburne Lodge
Killarney, Earls Court
Listowel, Allo's Bar & Bistro

County Kildare
Straffan, The K Club

County Kilkenny
Freshford, Kilrush House
Inistoge, Berryhill
Kilkenny, Dunromin
      Zuni

County Kilkenny (cont.)
Maddoxtown, Blanchville House
Thomastown, Mount Juliet

County Laois
Abbeyleix, Preston House

County Leitrim
Carrick-on-Shannon, Glencarne House
       Hollywell

County Limerick
Adare, Adare Manor
       Dunraven Arms
       Glenelg House
Ballingarry, The Mustard Seed at Echo
       Lodge
Glin, Glin Castle
Kilmallock, Flemingstown House
Rockhill, Ballyteigue House

County Londonderry
Coleraine, Greenhill House

County Mayo
Ballina, Ashley House
Cong, Ashford Castle
Crossmolina Enniscoe House
Rosturk, Rosturk Woods

County Meath
Kells, Boltown House

County Monaghan
Clones, Hilton Park

County Offaly
Fivealley, Parkmore Farmhouse

County Sligo
Ballymote, Temple House
Collooney, Markree Castle
Riverstown, Coopershill

County Tipperary
Bansha, Bansha House
Cashel, Legends Townhouse
Dualla, Dualla House
Nenagh, Ashley Park House
Newcastle, Kilmaneen Farmhouse
Terryglass, Tir na Fiúise
Thurles, Inch House

County Tyrone
Dungannon, Grange Lodge

County Waterford
Annestown, Annestown House
Cappoquin, Richmond House
Four-Mile Water, Glasha
Glencairn, Buggy's Glencairn Inn
Millstreet, Castle Farm
Nire Valley, Hanora's Cottage Guesthouse
Waterford, Brown's
       Foxmount Farm

County Westmeath
Moate, Temple Country House & Spa
Mullingar, Crookedwood House
        Lough Owel Lodge
        Mornington House

County Wexford
Arthurstown, Dunbrody House
Ballymurn, Ballinkeele House
Campile, Kilmokea
Ferns, The Old Deanery
Gorey, Marlfield House
Killinierin, Woodlands House
New Ross, Creacon Lodge Hotel
Wexford, Clonard House

County Wicklow
Annamoe, Carmel's Bed & Breakfast
Ashford, Ballyknocken House
Dunlavin, Rathsallagh House
Rathnew, Hunters Hotel
        Tinakilly House

Self-Catering Accommodation

Places in this guide that offer self-catering accommodation.

Bagenalstown, Kilgraney House
Ballinacurra, Rathcoursey House
Ballylickey, Sea View House Hotel
Bansha, Bansha House
Bantry, Dunauley
Beaufort, Beaufort House
Caherlistrane, Lisdonagh House
Campile, Kilmokea
Castlelyons, Ballyvolane House
Clifden, The Quay House
Clifden, Rock Glen Hotel
Corofin, Fergus View
Crossmolina, Enniscoe House
Farran, Farran House
Ferns, The Old Deanery
Kanturk, Glenlohane
Kinsale, The Old Presbytery
Leenane, Delphi Lodge
Maddoxtown, Blanchville House
Newcastle, Kilmaneen Farmhouse
Portsalon, Croaghross
Ramelton, Ardeen
Rosturk, Rosturk Woods
Straffan, The K Club
Terryglass, Tir na Fiúise

Thomastown, Mount Juliet
Youghal, Aherne's

Places to Stay with Handicap Facilities

We list all the places to stay that have ground-floor rooms, or rooms specially equipped for the handicapped. Please discuss your requirements with them to determine if they have accommodation that is suitable for you.

Adare, Dunraven Arms
Annestown, Annestown House
Arthurstown, Dunbrody House
Ballina Killaloe, Waterman's Lodge
Ballinacurra, Rathcoursey House
Ballylickey, Sea View House Hotel
Ballingarry, The Mustard Seed at Echo Lodge
Ballyvaughan, Gregans Castle
Bushmills, Bushmills Inn
Campile, Kilmokea
Caragh Lake, Caragh Lodge
Cashel, Cashel House
Castlelyons, Ballyvolane House
Clifden, The Quay House
Clifden, Rock Glen Hotel
Cork, Seven North Mall
Dingle, Greenmount House
Dublin, Cedar Lodge
Dublin, Harrington Hall
Dublin, The Merrion
Dublin, Mespil Hotel
Dublin, Raglan Lodge
Ferns, The Old Deanery
Gorey, Marlfield House

Kenmare, The Lodge
Kenmare, The Park Hotel Kenmare
Letterfrack, Rosleague Manor
Maddoxtown, Blanchville House
Newmarket-on-Fergus, Thomond House
Portaferry, The Narrows
Portsalon, Croaghross
Rathnew, Hunters Hotel
Rathmullan, Rathmullan House
Rosturk, Rosturk Woods
Shanagarry, Ballymaloe House
Thomastown, Mount Juliet

Members of Hidden Ireland 2001

Listed alphabetically by house

Ardnamona House, Lough Eske
Ballinkeele House, Ballymurn
Ballyvolane House, Castlelyons
Bantry House, Bantry
Blanchville House, Maddoxtown
Boltown House, Kells
Carnelly House, Clarecastle
Creagh House, Doneraile
Delphi Lodge, Leenane
Enniscoe House, Crossmolina
Farran House, Farran
Glenlohane, Kanturk
Hilton Park, Clones
Kilmokea, Campile
Kilgraney House, Bagenalstown
Lorum Old Rectory, Borris
Mornington House, Mullingar
Number 31, Dublin
The Quay House, Clifden
Simmonstown House, Dublin
Temple House, Ballymote

Members of Ireland's Blue Book 2001

Listed alphabetically by house

Aherne's, Youghal
Bushmills Inn, Bushmills
Ballymaloe House, Shanagarry
Caragh Lodge, Caragh Lake
Cashel House, Cashel
Coopershill, Riverstown
Crookedwood House, Crookedwood, Mullingar
Currarevagh House, Oughterard
Dunbrody House, Arthurstown
Enniscoe House, Crossmolina
Glin Castle, Glin
Gregans Castle, Ballyvaughan
Hunters Hotel, Rathnew
The K Club, Straffan
Lisdonagh House, Caherlistrane
Longueville House, Mallow
Marlfield House, Gorey
Moy House, Lahinch,
Mustard Seed at Echo Lodge, Ballingarry
Park Hotel, Kenmare
Rathmullan House, Rathmullan
Rosleague Manor, Letterfrack
St. Clerans, Craughwell
St. Ernan's House Hotel, Donegal
St. John's Country House, Fahan
Tinakilly House, Rathnew

Index

E

Earls Court, Killarney, 194
Electricity (Introduction), 14
Enniscoe House, Crossmolina, 145, 251, 253, 254
Enniscorthy, 35
Enniskerry, 33
Enniskillen, 77
Eyeries, 48

F

Fahan
    St. John's Country House, 174, 254
Farran
    Farran House, 251, 253
Fergus View, Corofin, 143, 251
Ferns
    The Old Deanery, 176, 251
Fivealley
    Parkmore Farmhouse, 177
Flemingstown House, Kilmallock, 197
Florence Court, 77
Four-Mile Water
    Glasha, 178
Foxmount Farm, Waterford, 238
Foyle Bridge, 82
Freshford, 39
    Kilrush House, 179
Fungi, 56

G

Gallarus Oratory, 58
Galway, 65
    Norman Villa, 180
Gap of Dunloe, Killarney, 53
Garinish, 48

Garinish Island, 47
Giant's Causeway, 83
    Giant's Causeway Centre, 83
Glasha, Four-Mile Water, 178
Glebe House and Gallery, 81
Glenariff Forest Park, 85
Glenarm, 85
    Glenarm Forest, 85
Glencairn
    Buggy's Glencairn Inn, 181
Glencarne House, Carrick-on-Shannon, 125
Glencolumbkille, 79
    Glencolumbkille Museum, 79
Glencree, 33
Glendalough, 34
Glenelg House, Adare, 91
Glengarriff, 47
Glenlohane, Kanturk, 185, 251, 253
Glenmacnass Waterfall, 34
Glens of Antrim, 85
Glenveagh National Park, 80
    Glenveagh Castle, 80
    Visitors' Centre, 80
Glin
    Glin Castle, 182, 254
Gorey
    Marlfield House, 183, 252, 254
Gortahawk, 81
Gougane Barra Lake, 46
Grange Lodge, Dungannon, 171
Great Blasket Island, 57
Great Island
    Kilmokea, 122
Greenhill House, Coleraine, 138
Greenmount House, Dingle, 148

Index

Enhance Your Guides

Online

www.karenbrown.com

- Hotel News
- Color Photos
- New Discoveries
- Currency Converter
- Corrections & Edits
- Property of the Month
- Postcards from the Road
- Links to Hotels & B&Bs

SHARE YOUR COMMENTS AND DISCOVERIES WITH US

Please share comments on properties that you have visited. We welcome accolades, as well as criticisms.

Also, we'd love to hear about any hotel or bed & breakfast you discover. Tell us what you liked about the property and, if possible, please include a brochure or photographs. We regret we cannot return photos.

Owner _____ Hotel or B&B _____

Address _____ Town _____ Country _____

Comments on places that are in the book and/or recommendations for your own *New Discoveries*.

Your name _____ Street _____

Town _____ State _____ Zip _____ Country _____

Tel _____ E-mail _____ Date _____

Do we have your permission to electronically publish your comments on our website? Yes _____ No _____

If yes, would you like to remain anonymous? Yes ___No ___, or may we use your name? Yes___ No___

Please send report to: Karen Brown's Guides, Post Office Box 70, San Mateo, California 94401, USA
tel: (650) 342-9117, fax: (650) 342-9153, e-mail: karen@karenbrown.com, www.karenbrown.com

SHARE YOUR COMMENTS AND DISCOVERIES WITH US

Please share comments on properties that you have visited. We welcome accolades, as well as criticisms.

Also, we'd love to hear about any hotel or bed & breakfast you discover. Tell us what you liked about the property and, if possible, please include a brochure or photographs. We regret we cannot return photos.

Owner _____ Hotel or B&B _____

Address _____ Town _____ Country _____

Comments on places that are in the book and/or recommendations for your own *New Discoveries*.

Your name _____ Street _____

Town _____ State _____ Zip _____ Country _____

Tel _____ E-mail _____ Date _____

Do we have your permission to electronically publish your comments on our website? Yes _____ No _____

If yes, would you like to remain anonymous? Yes ___No ___, or may we use your name? Yes___ No___

Please send report to: Karen Brown's Guides, Post Office Box 70, San Mateo, California 94401, USA
tel: (650) 342-9117, fax: (650) 342-9153, e-mail: karen@karenbrown.com, www.karenbrown.com

Become a Karen Brown Preferred Reader

Name _____

Street _____

Town _____

State _____ Zip _____ Country _____

Tel _____ Fax _____

E-mail _____

We'd love to welcome you as a Karen Brown Preferred Reader. Send us your name and address and you will be entered in our monthly drawing to receive a free set of Karen Brown guides. As a preferred reader, you will receive special promotions and be the first to know when new editions of Karen Brown guides go to press.

Please send to: Karen Brown's Guides, Post Office Box 70, San Mateo, California 94401, USA
tel: (650) 342-9117, fax: (650) 342-9153, e-mail: karen@karenbrown.com, website: www: karenbrown.com

KB Travel Service

❖ **KB Travel Service** offers travel planning assistance using itineraries designed by *Karen Brown* and published in her guidebooks. We will customize any itinerary to fit your personal interests.

❖ We will plan your itinerary with you, help you decide how long to stay and what to do once you arrive, and work out the details.

❖ We will book your airline tickets and your rental car, arrange rail travel, reserve accommodations recommended in *Karen Brown's Guides,* and supply you with point-to-point information and consultation.

Contact us to start planning your travel!

800.782.2128 ext. 328 or e-mail: info@kbtravelservice.com

Service fees do apply

KB Travel Service
16 East Third Avenue
San Mateo, CA 94401 USA
www.kbtravelservice.com

Independently owned and operated by Town & Country Travel
CST 2001543-10

auto ⊕ europe.

Karen Brown's

Preferred Car Rental Service Provider

When Traveling to Europe
for

International Car Rental Services
Chauffeur & Transfer Services
Prestige & Sports Cars
Motor Home Rentals

800-223-5555

Be sure to identify yourself as a Karen Brown Traveler.
For special offers and discounts use your
Karen Brown ID number 99006187.

Need a dual voltage hair dryer, a wrinkle-free blazer, quick-dry clothes, a computer adapter plug? TRAVELSMITH has them all, along with an enticing array of everything a Karen Brown traveler needs.

Karen Brown recommends TRAVELSMITH as an excellent source for travel clothing and gear. We were pleased to find quality products needed for our own research travels in their catalog—items not always easy to find. For a free catalog call TRAVELSMITH at 800-950-1600.

When placing your order, be sure to identify yourself as a Karen Brown Traveler with the code TKBX1 and you will receive a 10% discount.* You can link to TRAVELSMITH through our website *www.karenbrown.com.*

*offer valid till December 2001

Seal Cove Inn

Located in the San Francisco Bay Area

Karen Brown Herbert (best known as author of the Karen Brown's guides) and her husband, Rick, have put 22 years of experience into reality and opened their own superb hideaway, Seal Cove Inn. Spectacularly set amongst wild flowers and bordered by towering cypress trees, Seal Cove Inn looks out to the distant ocean over acres of county park: an oasis where you can enjoy secluded beaches, explore tidepools, watch frolicking seals, and follow the tree-lined path that traces the windswept ocean bluffs. Country antiques, original watercolors, flower-laden cradles, rich fabrics, and the gentle ticking of grandfather clocks create the perfect ambiance for a foggy day in front of the crackling log fire. Each bedroom is its own haven with a cozy sitting area before a wood-burning fireplace and doors opening onto a private balcony or patio with views to the park and ocean. Moss Beach is a 35-minute drive south of San Francisco, 6 miles north of the picturesque town of Half Moon Bay, and a few minutes from Princeton harbor with its colorful fishing boats and restaurants. Seal Cove Inn makes a perfect base for whale-watching, salmon-fishing excursions, day trips to San Francisco, exploring the coast, or, best of all, just a romantic interlude by the sea, time to relax and be pampered. Karen and Rick look forward to the pleasure of welcoming you to their coastal hideaway.

Seal Cove Inn • 221 Cypress Avenue • Moss Beach • California • 94038 • USA
tel: (650) 728-4114, fax: (650) 728-4116, e-mail: sealcove@coastside.net, website: sealcoveinn.com

KAREN BROWN wrote her first travel guide in 1976. Her personalized travel series has grown to fourteen titles which Karen and her small staff work diligently to keep updated. Karen, her husband, Rick, and their children, Alexandra and Richard, live in Moss Beach, a small town on the coast south of San Francisco. They settled here in 1991 when they opened Seal Cove Inn. Karen is frequently traveling, but when she is home, in her role as innkeeper, enjoys welcoming Karen Brown readers.

CLARE BROWN, CTC, was a travel consultant for many years, specializing in planning itineraries to Europe using charming small hotels in the countryside. The focus of her job remains unchanged, but now her expertise is available to a larger audience—the readers of her daughter Karen's country inn guides. When Clare and her husband, Bill, are not traveling, they live either in Hillsborough, California, or at their home in Vail, Colorado, where family and friends frequently join them for skiing.

JUNE BROWN'S love of travel was inspired by the *National Geographic* magazines that she read as a girl in her dentist's office—so far she has visited over 40 countries. June hails from Sheffield, England and lived in Zambia and Canada before moving to northern California where she lives in San Mateo with her husband, Tony, their daughter Clare, their German Shepherd, and a Siamese cat.

BARBARA TAPP, the talented artist who produces all of the hotel sketches and delightful illustrations in this guide, was raised in Australia where she studied in Sydney at the School of Interior Design. Although Barbara continues with freelance projects, she devotes much of her time to illustrating the Karen Brown guides. Barbara lives in Kensington, California, with her husband, Richard, their two sons, Jonothan and Alexander, and daughter, Georgia.

JANN POLLARD, the artist responsible for the beautiful painting on the cover of this guide, has studied art since childhood, and is well-known for her outstanding impressionistic-style watercolors which she has exhibited in numerous juried shows, winning many awards. Jann travels frequently to Europe (using Karen Brown's guides) where she loves to paint historical buildings. Jann lives in Burlingame, California, with her husband, Gene.

Travel Your Dreams • Order your Karen Brown Guides Today

Please ask in your local bookstore for Karen Brown's Guides. If the books you want are unavailable, you may order directly from the publisher. Books will be shipped immediately.

_____ *Austria: Charming Inns & Itineraries* $19.95

_____ *California: Charming Inns & Itineraries* $19.95

_____ *England: Charming Bed & Breakfasts* $18.95

_____ *England, Wales & Scotland: Charming Hotels & Itineraries* $19.95

_____ *France: Charming Bed & Breakfasts* $18.95

_____ *France: Charming Inns & Itineraries* $19.95

_____ *Germany: Charming Inns & Itineraries* $19.95

_____ *Ireland: Charming Inns & Itineraries* $19.95

_____ *Italy: Charming Bed & Breakfasts* $18.95

_____ *Italy: Charming Inns & Itineraries* $19.95

_____ *New England: Charming Inns & Itineraries* $19.95

_____ *Portugal: Charming Inns & Itineraries* $19.95

_____ *Spain: Charming Inns & Itineraries* $19.95

_____ *Switzerland: Charming Inns & Itineraries* $19.95

Name _____ Street _____

Town _____ State_____ Zip _____ Tel _____

Credit Card (MasterCard or Visa) _____ Expires: _____

For orders in the USA, add $4 for the first book and $1 for each additional book for shipment. California residents add 8.25% sales tax. Overseas orders add $10 per book for airmail shipment. Indicate number of copies of each title; fax or mail form with check or credit card information to:

KAREN BROWN'S GUIDES
Post Office Box 70 • San Mateo • California • 94401 • USA
tel: (650) 342-9117, fax: (650) 342-9153, e-mail: karen@karenbrown.com
You can also order directly from our website at www.karenbrown.com.